Cruising New Hampshire History:

A Guide to New Hampshire's Roadside Historical Markers

Michael A. Bruno

DEDICATION

This book is dedicated to my father, John Bruno who shared with me his vast knowledge of this beautiful State. To my mother, Elizabeth who offered words of support. I would also like to dedicate this work to my children Danielle, Evan, and Rachel who had to live with my constant soapbox sermon of New Hampshire's beauty and "Live Free or Die" way of life. Timing is everything. In the two years of working on this project, the day I completed writing the final marker was the day my first grandchild was born. Therefore, I would also like to dedicate this book to my granddaughter Savannah Marie Matteson.

I could not have taken on this endeavor without the encouragement of my wife, cheerleader, counselor, pro-bono editor and best friend Kristin. The effort to compile the research and the time to put pen to paper could not have been possible without her support. She was my inspirational coach in making this book a reality. Without my family support, this endeavor would not have been possible.

CONTENTS

ACKNOWLEDGMENTS

Many others have given me encouragement and suggestions. I would like to acknowledge the support of my peers at the White Mountains Regional High School. I cannot count the number of trips I made to the school's New Hampshire reference room to find resources. I also would like to extend my appreciation and gratitude to William "Bill" Jones of Whitefield who provided a great deal of information and artifacts for my research. Bill is a wealth of knowledge of North Country history.

Thank you to the Grafton NH Historical Society for providing artifacts for their two new markers in town. I would like to thank Dr. Ronald Mills, Sr. of Tilton, NH who provided me artifacts and photos of the *House by the Side of the Road* where Sam Walter Foss resided. Dr. Mills is a lifelong family friend. To everyone who has supported me in this venture, thank you.

Preface

As a native Granite-Stater, I have always been intrigued and passionate about the history of New Hampshire. Why not? New Hampshire is one of the original colonies to sign the Declaration of Independence and ninth state to ratify the U.S. Constitution. The State is home to noteworthy Granite State citizens that includes the 14th President of the United States, a U.S. Vice-President, U.S. Supreme Court justices to include two Chief Justices, ambassadors and Cabinet secretaries, legendary authors and poets, Hall of Fame athletes, comedians, actors, and inventors. The Granite State also earns national notoriety each presidential election cycle with the First in the Nation Primary. The Granite State is rich in history, notable figures, and beautiful scenery.

Growing up in New Hampshire, I enjoyed riding my motorcycle every chance I could. My friends may not have shared in my passion for New Hampshire history, but my friends did enjoy riding. While riding my motorcycle around the state, I would stop and read the historical markers that dotted the highways. I never knew where they were beforehand. I would simply spot one, stop and read about the historical significance of that site. Now more than thirty years later, I have made the commitment to visit, photograph and share some information of each historical marker. Lastly, I have included Global Positioning System (GPS) coordinates for each location so Geocache enthusiasts may plan their trip with accuracy. At the time of publishing this book, there are 255 roadside markers with more added each year.

With the accessibility of the Internet, I was curious if there was a central website to locate information about these historical markers. I was excited to find the webpage of the New Hampshire Division of Historical Resources with a tab for historical markers. For further information, please visit their webpage at ww.nh.gov/nhdhr/markers/. While the page lists more than two hundred markers, it simply depicts a photo of the marker. With this book, I have categorized the NH historical markers by region, and included additional information for each marker, and surrounding area that I hope you find as interesting as the marker itself.

The excitement of putting this book together is a compilation of learning the vast richness of the history of New Hampshire. From marker number 0001 in the northernmost town of Pittsburg installed in 1958, to the most recent (at the time of publication) marker number 0255 in Berlin installed in 2016, the Granite State has deep history displayed conveniently with these roadside markers.

I hope this book is a useful tool for newcomers to the Granite State, longtime lovers of New Hampshire history, or just the curious sightseeing enthusiast. My goal was to take in the unique and picturesque scenery and enjoy riding around the State where Poet Laureate Robert Frost penned, *"Two roads diverged in a wood, and I—I took the one less traveled by, and that has made all the difference."*

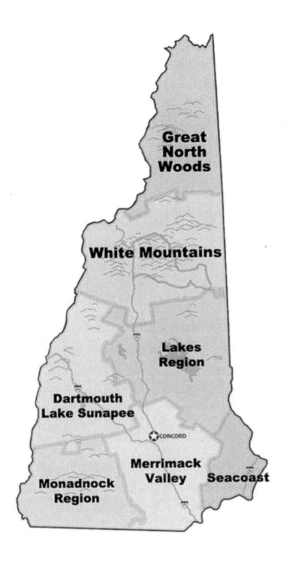

Image courtesy of NH Division of Travel & Tourism

Along your travels, you may encounter one of these helpful signs alerting you to the roadside marker ahead. I found that about one in ten markers had this sign. Traveling along the highways, these were also helpful because they point to which side of the road the marker is located. If you like treasure hunting, then these markers were exciting to see, letting you know that your destination is just ahead. Happy exploring!

Chapter One

The Great North Woods Region of New Hampshire is a unique destination. The area is best known as the wilderness of northern New Hampshire. This region is comprised of the majority of Coös County (pronounced Koe-ahs). The name is derived from the Abenaki dialect for "small pines". The region is a year-round destination for anglers, hunters (especially those hunting moose), hikers, snowmobilers, photographers and anyone who loves nature. From foliage seekers to vistas that span miles without sign of development, this region is truly a special place.

The Great North Woods Region is also home to the communities that lay claim to casting the first ballots for the presidential First in the Nation Primary. Dixville Notch is the home of the Balsams Grand Hotel and Resort that begins casting ballots in the infamous Ballot Room at midnight. The first ballots are cast by the approximately two dozen residents. At the time of the writing of this book (2016), New Hampshire is celebrating its' 100th anniversary of the presidential First in the Nation Primary status.

Another North Country community also casts their ballots at midnight on Primary Day. The unincorporated town of Millsfield, New Hampshire will again cast their Nation's first primary ballots in 2016 at midnight. Records show that Millsfield historically was the first New Hampshire town to cast their published on November 10, 1952 that the residents of Millsfield cast the nation's first presidential primary votes. Of the 16 residents, 7 voters cast their votes at the home of Mrs. Genevieve N. Annis at the stroke of midnight. The ballots were casts by 12:02am.

In 2015, New Hampshire state law included Millsfield in addition to Dixville Notch and Hart's Location as the towns authorized to open balloting at midnight. The town of Millsfield's population is approximately twenty-one registered voters. In years past, Millsfield residents gathered at a local farm to cast their ballots. Millsfield now casts their ballots at the Log Haven restaurant.

The Great North Woods Region of New Hampshire is steep in history and folklore. There are many websites that provide additional information for this unique area. A helpful website that includes excellent information for this region is *The Coos County, New Hampshire Genealogy & History* which can be accessed at http://www.nh.searchroots.com/coos.html.

Great North Woods

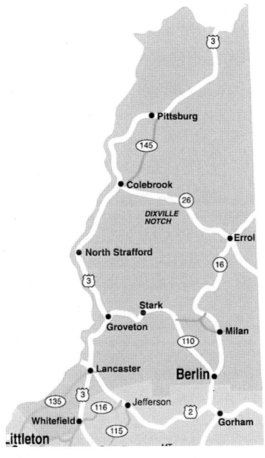

Berlin- Marker #0159: Boom Piers

Berlin – Marker #0215: Maynesborough's First Residence

Berlin- Marker #0254: The City that Trees Built

Berlin- Marker #0255: "The Avenues" Neighborhood

Clarksville- Marker #0115: 45th Parallel

Dixville- Marker #0171: Dixville Notch "First in the Nation"

Lancaster- Maker #0084: Wilder-Holton House

Lancaster- Marker #0173: Lake Coos and the Presidential Range

Lancaster- Maker #0219: The Weeks Act 1911

Milan- Marker #0227: Nansen Ski Jump

Pittsburg- Marker #0001: Republic of Indian Stream

Stark- Marker #0150: Camp Stark German Prisoner of War Camp

Stewartstown- Marker #0047: Metallak

Stewartstown- Marker #0064: 45th Parallel

Stratford- Marker #0034: Log Drives

Berlin

Marker #0159: Boom Piers

Location: NH Route 16 & 10th Street (across from 1575 Main St)

Sign Installed: 1989

GPS Coordinates- N 44° 30'.646″ W 71° 09'.185″

"The small man-made 'islands' in the river were used to secure a chain of boom logs which divided the Androscoggin River during the colorful and dramatic annual log drives, when the Brown Paper Company and the International Paper Company shared the river from the forests far upriver to the mills at Berlin. The logs were stamped on the ends with a marking hammer to identify their ownership, and they were sorted at a 'sorting gap' further upriver. The log drives ended in 1963. The old piers continue to serve as a reminder of North Country heritage."

The "City that trees built" was centered around the lumber and paper industry. The first river-powered sawmill was believed to have been built here in the 1820's. The Androscoggin River is the lifeblood of this community. The river was used to move the logs from the northern woods to the paper mills of Berlin and Gorham. The Brown Paper company was established in the late 1800's and was the largest paper producer in the world. From Berlin's early industrial time, this city was a company town where most businesses were owned by the Brown company.

The boom piers are small man-made islands situated on the Androscoggin River from north of Milan Village to the dam at the Northern Forest Heritage Park. This park was founded in 1994 to showcase the history of the logging and paper industry as well as the inter-cultural legacy which built this community. During the annual log drive, barriers were in place between the boom piers to separate the logs for the two major companies. Today, Berlin celebrates its log drive history with the RiverFire Festival. This annual event is a family-friendly weekend each October which culminates in an evening spectacle of bonfires on each boom pier from the 12th Street bridge to the Northern Forest Heritage Park.

Berlin New Hampshire has a deep cultural history. The largest ethnic group to settle in the area were French-Canadian immigrants to work in the lumber and pulp industry. The city also had a large Scandinavian influence as well. Today, the city is a hub for outdoor enthusiasts who enjoy hunting, fishing, hiking and snowmobiling. A major draw to the area is ATV riders to Jericho State ATV park on NH Route 110 in Berlin.

Berlin

Marker #0215: Maynesborough's First Residence 1824

Location: 131 East Milan Rd (left hand side of road between two white barns)

Sign Installed: 2009

GPS Coordinates- N 44° 30'.646″ W 71° 09'.185″

"On the knoll north of this site, William Sessions and his nephew, Cyrus Wheeler erected "the first building that could be honored with the name of house" in what is now Berlin, NH. Sessions helped clear many other farms in the area. In the 20th century, the property was the Brown Company farm. The two barns still extant housed draft horses for the logging side of the business; the larger was moved about ¼ mile south from W. R. Brown's Arabian horse stud-farm in 1947".

The first house built in Berlin (then known as Maynesborough) was on this site and built in 1824 by William Sessions. The two barns located at this site were used for housing the draft horses used in retrieving logs from the woods. The barns are the Thompson barn and Maynesborough Stud barn. The Thompson barn was named for Benjamin Thompson whose family purchased this property from William Sessions in 1827 and resided here until the property was purchased by the Brown Paper Company in 1891. At the time, the property consisted of a house, two barns and 450 acres. The Brown Paper Company owned more than 900 draft horses which were housed here and in other barns in the area.

Most travelers to the area miss the opportunity to travel this side (east) of the Androscoggin River. The road parallels the river north to Milan. It is worth the trip to make the loop and come back to check out the historical city of Berlin. For additional information for this area, check out the Berlin and Coos County Historical Society at: http://berlinnhhistoricalsociety.org/.

The city of Berlin was originally granted and settled as Maynesborough on December 31, 1771. On July 1st, 1829, Maynesborough was renamed Berlin. Researchers cannot agree as to the reason this community was renamed Berlin. However, the residents pronounce their hometown as "BUR-lin" and not "Ber-LIN". The pronunciation took root during the First World War as a patriotic stance against Germany.

Berlin

Marker #0254: The City That Trees Built

Location: NH Route 110 & Gilbert St. (In front of Police Dept.)

Sign Installed: 2016

GPS Coordinates- N 44° 28'.178″ W 71° 11'.125″

"Berlin became known as "The City that Trees Built" after innovations in the 1870s replaced rags with wood pulp in paper manufacturing. As the paper industry expanded Berlin's population grew from 8,886 in 1900 to 20,018 in 1930. The Brown Company research laboratory, associated with a prominent mill company, held some 500 patents. While pulp, newsprint, and kraft shipping paper were major products, Brown Company manufactured many other wood-based items including chloroform, Kream Krisp shortening, Nibroc paper towels, and Bermico sewer plates."

This northern stretch of land along the Androscoggin River was dense forest. The Grand Trunk Railway was constructed in 1851 to move logs to the shipyards in Portland Maine. In 1852, the H. Winslow & Company mill was built along the falls in Berlin. This was the start of the worldwide influence of the Brown Paper Company.

The Berlin Mills Company was formed in 1866 and with it began the company town of Berlin, New Hampshire. History of Berlin depicts that the Brown Company practically built the mill town.

Any goods or services needed by the residents were available at company-owned businesses.

With the vast natural resources of pulpwood, hydropower, and moving logs down the river from northern reaches, this region became an industry leader in the manufacturing of paper. Wood pulp was abundant and less expensive than cloth rags in paper production. As a child in the early 1970's, I recall the paper towel dispensers in the school bathrooms imprinted with "Brown Paper Co.- Berlin NH".

The Brown Company built this town. The trees and the river provided the resources to make this city known world-wide. However, the influence of the mills came to an end in 2001. The city of Berlin has been working diligently ever since to rebrand itself. Now the City that Trees Built is a city that showcases recreational activities in Northern New Hampshire.

Berlin

Marker #0254: The Avenues

Location: NH Route 110 & 3rd Ave

Sign Installed: 2016

GPS Coordinates- N 44° 28'.419″ W 71° 11'.238″

"The Avenues," a large neighborhood with small lots, was named for its north-south avenues, 1st to 6th. Housing construction was fueled by the booming paper industry and the arrival of the Berlin Street Railway in 1902. Over the next 30 years, many working-class immigrant families built single and multi-family houses in this ethnically-diverse neighborhood, which included many French-Canadian families, as well as those from Russia, Poland, Ireland, and Italy."

Located in the southwestern part of the city. "The Avenues" is comprised of six avenues which run parallel with the Androscoggin River. This development was created between 1890 and 1920 to house the influx of immigrant mill workers moving to Berlin. Within this development, there were two subdivisions. The Berlin Heights was the first and began in 1892 and the Green Aqueduct additions in 1893-1894. The Avenues were considered a prime location for the development of single family and multi-family homes due to its proximity to the mills and relatively flat terrain.

The paper mills were bustling, and new workers were in high demand. Immigrant families settled here from Russia, Canada, Scotland, Ireland, Italy, Poland and Scandinavian countries. Berlin's large immigrant population played a vital role in the future of the city. Today, visitors can see the Russian Orthodox church near 4th Avenue and Petrograd Street.

Many streets and schools in the area reflect the influence of French-speaking Canadian immigrants. Italian immigrants settled in what is known as Cascade Flats. It is believed by 1900, most residents of The Avenues were foreign-born. Today, The Avenues is admired for its historical significance to the heritage of the city.

Clarksville

Marker #0115: 45th Parallel

Location: NH Route 145 and West Road (7/10 mile north of Clarksville town line)

Sign Installed: 1977

GPS Coordinates- N 44° 59'.980″ W 71° 25'.168″

"At this point you stand on the 45th parallel, halfway between the Equator and the North Pole. At this point you stand also at longitude 71 degrees, 24' West from Greenwich, England. A line from this point through the center of the earth would emerge in the Indian Ocean 982 miles southwest of Perth, Australia."

Clarksville is a small community that was incorporated in 1853. Originally, the land was part of the Dartmouth College Grant deeded by the New Hampshire legislature in 1789. The land was sold by Dartmouth College to two of their graduates, Joseph Murdock and Benjamin Clark. The Clark family settled on this land; thus, the namesake of Clarksville. The town of Clarksville is also the second most northern incorporated town in New Hampshire with Pittsburg being the most northern incorporated town. The 2014 estimated U.S. Census data for Clarksville is 315 residents. The predominant industry for Clarksville has been timber. With the loss of major paper mills in the north country, the town is frequently visited for recreation. ATV travel, snowmobilers, and those who enjoy fishing and hunting comprise many visitors to this town. Clarksville extends from the southernmost shore of Lake Francis and to the Connecticut River to the west near Beecher Falls, Vermont and south to Colebrook.

The drive/ride along NH Route 145 from Pittsburg to Colebrook is very picturesque. The road is lightly traveled, and there are many old farms with scenic vistas along this route. My preference is to travel south along this road for the best views. Consider stopping at Beaver Brook Falls State Natural Area. This is a great place to admire the waterfall as well as explore along the pools and stream. This is also a nice spot for a picnic with tables and bathroom facilities on site.

Dixville

Marker #0171: Dixville Notch "First in the Nation"

Location: NH Route 26 at the Balsams Grand Hotel entrance

Sign Installed: 1998

GPS Coordinates- N 44° 51'.984″ W 71° 18'.156″

"New Hampshire has held the first-in-the-nation presidential primaries since 1920. With the first presidential "beauty contest" in 1932, our citizens have personally met the candidates and by popular ballot have declared their preference for their party's nominee. Since 1960, Dixville has been the first community in the state and country to cast its handful of votes in national elections. On election eve 100% of the eligible voters gather in the ballot room of The BALSAMS. At midnight polls open and a few minutes later promptly close. The results are broadcast around the world."

Dixville Notch, and notably the Balsams Grand Resort Hotel is a picturesque hamlet nestled along NH Route 26. The most impressive vantage point is when you travel westerly from Errol to Colebrook. As you travel through and crest the steep and narrow Dixville notch, the viewpoint is stellar with Lake Gloriette in the forefront, and the cliff face of Abeniki Mountain in the background. While standing at the historical marker, turn to your left and look up to the cliff face across Route 26. Table Rock is a popular vantage point 700 feet above the highway. Table Rock is situated along the Cohos Trail that runs 165 miles from Crawford Notch to Canada.

The Balsams Grand Resort Hotel is comprised of more than 11,000 acres that includes an alpine ski area, Nordic center, and a 9-hole Donald Ross designed golf course. Major renovations are taking place to make the Balsams an exclusive four-season resort. While stopping at this marker, it is a must to go to the resort and visit the infamous Ballot Room. It is worth it to see all the political history that begins in this small community. At the time of publication, the resort is under major renovations with plans to open with 21st century amenities with the pristine details of the 19th century grand hotel era.

Lancaster

Marker #0084: Wilder-Holton House

Location: North side of U.S. Route 2 & U.S. Route 3 traffic circle (Lancaster Historical Society)

Sign Erected: 1972

GPS Coordinates- N 44° 29'.824″ W 71° 34'.604″

"This structure, erected by Major Jonas Wilder, from boards planed and nails wrought on the site, originally possessing a four-fireplace chimney and Indian shutters, is Coos County's first two-story dwelling. Construction was initiated on the noted 'Dark Day' of May 19, 1780, which caused work to cease temporarily. Successively a home, a tavern, a church, and a meeting place, it is now a museum".

Local historian, Lancaster native, colleague, and friend Tim Phillips shared with me the history of the Wilder-Holton house. The "Dark Day" of May 19, 1780 was an eclipse which darkened the north country sky. Builders were frightened that the event was a curse on them for constructing on a possible Indian burial ground. Folklore for this building also suggests that it was a stop on the "underground railroad" for providing shelter to escaped slaves traveling to Canada. The building remained a family home until 1965 when it was purchased by the Lancaster Historical Society.

Lancaster is also referred to as the "Gateway to the Great North Woods". This community was originally chartered in 1763.

Predominantly, this community's mainstay was farming due to its rich soils replenished by the Connecticut River. Lancaster has a picturesque downtown with many quaint shops for visiting. Lancaster is also the home of the Kilkenny Cup. This is the oldest snowmobile race in the United States. The first race was held in 1962. The local snowmobile club (Lancaster Snow Drifters) is the oldest snowmobile club in the country established in 1962.

In the summer, be sure to visit the weekly flea markets on site of the Wilder-Holton House property. The Wilder-Holton House was added to the National Register of Historic Places in 1975. There is also a museum on site sponsored by the Lancaster Historical Society. During Labor Day week, spend some time at the Lancaster Fair where you still can enjoy a vintage agricultural fair.

Lancaster

Marker #0173: Lake Coos and the Presidential Range

Location: U.S. Route 2 (Mile Marker 3.6) East across from Rogers Campground.

Sign Installed: 1999

GPS Coordinates- N 44° 28'.067" W 71° 32'.600"

"Lancaster, founded in 1763, lies on the bed of glacial Lake Coos, formed as the glaciers receded 14,000 years ago. Today, the Connecticut, and American Heritage River, flows along the bottom of the ancient lake.

You stand at a gateway to The Great North Woods Region. To the east, aligned from north to south, are Mounts Madison, Adams, Jefferson, and Washington, at 6288 feet, is the highest in the Northeast. The strongest winds ever recorded, 231 miles per hour, were measured on its summit on April 12, 1934".

This historical marker has a magnificent view of the White Mountains to the east and the Kilkenny Range to the north. As the marker depicts, the glacial Lake Coos (pronounced Koe-ahs) and the Connecticut River are what made this area prime for farming and agriculture.

Glacial Lake Coos once filled this valley during the Ice Age. Geologists believe the extended lakebed of Lake Hitchcock extended from the State of Connecticut to Lyme, NH. Smaller Lake Upham and Lake Coos extended north to St. Johnsbury, Vermont. It is believed this glacial lake existed for more than four-thousand years and was the last remnant of the glacial ice shelf in the region. Evidence of glacial erosion is evident in both Franconia and Crawford Notches. These passageways depict the carving of the landmass from the massive ice sheet.

Today, we get to enjoy the spectacular scenery of rugged cliffs and peaks of the White Mountains. The White Mountains to the east and south of this marker are the highest peaks in New Hampshire. The peaks are named for the presidents in order of succession in relation to the elevation of the peak. The one exception is Mount Monroe is twenty-two feet higher than Mt. Madison. This was a result of a surveying error.

Lancaster

Marker #0219: The Weeks Act of 1911

Location: U.S. Route 3 (Mile Marker 163) at the entrance to Weeks State Park.

Sign Installed: 2009

GPS Coordinates- N 44° 27'.181″ W 71° 34'.672″

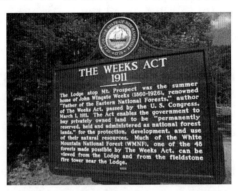

"The lodge atop Mt. Prospect was the summer home of John Wingate Weeks (1860-1926), renowned "Father of the Eastern National Forests," author of the Weeks Act, passed by the U.S. Congress, March 1, 1911. The Act enables the government to buy privately owned land to be "permanently reserved, held and administered as national forest lands," for the protection, development and use of their natural resources. Much of the White Mountain National Forest (WMNF), one of the 48 forests made possible by the Weeks Act, can be viewed from the Lodge and from the fieldstone fire tower near the Lodge".

John Wingate Weeks is considered the Father of the eastern National Forests. Prior to the Weeks Act, these lands were unprotected from the ravishes of development and logging. Without the protections, much of the wilderness was stripped of its resources and left unmanaged. The Weeks Act put into place the protections that gives us the treasures of the National Forest system.

This historical site is a favorite of mine. After visiting the marker, take the time to go up the driveway (on foot is best) for viewing options; there is limited parking at the top. This roadway is approximately 1.5 miles long. The Weeks Lodge is filled with exceptional New Hampshire history. The Lodge is still decorated in the era of its use. On display are collectibles of John Week's political career as a US Congressman, US Senator, and Secretary of War. The upstairs boasts a great room where President Teddy Roosevelt gifted a bull moose head that is mounted on the wall. If you are a history buff, the visit is worth the trip.

On one of my last visits to the Week's State Park, the grandson of John Wingate Weeks was on the property. He enthusiastically spoke of the accomplishments of his grandfather, as well as the impact on our environment through the Weeks Act. A stroll through the Week's summer cottage and the Top of the Stone observatory and Fire Lookout tower onsite is a great opportunity to take in the splendid views of Lancaster and points north.

Milan

Marker #0227: Nansen Ski Jump

Location: NH Route 16 north of Berlin/Milan Town line on left side of road.

Sign Installed: 2011

GPS Coordinates- N 44° 31'.937 W 71° 10'.073"

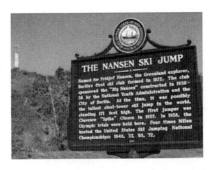

"Named for Fridjof Nansen, the Greenland explorer, Berlin's first ski club formed in 1872. The club sponsored the "Big Nansen" constructed in 1936-38 by the National Youth Administration and the City of Berlin. At the time, it was possibly the tallest steel tower ski jump in the world, standing 171 feet high. The first jumper was Clarence "Spike" Oleson in 1937. In 1938, the Olympic trials were held here. Four-time Milan hosted the United States Ski Jumping National Championships: 1940, '57. '65. '72."

This structure is quite impressive. The ski jump structure had been in a state of disrepair for decades. Recent work started in 2015 has brought this jump back to life. The local Nansen Ski Club is fundraising to bring this structure back to its' original glory. During the 1940's through 1960's, this ski jump was the premier ski jump structure in the country and a major attraction to the region. The last jump was made in 1983 and it was closed in 1988. Renovation plans include the ski jump as well as the judges stand. In its' heyday, ski jump competitions would draw hundreds of spectators.

The Friends of Nansen Ski Jump have begun revitalizing the site. To date, efforts have been made to clear the brush, replace the steps up to the top of the jump and in December 2016 completed the planking of the ski jump. On March 4, 2017 US Olympian and 2013 World Champion Sarah Hendrickson completed the first jump off Nansen in 32 years. At this time, the New Hampshire State Park system is working collaboratively with the Nansen Ski Club to get this structure listed on the National Register of Historic Places as a National Historic Landmark.

Photo courtesy of Berlin NH & Coos County Historical Society.

Pittsburg

Marker #0001: Republic of Indian Stream

Location: U.S. Route 3 at the intersection Back Lake Rd (on the Village Green)

Sign Installed: 1958

GPS Coordinates- N 45° 03'.081" W 71° 23'.219"

Indian Stream Republic marker US. Route 3 & Hill Rd

GPS Coordinates- N 45° 03'.445" W 71° 20'.753"

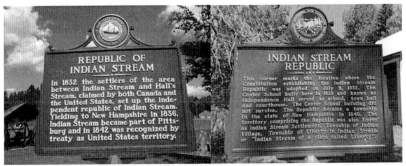

"In 1832 the settlers of the area between Indian Stream and Hall's Stream, claimed by both Canada and the United States, set up the independent republic of Indian Stream. Yielding to New Hampshire in 1836, Indian Stream became part of Pittsburg and in 1842 was recognized by treaty as United States territory."

"This corner marks the location where the Constitution establishing the Indian Stream Republic was adopted on July 9, 1832. The Center School built here in 1828 and known as Independence Hall served as school, town hall and courthouse. The Center School building did not survive. The Republic became a township in the state of New Hampshire in 1840. The territory comprising the Republic was also known as Indian Stream Settlement, Township of Indian Village, Township of Liberty in Indian Stream or "Indian Stream of a place called Liberty".

This marker was the first to be installed by the State in 1958. The Republic of Indian Stream history depicts the independent spirit of early settlers. While the land known as "Indian Stream Territory" was claimed by both Canada and the United States, the settlers claimed their independence as a Sovereign Nation in 1832 as the Republic of Indian Stream. As found in the *"History of Coos County New Hampshire*; (1888) by Georgia Drew Merrill, the citizens created their own Bill of Rights, established a judicial system, and the citizens of the Republic comprised the legislative body. Records report that the Republic also had a small militia. While the Republic was short-lived, the independent spirit of the settlers depicts the tenacity of the citizens of Indian Stream to be self-regulated. This independent spirit is still prevalent in the Great North Woods of New Hampshire. Another great book, *Indian Stream Republic, Settling a New England Frontier 1785-1842* by Daniel Doan (1997) is an excellent read. It is a wonderful blend of history and fiction of life in the New Hampshire frontier. While visiting this marker, continue north on U.S. Route 3 through the village of Pittsburg. The second marker sign is located approximately 3 miles north of the Village Center at US Route 3 and Hill Rd. This marker denotes the location where the Indian Stream Republic was ratified by the residents on July 9, 1832.

This town is a premier destination for outdoor enthusiasts. Pittsburg is truly a four-season community. Along the drive, you will pass Lake Francis and the Connecticut lakes, and enter what is infamously known as "Moose Alley". This stretch of highway runs twenty-two miles from the village to the U.S./Canada border. If you are going to see a moose, it is here. So, stay alert and enjoy the wildlife. Pittsburg also holds claim to be being NH's largest landmass township with the town boundaries encompassing more than 283 square miles. A unique fact of Pittsburg is that it borders two states (Vermont & Maine) and the Province of Quebec Canada to the north.

Stark

Marker #0150: Camp Stark German Prisoner of War Camp

Location: NH Route 110 approximately 1.6 miles east of Stark Village covered bridge

Sign Installed: 1985 & 1990

GPS Coordinates- N 44° 37'.113″ W 71° 23'.249″

"In the spring of 1944 a high fence and four guard towers transformed a former Civilian Conservation Corps camp on this site into New Hampshire's sole World War II prisoner of war camp. Approximately 250 German and Austrian soldiers, most captured in North Africa and Normandy, lived in Camp Stark while working in the forest cutting pulpwood vital to wartime industry. The camp closed in the spring of 1946 when the prisoners of war were returned to their homeland. Several maintained the new friendships they had formed with local residents. Germans and Americans attended a reunion here in 1986".

Stark is a picturesque village with the quintessential New England charm. Chartered in 1774 as Percy and was incorporated in 1795. The town was renamed in 1832 in honor of its' namesake, General John Stark, the famous New Hampshire Revolutionary War leader at the Battles of Bunker Hill and Bennington. The New Hampshire motto of "Live Free or Die" is credited to a statement made by General Stark. A notable fact is that there are no records of General Stark ever visiting the village of Percy.

The site of the German POW camp is overgrown but there are remains of a couple of chimneys on site. If you find this site interesting, I highly encourage reading *"Stark Decency: German Prisoners of War in a New England Village"* written by Allen V. Koop. It is an excellent portrayal of what life was like for the prisoners, guards, and the citizens of Stark during World War II. Camp Stark opened in 1944 and was closed by 1946. It was the only Prisoner of War camp in New Hampshire during World War Two.

The 250 prisoners of war who were encamped here were not Nazis. The Camp Stark prisoners were conscripted, and many were professional artisans in Germany prior to the war. The prisoners were brought here as laborers to cut pulpwood to supply the Brown Company mill. This was needed since most male mill workers were serving overseas in the war. The book, *Stark Decency* goes into detail of the lives of the prisoners, escape attempts, and their reunion back in Stark in 1986.

Stewartstown

Marker #0047: Metallak

Location: U.S. Route 145 and Creampote Rd, One mile north of Stewartstown Village

Sign Installed: 1967

GPS Coordinates- N 44° 58'.508″ W 71° 26'.018″ (marker)

N 44° 58'.490″ W 71° 25'.240″ (gravesite)

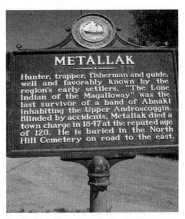

"Hunter, trapper, fisherman and guide, well and favorably known by the region's early settlers, "The Lone Indian of the Magalloway" was the last survivor of a band of Abnaki inhabiting the Upper Androscoggin. Blinded by accidents, Metallak died a town charge in 1847 at the reputed age of 120. He is buried in the North Hill Cemetery on the road to the east."

The town's most revered and popular resident was an Abenaki native named Metallak. Ernest Hebert authored an article entitled, Metallak: A Life in *Beyond the Notches, Stories of Place in New Hampshire's North Country* (2011). Hebert depicts larger-than-life folklore of Metallak. One story claims that Metallak jumped on the back of a moose and attempted to kill it with nothing more than bravery and a knife. While the moose bucked and kicked, ultimately it was Metallak that was the victor. Another story of lore is when Metallak's wife Molly Molasses died during the dead of winter. Far into the wilderness and without means to transport her body, Metallak used his skills as an outdoorsman to build a coffin frame and smoke her body to preserve it through the winter.

While the folklore of Metallak is just that, it does depict the unique rugged life in the Great North Woods of New Hampshire. Metallak was revered by the townspeople and looked after his welfare. His grave still displays the number of tokens that visitors leave for him. I suggest the extra few minutes to visit his resting place.

Take the dirt road next to the sign (Creampote) and follow to the "T" in the road. Take a right onto N. Hill Rd and the cemetery is just down on your right side. Metallak's distinctive grave marker is in the corner of the cemetery. North Hill Rd is a Class 6 road and is not maintained in winter.

Stewartstown

Marker #0064: 45th Parallel

Location: U.S. Route 3 (Mile Marker 210.2) ½ mile north of West Stewartstown.

Sign Installed: 1970

GPS Coordinates- N 45° 00'.022″ W 71° 23'.249″

"As you stand at this point on the 45th parallel you are halfway between the Equator and the North Pole."

The territory which makes up Stewartstown was originally chartered by New Hampshire colonial Governor John Wentworth in 1770. The town incorporated as Stuart in 1795, but the legality of the incorporation was challenged, and the town incorporated as Stewartstown in 1799. During the 18th and early 19th century, Stewartstown was the northernmost incorporated town along the Connecticut River. This was a river port for goods to travel south throughout New Hampshire and New England, as well as a port for goods traveling north.

While Stewartstown and West Stewartstown are one township, they are both distinct and unique. West Stewartstown borders the Connecticut River and is more populated. Travel along NH Route 145 in Stewartstown (also known as the Hollow Road) is more rural. While traveling on Route 145, it is worth a visit to the Poore Family Farm Foundation for North Country Conservancy. This is a historical homestead which was featured in Yankee magazine in March 2013. This homestead is a living museum of what life was like in the 1830's to early 20th century. Most visitors find it intriguing how frugal and resourceful folks lived up here in the north country during this era.

Stratford

Marker #0034: Log Drives

Location: U.S. Route 3 (Mile Marker 187.1) 1.7 miles south of North Stratford

Sign Installed: 1965

GPS Coordinates- N 44° 43'.852" W 71° 23'.249"

"The dramatic process of conveying lumber logs and pulpwood from northern New Hampshire forests to manufacturing centers, by driving them down the Connecticut River, spanned the turn into the Twentieth Century. Hardy crews of "white-water men" risked life and limb in the hazardous work of the annual spring drives"

The town of Stratford was first settled in 1762 and incorporated in 1773. The town website claims that this community was predominantly farms until the late 1880's. At that time, logging became a major industry in the area. With an abundance of forests, the Connecticut River and the railroad made this area a major timber producer. Saw and grist mills were prevalent in this community with the availability of hydropower from surrounding streams. Secondly, the location along the Connecticut River made it suitable for transport downstream to mills along the river.

The lifeblood of northern New Hampshire was logging. According to the north country subject matter expert and author of *Log Drives of the Connecticut River*, (2003) Bill Gove wrote, *"North Stratford, New Hampshire, had been a small but active railroad village since 1850, before the era of the log drives; it became a booming community afterward, the log driving center for Vermont's Essex County and New Hampshire's Coos County (p. 89).*

Today, Stratford is popular with outdoor enthusiasts who enjoy hunting, fishing, snowmobiling, and ATV riding. Stratford has access to the popular Nash Stream Wilderness area. The town library and museum are located in a renovated train depot on Route 3. A short drive south on Route 3 will lead you to Stratford Hollow Rd on the left to the historical society in the former Methodist church.

Chapter Two

White Mountains Region

The White Mountains region of New Hampshire is a premier tourist destination for visitors worldwide. At the heart of this region, is the White Mountains National Forest which spans more than 1,200 square miles of mountains, quaint villages, and four-season recreational activities. Interestingly, the White Mountains National Forest came about due to the Weeks Act of 1911 (see Marker #0219 in Lancaster, NH). Prior to the enactment of the Weeks Act, much of this pristine wilderness we now enjoy in the White Mountains was owned and timbered by major lumber companies.

The White Mountains region is famous for being the home to the highest peak in the northeast; Mount Washington (6,288 ft). Mount Washington is also infamous for some of the most dangerous weather on earth. The highest recorded wind speed on earth was measured at 231 mph on April 12, 1934.

The Appalachian Trail traverses the heart of this region for more than 100 miles. It is common to see AT thru-hikers in the summer and fall months. Also, the highest peaks found along the Appalachian Trail are in this region. For hikers, many determined "peak baggers" attempt to complete all the New Hampshire forty-eight peaks with an elevation of 4,000 ft. or higher.

I believe this region has the most scenic vistas in the eastern United States. From the famous "notches" formed by Ice-Age glaciers, the pristine bodies of water and the Grande Dame Mount Washington Hotel. A trip through the White Mountains region will require multiple stops to view scenic vistas, take short hikes up trails to mountain lakes, sample local cuisine, and multiple opportunities to take photos. Enjoy the beauty of the White Mountains!

Growing up in New Hampshire, one of my most favorite trips was traveling through Franconia Notch and to view the Old Man of the Mountain. This iconic symbol of New Hampshire epitomized the pride I felt growing up here. This majestic figure towering 1,200 feet above Profile Lake kept watch over the state. Sadly, the Great Stone Face collapsed May 3, 2003.

On the northern shore of Profile lake is a commemorative viewing spot to learn of the glacial formation and the history of this lost landmark. This is a worthwhile stop while traveling through Franconia Notch. One of my most vivid memories of visiting the "Old Man" was a sign posted at the shore of Profile Lake, which included a verse from Daniel Webster:

"Men hang out their signs indicative of their respective trades; shoemakers hang out a gigantic shoe; jewelers a monster watch, and the dentist hangs out a gold tooth; but up in the Mountains of New Hampshire, God Almighty has hung out a sign to show that there He makes men."

White Mountains Region

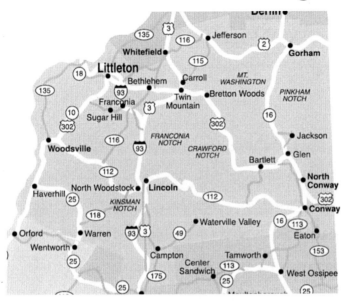

Bartlett- Marker #0109: Lady Blanche House

Bath- Marker #0121: Bath, New Hampshire

Bath- Marker #0217: Bath Bridge

Bean's Grant- Marker #0045: Mount Washington Cog Railway

Benton- Marker #0245: Beginning of White Mountains National Forest

Bethlehem- Marker #0198: Alderbrook

Bethlehem- Marker #0218: Pierce Bridge

Campton- Marker #0196: Blair Bridge

Carroll- Marker #0030: The Crawford Family

Carroll- Marker #0087: Crawford House

Carroll- Marker #0122: Mount Washington Hotel/Bretton Woods Monetary Conference

Carroll- Marker #0233: Zealand and James Everell Henry

Conway- Marker #0038: White Mountain School of Art

Easton- Marker #0200: Wildwood

Franconia- Marker #0009: Stone Iron Furnace

Harts Location- Marker #0186: Sawyer's Rock/Crawford Notch Road

Harts Location- Marker #0213: Frankenstein Trestle

Haverhill- Marker #0056: Rogers Rangers

Haverhill- Marker #0104: Ebenezer Mackintosh (1737-1816)

Haverhill- Marker #0136: The Bedell Bridge

Haverhill- Marker #0160: Haverhill Corner Historic District

Haverhill- Marker #0190: Haverhill-Bath Bridge

Jefferson- Marker #0019: Thaddeus S.C. Lowe (1823-1913)

Jefferson- Marker #0152: Cherry Mountain Slide

Jefferson- Marker #0229: Granny Stalbird (1755-1845)

Lincoln- Marker #0224: Betty and Barney Hill Incident

Lisbon- Marker #0070: Old Coal Kiln

Littleton- Marker #0071: Kilburn Brothers Stereoscopic View Factory

Littleton- Marker #0185: Willowdale Settlement

Madison- Marker #0207: Granville Homestead

Pinkham's Grant- Marker #0011: First Ascent of Mount Washington

Randolph- Marker #0220: The Ravine House

Rumney- Marker #0055: Baker River

Rumney- Marker #0174: Loveland Bridge

Sugar Hill- Marker #0073: First Ski School in America

Thornton- Marker #n/a: Andrew C. Robertson Memorial Bridge (1892-1980)

Warren- Marker #0231: Norris Cotton, Statesman (1900-1989)

Bartlett

Marker # 0109: Lady Blanche House

Location: West Side Road 3.3 miles south from US Route 302 (sign on left side of road)

Use Caution- limited shoulder and sign is located on a curve.

Sign Installed: 1976

GPS Coordinates- N 44° 05'.109″ W 71° 09'.938″

"This rustic cottage was once the home of Thomas Murphy and his wife, Lady Blanche, daughter of the Earl of Gainsborough. Thomas was the organist at the church on the Earl's estate. The commoner and lady eloped to America, where Thomas taught at the Kearsarge School for Boys in North Conway. Lady Blanche, a noted writer and contributor to such publications as Harper's and The Atlantic Monthly, died here in 1881."

Lady Blanche Elizabeth Annunciata Noel was of English nobility. She was born March 25, 1845, the daughter of the 2nd Earl of Gainsborough. She was also the godchild of England's Queen Victoria. She married an Irish commoner against her parents' wishes. Deeply in love, the sixteen-year-old Blanche and Thomas Murphy eloped from England and sailed on a ship in the steerage section to America to live their lives together in New York. They saved their measly earnings and set north to New Hampshire in 1880 and purchased this home.

As the sign depicts, Lady Blanche's husband Thomas taught music and French at the Kearsarge School for Boys. Lady Blanche and Thomas purchased the home, known at the time as the Ledge Farm in 1880 and she died eleven months later in 1881. Records state that she loved the beauty of the region and used it to inspire her writings. She wrote for the *Atlantic Monthly* and for *Galaxy.* Her works were popular, and she was considered the most sought-after female writer of her time.

A local newspaper article shares the insight of Mr. Dick Goff, the current owner of the Lady Blanche House. In his interview with the *Mountain Ear* newspaper, Mr. Goff states the property includes 32 acres which borders the Saco River with the view of Humphrey's Ledge. Notably, the vantage point is so stunning, a photograph from the river towards the home and Humphrey's Ledge was selected the winner of the 1893 World's Fair photo competition.

Bath

Marker # 0121: Bath, New Hampshire

Location: US Route 302 (Mile Marker 4.5) ½ mile south of Bath Village on west side of road

Sign Installed: 1978

GPS Coordinates- N 44° 09'.575" W 71° 57'.930"

"Settled in 1766 by Jaasiel Harriman whose cabin was near the Great Rock. His nine-year-old daughter Mercy carried dirt in her apron to the top of this unique rock formation. Here she planted corn, pumpkins, and cucumbers, making the first garden in town.

Three well-preserved covered bridges are to be found here. Among its many fine homes is the Federal mansion built by Moses P. Payson in 1810."

I consider this historical marker a gem of a find. I live within twenty minutes of this site and have traveled by it numerous times. The parking space where this marker is located lacks appeal. While working on this project, I stopped to read this marker and pay more attention to my surroundings. To the immediate right of this marker is a small, yet discreet marker showing the way on "Mercy's Path" to the original garden spot. This short walk ended at a large rock outcropping with a plaque identifying the original garden spot. To this day, the Bath

Historical Society maintains a garden atop the same rock outcropping. This is a fun find and worth the few minutes walk along "Mercy's Path".

While you are in Bath, a short ride north on Route 302 takes you to Bath Village. There is a picturesque covered bridge over the Ammonoosuc River as well as the oldest general store in the United States. The Bath General Store is listed on the National Register of Historic Places.

Bath

Marker # 0217: Bath Bridge

Location: Intersection of US Route 302 & NH Route 10/NH Route 112

Sign Erected: 1978, 2009

GPS Coordinates- N 44° 09'.147″ W 71° 58'.526″

"Erected in 1928, this riveted steel Warren truss span was built to replace a wooden span destroyed in the 1927 flood. This efficient truss design is based on a series of equilateral triangles with verticals added for strength. Boston Bridge Works fabricated the structure in Elmira, NY. Reflecting recent improvements in steel technology, the bridge incorporates rolled I-beams that minimized shop time and eased assembly in the field. This standard plan was also used in Bethlehem Hollow."

This historic Warren truss span bridge straddles the Wild Ammonoosuc River which is popular destination for gold prospectors and anglers. For those who appreciate scenic roadways, traveling east on NH Route 112 affords a windy highway that follows the river through Swiftwater New Hampshire and beyond to the Kinsman Mountain range. This route also offers scenic vistas and New Hampshire's famous Lost River attraction.

This now untraveled bridge was the main north/south route along the Connecticut River. The Bath Bridge is constructed with the same design as the bridge spanning the Ammonoosuc River located on NH Route 142 (Maple Street) in Bethlehem Hollow. Another Warren Truss bridge is commemorated with a New Hampshire roadside marker. The Cork Plain Bridge in Antrim (marker # 0228) details the bridge as well as the Second New Hampshire Turnpike.

Bean's Grant

Marker # 0045: Mount Washington Cog Railway

Location: Base Station Rd- 5.9 miles east of US Route 302 intersection

Sign Erected: 1965

GPS Coordinates- N 44° 16'.081″ W 71° 21'.247″

"Completed in 1869 for $139,500, this unique railway was built through the genius and enterprise of Herrick and Walter Aiken of Franklin and Sylvester Marsh of Campton. Over three miles long, the average grade to the 6,293-foot summit is one foot in four. Made safe by toothed wheel and ratchet, it is the second steepest in the world and the first of its type."

The Mount Washington Cog Railway has been a tourist destination for nearly 150 years. In the early 19th century, visitors sought a means to summit the great mountain. When Sylvester Marsh solicited the New Hampshire legislature for interest in building the cog railway, they laughed him out with "you might as well build a railway to the moon". The ridicule did not stop Marsh who worked tirelessly on this project starting in 1866. On July 3, 1869, the first steam-driven engine "Old Peppersass" climbed to the summit. "Old-Peppersass" is still on display at the base station of the Cog Railway. The original steam engine "Old Peppersass" earned its name from its shape that resembles a pepper bottle. If you do not pursue the adventure (which is truly an experience), stop in to visit the on-site cog railway museum. This is a stop worth making for New Hampshire history and railroad enthusiasts. Don't forget to check the history of the "Devil's shingle".

The Mount Washington Cog railway is the oldest cog railway still in operation in the world. In 1869, while President Ulysses S. Grant was visiting northern New Hampshire, he rode to the summit of Mount Washington on the cog railway. President Grant was a bit of a daredevil!

As you travel back to US Route 302, take a moment to stop and visit the Upper Falls of the Ammonoosuc River. This is a popular swimming hole for locals and tourists alike. The water is crystal clear. Beware of the dangers of cold spring mountain water and current. Follow the safety rules posted onsite. This stop is located 3.7 miles west of the Cog Railway marker on Base Station Rd.

Benton

Marker # 0245: Pike Tract, Beginning of the White Mountains National Forest

Location: NH Route 25 (Mt Moosilauke Highway) Mile Marker 14.6

Sign Erected: 2015

GPS Coordinates- N 44° 00'.210″ W 71° 55'.894″

"The US Forest Service purchased 7,022 acres of timber-covered mountain slopes, cliffs, streams, ponds, and abandoned farmland from Haverhill businessman E. Bertram Pike on January 2, 1914. The purchase was the first acquisition towards the establishment of the White Mountains National Forest in 1918, a significant accomplishment to restore and protect lands and watersheds from the impact of years of destructive practices. The nearly 800,000-acre WMNF is carefully managed as a working forest, sustaining the health, beauty, and productivity of natural resources."

The drive on NH Route 25 is picturesque with farmlands meeting the mountains with the highest being 4,802-foot Mount Moosilauke. Approaching this marker from the village of Pike, you will see the cliff face of Owl's Head. This is a popular site for adventurous rock climbers. At the marker, is Oliverian Pond. This is a favorite spot for local fishermen. Traveling east on the Mount Moosilauke highway towards Warren, you will cross the

Appalachian Trail. Do not be surprised to see some weary thru-hikers along the way.

The town of Benton was founded on January 31, 1764 and named Coventry for the large number of settlers who were from Coventry, Connecticut. The town was renamed on December 4, 1840 in honor of Missouri Senator Thomas Hart Benton. Benton championed the ideal of the United States westward expansion.

An interesting tidbit of history shared by New Hampshire celebrity historian, Fritz Wetherbee is that Benton is the only town in New Hampshire history to have raised taxes to buy out Civil War draftee fees to be exempt from service. The story continues that a Benton resident was drafted before the town approved tax money to pay the exemption fee. He was so disheartened and determined to not serve in the Army that he cut off his own thumb to disqualify him from service in the Army. One week later, the town authorized funding for future draft exemptions through taxation. The man never served and was nicknamed "Thumby".

Bethlehem

Marker # 0198: Alderbrook

Location: NH Route 116 (Whitefield Rd) & Alderbrook Gun Club access road

Sign Erected: 2006

GPS Coordinates- N 44° 19'.630″ W 71° 42'.119″

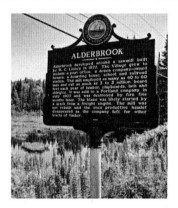

"Alderbrook developed around a sawmill built by H.C. Libbey in 1877. The village grew to include a post office, a dozen company-owned houses, a boarding house, school and railroad station. The mill employed as many as 40 to 60 men and cut as much as 3 to 5 million board feet each year of lumber, clapboards, lath and shingles. It was sold to a Portland company in July 1909 and was destroyed by fire five months later. The blaze was likely started by a spark from a freight engine. The mill was not rebuilt, and the once productive hamlet disappeared as the company left for other tracts of timber."

The town of Bethlehem was granted as Lloyds Hills by colonial Governor John Wentworth in 1774. Lloyds Hills was the last provincial grant in the state. After the Revolution, records could not be found. On December 25th, 1799 the town was renamed Bethlehem. The town has many notables to list. Bethlehem is the highest elevated town east of the Rockies. The town is also listed as the Poetry Capital of New Hampshire and gained popularity in the 19th and 20th century as a tourist destination. It was believed that the pure mountain air of Bethlehem was beneficial for sufferers of allergies and hay fever.

In the early 20th century, Bethlehem became a major destination for people escaping the sweltering summer conditions of eastern U.S. cities. Many summer residents who owned summer "cottages" were major leaders of business. Names such as Woolworth, Glessner, and Chicago Symphony Conductor Theodore Thomas are just a sample. The town is also a popular destination for Jewish visitors. Many orthodox Jewish families find Bethlehem a favored vacation destination. The Hebrew Hay Fever Relief Association was established in Bethlehem in 1919.

Bethlehem "The star of the White Mountains" was also the home to nearly 30 grand hotels. To date, only the Maplewood remains. However, in 2016 the Arlington hotel, a kosher boutique hotel was rebuilt to continue its' storied history of hospitality. The Bethlehem community is a jewel to visit. When in town, stop by the Bethlehem Heritage Center on Main street and enjoy the many keepsakes of this fascinating town. You will be impressed.

Bethlehem

Marker # 0218: Pierce Bridge

Location: US Route 302 & River Rd (next to the Wayside Inn)

Sign Erected: 2009

GPS Coordinates-N 44° 16'.296″ W 71° 37'.838″

"By 1920 the adjacent road, Rt. 302 was part of the Teddy Roosevelt (TR) Trail, which ran from Maine to Oregon. It was an important way for tourists to access the White Mountains. After the 1927 floods, many bridges needed to be quickly replaced. With vertical members in compression and diagonals in tension, the High Pratt truss was strong and easy to construct, making it a favorite of the state highway engineers. This riveted steel span was erected in 1928, keeping this important crossing in use."

The early 20th century was a boom for this region. Major train lines provided easy access to White Mountains destinations. This location is still considered Bethlehem Junction. A major stop for tourists to enjoy the grandeur of the White Mountains from far away cities such as Boston, Hartford, Providence, New York, Hartford, to name a few. With the invention of the car, more visitors opted to travel by automobile.

While in Bethlehem, take some time to enjoy the downtown just a few miles west of this location. Many artisan shops as well as the Colonial Theater which opened in 1914. Further east of downtown is the Rocks Estate. This 1,400-acre property is owned by the Society for the Protection of New Hampshire Forests. It was purchased by John Glessner, co-founder of Chicago-based International Harvester equipment in 1882. The Glessner family owned the property until 1978 when they donated it to the SPNH. John Glessner's daughter, Frances Glessner Lee is considered the pioneer of forensic criminology with, *The Nutshell Studies of Unexplained Death*". Her famous crime scene dioramas are still used today to train forensic scientists. The only crime scene diorama available for the public to view is located at the Bethlehem Historical Society building on Main street. The Rocks Estate is also home to the New Hampshire Maple Experience Museum.

This author researched and proposed a New Hampshire historical marker for "The Mother of Forensic Science"- Frances Glessner Lee. The marker was approved and will be installed during the summer of 2018. Come visit one of the newest markers at the intersection of US Rte 302 & Glessner Rd.

Campton

Marker # 0196: Blair Bridge

Location: Blair Bridge Rd & US Route 3 (near exit 27 I-93)

Sign Erected: 2005

GPS Coordinates- N 43° 48'.621″ W 71° 40'.000″

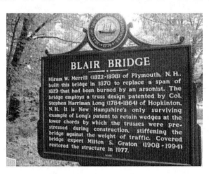

"Hiram W. Merrill (1822-1898) of Plymouth, N.H., built this bridge in 1870 to replace a span of 1829 that had been burned by an arsonist. The bridge employs a truss design patented by Col. Stephen Harriman Long (1784- 1864) of Hopkinton, N.H. It is New Hampshire's only surviving example of Long's patent to retain wedges at the lower chords by which the trusses were pre-stressed during construction, stiffening the bridge against the weight of traffic. Covered bridge expert Milton S. Graton (1908-1994) restored the structure in 1977."

In researching Blair Bridge, a notable distinction is this bridge is more than 292 feet long, the second longest covered bridge entirely within one state. This bridge spans the Pemigewasset River which originates in Franconia Notch and flows south to Franklin, NH. The Cornish-Windsor covered bridge (marker #0158) is the longest span at more than 449 feet and spans from New Hampshire to Vermont. The Bath covered bridge is the largest span within the boundaries of New Hampshire of 374 feet. Campton is home to three covered bridges. The other two Campton covered bridges are Turkey Jim's bridge on Old Stephans Rd, and the Bump covered bridge on Bump Rd.

Campton was granted by colonial Governor Benning Wentworth in 1761 to Captain Jabez Spencer. Captain Spencer died before the terms of the grant could be made which required fifty families to settle. The land was granted under a new charter by colonial Governor John Wentworth to two families in 1767. The town's name came to be when the two families (Fox and Taylor) camped here to survey the land.

Campton is the gateway to the White Mountains region. This beautiful town is loaded with amenities to satisfy travelers to the White Mountains Today, Campton is a destination for outdoor enthusiasts with access to hiking, snowmobiling, and climbing trails nearby.

Carroll

Marker # 0030: The Crawford Family

Location: US Route 302 and Base Station Rd (Fabyans Restaurant) Mile Marker 39.2

Sign Erected: 1965/1998

GPS Coordinates- N 44° 15'.790″ W 71° 27'.475

"For whom the Notch is named, included Abel and his sons, Thomas J. and Ethan Allen. They established the first regional hotels and pioneered in opening the White Mountain area to the public. Ethan and his wife, Lucy Howe Crawford, author of an 1846 history of the region, are buried in a nearby cemetery."

The Crawford family first settled this wilderness north of the notches when patriarch Abel Crawford built his first log cabin on this site in 1792. Abel Crawford sold this cabin to his father- in-law Eleazar Rosebrook and resettled his family on the southside of White Mountain Notch (now known as Crawford Notch).

Over the years, travelers would stay at the homes of both Rosebrook and Crawford. As early as 1819, Abel and his son, Ethan Allen began construction of a carriage path to allow access to the summit of Mount Washington. To this day, the path is known as Crawford Path and has a trailhead across from the Appalachian Mountain Club's Highland Center at the summit of Crawford Notch on US Route 302.

By 1830, the Crawford family homes at White Mountain Notch (now the AMC Highland Center), here at Fabyan, and Eleazer Rosebrook's home in Hart's Location became a chain of family homes which were open to travelers. Many visitors came and stayed at "houses" of the Crawford Family and were guided up to the summit of Mount Washington by Ethan Allen Crawford. The Crawford family were the first full- service resort operators in the region.

Crawford Notch is one of the most beautiful of the notches to travel in New Hampshire. Traveling this route in any season is picturesque and breathtaking. Be sure to stop and take in the vistas. It is worth the trip. Winter provides world class ice-climbing, fall is the premier season with stellar foliage. All seasons draw hikers to enjoy the many trails.

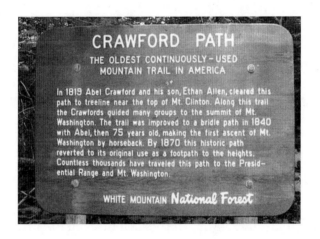

Carroll

Marker # 0030: Crawford House

Location: US Route 302 at the Appalachian Mountain Club's Highland Center (Summit of Crawford Notch)

Sign Erected: 1972

GPS Coordinates-N 44° 13'.082″ W 71° 24'.662″

"Abel Crawford and his son, Ethan Allen Crawford, built the first Crawford House in 1829. It was run by Ethan's brother, Thomas, until sold in 1852. Fires in 1854 and 1859 destroyed the original inn and a replacement. Col. Cyrus Eastman erected the third and present Crawford House. It opened July 1859 to continue a tradition of hospitality to White Mountain visitors. Among them have been Daniel Webster, Nathaniel Hawthorne, John Greenleaf Whittier and Presidents Pierce, Grant, Hayes, Garfield and Harding."

The Crawford family history in this region is deeply rooted. As stated on this marker, two former Crawford House inns have been destroyed by fire. The marker states the present Crawford House was rebuilt and opened in 1859. However, the marker was installed in 1972. On November 20, 1977 the Crawford House built by Colonel Cyrus Eastman burned to the ground. The current building is the Appalachian Mountain Club (AMC) Highland Center which was built in 2007 and located on the grounds of the former Crawford House. The Highland center offers lodging, dining, outdoor merchandise and history adorning its walls. If you visit during the summer and fall months, the Crawford Notch depot is also open with a visitor's center.

A few miles south on US Route 302 (mile marker 46) is the Willey House which is operated by the New Hampshire State Park system. The Willey family operated an inn open for travelers at the foot of what is now Mount Willey. After a rain-soaked summer, a landslide engulfed their property killing Samuel Willey, his wife, their five children and two hired hands. Ironically, the house was spared any damage due to boulders uphill from the home diverting the debris. The family left the home for safety and perished. Folklore states that the interior of the home was unscathed. Once the tragedy was reported in distant cities, curiosity seekers traveled to Crawford Notch to witness the remains of the Willey home. The current location has a marker noting the spot of the home and the boulders that diverted the debris are marked.

THE CRAWFORD HOUSE AND SACO LAKE FROM ELEPHANT'S HEAD. At Crawford's Notch in the White Mountains a huge boulder shaped like the head of an elephant towers 100 ft. above the roadway. One of New Hampshire's natural curiosities.

Carroll

Marker # 0122: Mount Washington Hotel/ Bretton Woods Monetary Conference

Location: US Route 302 at the scenic view turnout (mile marker 40)

Sign Erected: 1978/2009

GPS Coordinates- N 44° 15'.209" W 71° 26'.927"

"Standing to the east, the Mount Washington Hotel was completed in 1902 as one of the largest, most modern grand hotels in the White Mountains, one of the few built in a single campaign. Designed by New York architect Charles Alling Gifford (1861-1937), the hotel was financed by Concord, N.H. native Joseph Stickney (1840-1903), an industrialist who had purchased 10,000 acres here in 1881. Served by as many as 57 trains a day, the Mount Washington Hotel became known as one of the most luxurious summer resorts in the United States. It was designated a National Historic Landmark in 1986."

"This site in the town of Carroll, named "Bretton Woods" in 1903 to recall the original land grant of 1772, was chosen in July 1944 as the location of one of the most important meetings of the 20th century. Convened by the allied nations before the end of WWII and attended by representatives of 44 countries, the Bretton Woods Conference established regulations for the international monetary system following the war. The conference created the

International Monetary Fund and the future World Bank and linked the exchange rate of world currencies to the value of gold."

The history of the Mount Washington Hotel and the amount of history associated with this property is astounding. This is by far my most favorite topic to share. Complete books have been written of the Grande Dame of the White Mountains. I know that I cannot cover enough to give it the credit it deserves. My advice is to take an hour to visit this New Hampshire gem. The interior is a living museum. The walls are full of photos and paintings of this property. A couple of "must see" points include the "Gold Room" where the Bretton Woods Conference agreement was signed. The room has many photos of that historic event. Another fun "must see" is the "Hole in the Wall" in the basement. This was a speakeasy during the prohibition.

Lastly, a building with the history of the Mount Washington also has its' own ghost stories. One is the spirit of Princess Carolyn Stickney, the bride of railroad magnate and builder Joseph Stickney. Mr. Stickney spared no expense in the construction of the hotel. In 1900, he hired Italian stoneworkers and other craftsmen to complete this magnificent hotel in 18 months. Sadly, Mr. Stickney died shortly after completion in 1903.

Carolyn Stickney operated the hotel and was considered an elegant and shrewd hotelier. While vacationing in southern France, Carolyn Stickney fell in love and married a French prince, and was affectionately known as Princess Stickney.

Princess Caroline lived in an apartment in the mezzanine level of the hotel. She sat behind a curtain at her balcony and observed the attire of the lady guests. Folklore states that she observed whether her guests had gowns more elegant than hers. She was believed to have changed her attire multiple times in one evening to have the most elegant. Near the check-in desk, visitors can look up and see a painting of Princess Stickney at a balcony looking down towards her guests (is she looking at you?)

As for ghosts, Princess Caroline is the most famous at this hotel. Her spirit is believed to be in room 314 (Princess Room). In this room is her four-post bed and some of her original furnishings. Caroline Stickney loved her four-post bed. So much so, that she slept in it every evening and even had it disassembled when she traveled. Princess Caroline Stickney died in Rhode Island in the bed which is now in room 314. Don't worry, they say her spirit is friendly! She is buried in Concord New Hampshire next to her first love, Joseph Stickney.

Carroll

Marker # 0233: Zealand and James Everell Henry

Location: US Route 302 (mile marker 37)

Sign Erected: 2013

GPS Coordinates- N 44° 15'.937″ W 71° 29'.953″

"The village of Zealand grew up in 1875 to serve the logging industry. Henry owned 10,000 acres in the heart of the White Mtns., with a 10-mile railroad to move logs from forest to sawmill. The village had a post office, school, store, housing, and charcoal kilns to eke out every bit of forest value. Depending on the season, the logging business employed 80-250 men. By 1885, Henry left the Valley moving on to Lincoln, leaving the area mostly clear cut. From 1886-1903, fires destroyed the valley and village."

It difficult to fathom that so much of the White Mountains National Forest was once clear-cut land. Zealand is one of many abandoned logging towns that existed solely for harvesting logs. A typical company-town, everything a worker needed from housing, schools, stores, were owned by the logging company to accommodate their workers. Much of what you see on-site now is the campground, trailheads to 4,000 ft peaks and numerous trails, and wilderness. If you explore the riverbed in front of you, do not be surprised if you find remnants of logging rail beds from a bygone era.

Much like the other abandoned logging towns such as Willowdale, Alderbrook, Wildwood (these are just those who have historic markers) once the land was stripped of the logs, the company uprooted and went to a new location. In the case of Zealand, when the timber was all harvested the Henry logging company moved to Lincoln Woods and set up logging operations in the Pemigewasset Wilderness area. Today, Lincoln Woods is part of the US Forest Service and has a popular trail along the former railbed of the logging railroad. Hikers will also recognize the railroad ties still embedded along the trail deep inside the Pemigewasset Wilderness Area. It is hard to believe this pristine wilderness area was once heavily logged and full of workers.

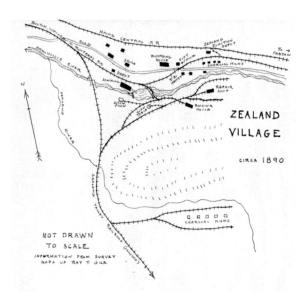

photo from book *White Mountain History*

Conway

Marker # 0038: White Mountain School of Art

Location: US Route 302/Route 16 (Intervale Scenic Vista Center)

Sign Erected: 1966

GPS Coordinates- N 44° 04'.533″ W 71° 08'.367″

"Since Thomas Cole's visit in 1828, New Hampshire's splendid scenery has been an enduring inspiration to countless landscape artists. From 1850 to 1890 this region was particularly favored for their easels. Benjamin Champney (1817-1907), New Hampshire-born painter, described the glorious era in "Sixty Years of Art and Artists"."

Champney's book, "*Sixty Years of Art and Artists*" (1900) illustrates the natural beauty that abounds in the New Hampshire White Mountains region. The easily accessible White Mountains became a favorite destination for artists seeking landscape favorable of their expression of nature's splendor. According to the website *White Mountain Art & Artists,* many artists learned of the beauty of the area during the tragedy of the Willey family in Harts Location. Curiosity seekers traveled north after the mountain landslide killed the Willey family and two hired men. Depicting the mountains in their art, hundreds of artists traveled to the White Mountains region to capture the wild and beauty of this newly settled wilderness.

Conway is a four-season destination for tourists, shoppers, and adventure seekers. Climbers are drawn to the world-class challenges of the Cathedral and Whitehorse ledges. Ice climbers are seen each winter in Crawford Notch. The Saco River is a magnet for rafting, fishermen, and canoeist. It is not uncommon to see hundreds of folks floating down the Saco River on a hot summer day on inner tubes.

Easton

Marker # 0200: Wildwood

Location: NH Route 112/Tunnel Brook Road 3/10 mile east of NH Route 116

Sign Erected: 2006

GPS Coordinates-N 44° 05'.532″ W 71° 49'.584″

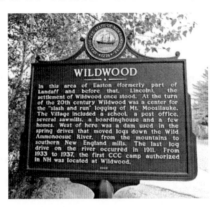

"In this area of Easton (formerly part of Landaff and before that, Lincoln), the settlement of Wildwood once stood. At the turn of the 20th century Wildwood was a center for the 'slash and run' logging of Mt. Moosilauke. The Village included a school, a post office, several sawmills, a boardinghouse and a few homes. West of here was a dam used in the spring drives that moved logs down the Wild Ammonoosuc River, from the mountains to southern New England mills. The last log drive on the river occurred in 1911. From 1933 to 1937, the first CCC camp authorized in NH was located at Wildwood."

This marker is the 200th to be installed in New Hampshire since the program's inception in 1955. According to the New Hampshire Department of Cultural Resources (www.nh.gov/nhculture), this marker was sponsored by Eunice Woods. Ms. Woods was 84-years old and is believed to be the last living person who remembers this settlement in its existence. Eunice shared with the gathered crowd stories expressed by the loggers of Wildwood. Eunice Woods grandfather was the owner of the general store at Wildwood. Ms. Woods shared how the logs were driven down the Wild Ammonoosuc to the Connecticut River where they were destined for sawmills further south.

If you travel east from this point, the views of rugged Kinsman Notch and famous local attraction Lost River. The Appalachian Trail crosses this highway (locally known as Lost River Rd) at Beaver Pond. If time allows, a stop at Lost River is worth the time. Owned by the Society for the Protection of New Hampshire Forests, this attraction has an intriguing history in its discovery, as well as the excitement of exploring this glacial creation that was first discovered by the Lyman brothers in 1852.

Franconia

Marker # 0009: Stone Iron Furnace

Location: NH Route 116 north of Franconia Village

Sign Erected: 1962

GPS Coordinates- N 44° 13'.802″ W 71° 45'.271″

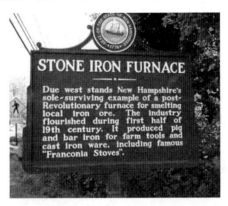

"Due west stands New Hampshire's sole surviving example of a post-Revolutionary furnace for smelting iron ore. The industry flourished during first half of 19th century. It produced pig iron and bar iron for farm tools and cast iron ware, including famous 'Franconia Stoves'."

Iron ore was first discovered in this area in 1805. Franconia had two iron ore smelters at the beginning of the 19th century. This location was known as "Lower Works". This smelter was in operation from 1807 to the 1880's. The iron ore was mined in neighboring Sugar Hill (at Ore Hill) and shipped here by oxen cart. It is believed this location was established due to its proximity to the mine as well as accessibility to water where a dam was made just upstream to power the bellows to fire this furnace. This smelter made pig iron which was commonly used by blacksmiths, as well as the rare Franconia cast iron stove, kettles and other metal ware. There is a small museum on site with interesting artifacts of this furnace. Please keep in mind that the furnace structure is on private property and visitors must remain on the marker side of the river.

Franconia is a lovely community to walk around, get a coffee and simply relax. Many visitors come to ski at Cannon Mountain or take the first tramway in the country to the summit of Cannon Mountain. At the tram parking lot is the New England Ski Museum. Just up NH Route 116 is the summer home of Poet Laureate Robert Frost. Each year, Dartmouth College has a poet-in-residence who summers in the home which is open to visitors. The Frost House is located at 158 Ridge Road. There a many accessible hiking trails within miles of this location. Take the time to explore this beautiful town.

Harts Location

Marker # 0186: Sawyer's Rock / Crawford Notch Road

Location: US Route 302 (mile marker 55.2 Sawyer Rock Picnic Area)

Sign Erected: 2003

GPS Coordinates-N 44° 04'.553″ W 71° 19'.684″

"In 1771, Timothy Nash of Lancaster and Benjamin Sawyer of Conway made a bargain with Governor John Wentworth to bring a horse through Crawford Notch in order to prove the route's commercial value. The pair succeeded by dragging and lowering the animal down rock faces. Sawyer's Rock is said to be the last obstacle they encountered before reaching the Bartlett intervales. Nash and Sawyer were rewarded with a 2,184-acre parcel at the northern end of the Notch. Sawyer's Rock symbolizes the determination and foresight that helped open and develop trade and travel into the White Mountains Region."

"Between 1771 and 1785, a rough road through Crawford Notch was constructed to facilitate trade and travel. In the early 1800's, the Tenth New Hampshire Turnpike was built along the old road, from Bartlett through the Notch. Spurred on by tourism in the White Mountains, the turnpike became Route 18, a part of the 1903 state highway system. During the 1920's, the state road was incorporated into the Theodore Roosevelt Highway, a

transcontinental roadway. Reminders are evident along today's US Route 302, which is part of the White Mountain Trail, a National Scenic Byway."

According to *"Hart's Location in Crawford Notch" (1997)* by Marion L. Varney, Sawyer's Rock was significantly large and required blasting to get a passable road through. Varney also claims that this rock was originally located closer to the Saco River. A view of the surrounding area will lead the observer to notice considerable rock on the east side of the road. Much of Sawyer rock has been removed to allow construction of the road. The site where this picnic area is located was built by the Civilian Conservation Corps in 1933.

Hart's Location holds the dubious title of New Hampshire's smallest town. Yankee magazine reporters visited the smallest towns in each of the New England states. At the time, Hart's Location had a population of 23 residents. Hart's Location is a popular four seasons destination. In the summer, many visitors stop along US Route 302 to swim in the popular pools of the Saco River. In the winter, many thrill seekers are seen ice climbing on the western cliffs of Crawford Notch. In the Fall, this drive through Crawford Notch has some of the most spectacular foliage in the entire State. Other popular destinations in Hart's Location are Arethusa Falls (New Hampshire's highest waterfall that is more than 200 feet drop (mile marker 48.5); and the Willey House Historic Site (mile marker 46).

Just north of this point is Sawyer River road. About 2 miles up this road is the ghost town of Livermore. Livermore was established in 1874, ceased operations in 1931 and the property ownership was transferred to the US government to be incorporated into the White Mountains National Forest in 1951. Once a thriving company town for logging, the only remnants that remain are cellar holes, train bridge abutments, powerhouse foundation, and machinery parts from the former saw mill. Additional information about this ghost town can be viewed on www.whitemountainhistory.org

Harts Location

Marker # 0213: Frankenstein Trestle

Location: US Route 302 (mile marker 48.7)

Sign Erected: 2009

GPS Coordinates- N 44° 09'.366″ W 71° 21'.811″

"The high steel trestle above was built in 1893 to replace a wrought iron trestle of 1875, and was strengthened in 1930 and 1950. Name for American artist Godfrey N. Frankenstein (1820-1873), the adjacent cliff and gulf were formidable barriers to completion of the Portland and Ogdensburg Railroad, later the Maine Central, which connected Portland, ME, and the Great Lakes. Trains used the trestle until 1983. It now carries excursion trains through Crawford Notch."

Creating a major rail line from the eastern seaboard to the Great Lakes was a major undertaking with significant financial costs of approximately three million dollars. The trestle and surrounding cliffs were named by Dr. Samuel Bemis who resided in the current Notchland Inn. He suggested the trestle and cliffs be named for his friend Godfry Frankenstein. Godfry Frankenstein immigrated from Germany to the United States in 1831. Frankenstein was an accomplished artist whose paintings included Niagara Falls, and local Crawford Notch scenery. Frankenstein was a noted artist at the White Mountain School of

Art (see Historical Marker #0038 in Conway) An interesting fact, Frankenstein never had the chance to visit the trestle or cliffs. He was aware of his friend Dr. Bemis' intent to name the trestle after him. He died in 1873, two years before its' completion.

The photo of the bridge above is of an antique postcard I have of the trestle. I have attempted to take appealing photos of the trestle and it was not as easy as I had anticipated. The Frankenstein Trestle is difficult to see from the vantage point of the marker with the leaves on the trees. The trestle is across the street from this marker. Access to this trestle can be made via the Frankenstein Cliff trail which passes underneath the trestle. Or, park at the Arethusa Falls lot and make the ½ hike to the trestle. The views are daunting, yet spectacular.

Haverhill

Marker # 0056: Rogers Rangers

Location: NH Route 10 (mile marker 121.2)

Sign Erected: 1968

GPS Coordinates- N 44° 07'.658″ W 72° 01'.986″

"The rivers junction two miles north was rendezvous for Rogers Rangers after their destruction of St. Francis, Que., October 4, 1759. Pursuing Indians and starvation had plagued their retreat and more tragedy awaited here. The expected rescue party bringing food had come and gone. Many Rangers perished and early settlers found their bones along these intervales."

Rogers Rangers was named for the colonial company of men under the command of Major Robert Rogers. Rogers Rangers were attached to the British Army during the French and Indian War (Seven Years War). Major Rogers training of his Rangers included "Rogers Rules of Ranging". These twenty-eight rules are the predecessor for the modern-day U.S. Army Rangers. Rogers training included wearing green uniforms as camouflage and using Indian fighting tactics.

The notoriety for Rogers Rangers were their skill as frontiersmen who specialized in unconventional warfighting methods. This form of warfighting is also known as guerilla or special operations warfare. New Hampshire hero General John Stark began his military career as a captain for Rogers Rangers.

In my research, the attack on the Indian encampment at St. Francis, Quebec was amplified when Major Rogers witnessed the hundreds of scalps collected by the Indians of St. Francis. After killing the Indians and destroying the village, Major Rogers Rangers endured countless Indian ambushes. The risk of death and lack of food and supplies is a story of enduring hardship.

Folklore suggests that nine rangers escaped back to northern New Hampshire after pillaging a 10-pound silver statue of the Virgin Mary and Christ child, plus other precious artifacts. Eight rangers died, and the lone survivor did not have any of the relics with him. Today, treasure hunters search for the missing relics known as the Lost Treasure of St. Francis.

Haverhill

Marker # 0104: Ebenezer Mackintosh (1737-1816)

Location: NH Route 10 (mile marker 119.5) & Horse Meadow Rd.

Sign Erected: 1975

GPS Coordinates- N 44° 06'.368″ W 72° 02'.142″

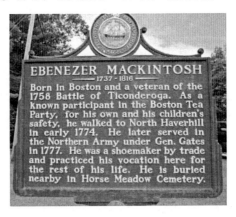

"Born in Boston and a veteran of the 1758 Battle of Ticonderoga. As a known participant in the Boston Tea Party, for his own and his children's safety, he walked to North Haverhill in early 1774. He later served in the Northern Army under Gen. Gates in 1777. He was a shoemaker by trade and practiced his vocation here for the rest of his life. He is buried nearby in Horse Meadows Cemetery."

Ebenezer Mackintosh was born June 20, 1737 and raised in the South End of Boston. He apprenticed and became a shoemaker which was regarded as a lower economic trade. Mackintosh gained fame and popularity as a voice for the common man of Boston. Mackintosh was a rebel leader against the infamous Stamp Act of 1765. As a mob leader against British oppression, Mackintosh built his reputation as common man's leader and led numerous riots against the British.

Ebenezer Mackintosh moved his family to North Haverhill for the safety of his family from the British and loyalists. He continued his trade as a shoemaker here in Haverhill and lived a relatively quiet life. The cemetery where Ebenezer Mackintosh is buried is close to this marker. Turn right at this sign and the older section of the cemetery is on the right.

The Town of Haverhill has significant history for this region. Incorporated in 1763, the settlement was the terminus of the colonial provincial road from the seacoast to points north and west. The fertile lands adjacent to the Connecticut river were prime for farming. The Connecticut river was the major route for shipping goods from southern New England to northern settlements. In 1773, Haverhill became the county seat for Grafton county. The town of Haverhill is comprised of six distinct villages with the largest being Woodsville. Woodsville was a major railroad center for the region throughout the 19th and early 20th century.

Haverhill

Marker # 0136: The Bedell Bridge

Location: Off NH Route 10 (mile marker 114)-dirt road (880 Meadow Lane) west to River follow signs for Bedell Bridge State Park.

Sign Erected: 1979/1980

GPS Coordinates- N 44° 02'.690″ W 72° 04'.406″

"The last of five 19th century bridges which have existed at this location was erected in 1866 by a local entrepreneur, Moody Bedell, who had operated a ferry service here prior to the first bridge in 1805. The 396-foot structure was the largest surviving example of a two-span covered bridge utilizing Burr truss and timber arch design. Following several years of human effort which corrected decades of deterioration, the newly-restored landmark was destroyed by a violent windstorm on September 14, 1979."

First, this marker is a bit tricky to locate. As you travel south on NH Route 10 turn right onto a dirt road (Meadow Lane). Follow signs to Bedell Bridge State Park. This State Park Historic site is a wonderful break area for a picnic. There is also a boat launch onsite. As I toured the state to find these markers, this is one of the few that is not installed directly along a New Hampshire highway shoulder.

This marker has a connection with the Republic of Indian Stream marker located in Pittsburg. Moody Bedell was one of first surveyors and title bearers for the settling of the land north of the 45th parallel, which is now Pittsburg. Moody Bedell was a local businessman who operated a ferry across the Connecticut River from this location to Bradford, Vermont. The charter for the construction of this bridge was made June 16, 1802 alongside Bedell's Ferry launch site. The New Hampshire State Parks website also states that The Bedell Bridge was at one time the second longest two-span bridge in the United States. The bridge was funded by the sale of one hundred shares which Moody Bedell owned thirty-five. Moody Bedell conveyed his rights to the ferry to the bridge company for $900.

Today, visitors can launch a canoe or kayak from this site. It is also a quiet spot for a picnic. The Bedell Bridge site was listed on the National Register of Historic Places in 1975.

Haverhill

Marker # 0160: Haverhill Corner Historic District

Location: NH Route 10 (mile marker 113.6) & Court St.

Sign Erected: 1990

GPS Coordinates- N 44° 02'.059″ W 72° 03'.813″

"National Register of Historic Places, 1987 Town of Haverhill Granted, 1763

"The Corner" was part of a mile-wide strip of land claimed by both Haverhill and Piermont, and finally divided between them. Haverhill Corner's architecture reflects its history as Grafton County seat (1793-1891), home of Haverhill Academy (founded 1794), and northern end of the first Province Road from the coast (later the Coos Turnpike, now Court Street). Col. Charles Johnston settled here in 1769 and promoted village growth. His house and Gov. John Page's still stand, with other notable dwellings, taverns, church, library, and school buildings."

One of the six villages of Haverhill, Haverhill Corner is always enjoyable to stop and appreciate for its beauty. The Corner is comprised of sixty-eight buildings within the district. The number of Georgian and Federal-style homes and buildings located in this small village are in wonderful condition. This village gives the visitor the idea what this community looked like in the late 18th and early 19th century. Once the terminus of the first Province Road that spanned from Durham at the seacoast through the Lakes Region (see Old Province Road marker in Gilmanton) to the Connecticut River. The Corner was inhabited by lawyers, doctors and other professionals. The first Province Road continued to be the major route for points west from the seacoast until the advent of the railroad. When the railroad network was built, the village of Woodsville became the new hub of activity for the town of Haverhill.

The former courthouse built in 1840 is now the public library. The Congregational church was built in 1827. The town was granted in 1763 by colonial Governor Benning Wentworth and was known as Lower Cohos. The village of Haverhill Corner was listed on the National Register of Historic Places on August 17, 1987.

Haverhill

Marker # 0190: Haverhill-Bath Bridge

Location: NH 135 & US Route 302 intersection (NH Covered Bridge #27) in Woodsville Village.

Sign Erected: 2005

GPS Coordinates- N 44° 09'.188″ W 72° 02'.200″

"Constructed in 1829 by the towns of Bath and Haverhill at a cost of about $2,400, this is one of the oldest covered bridges in the United States. Built with 3-by-10-inch planks that were probably sawn at an adjacent mill, the span is the earliest surviving example of the lattice bridge truss that was patented in 1820 by Connecticut architect Ithiel Town (1784-1844). The bridge was strengthened with laminated wooden arches in 1921-22, and the upstream sidewalk was added at about the same time. The 256-foot-long bridge carried traffic for 170 years before being bypassed in 1999."

One of the wonderful aspects of living in New Hampshire is the many covered bridges. The Haverhill-Bath bridge is a nice place to stop and watch the water of the Ammonoosuc River pass over the rocks during the spring runoff, or in the fall with the colorful backdrop. According to the New Hampshire Department Natural and Cultural Resources, this is the only bridge built at this location and remains generally the same as originally built. The bridge built at the confluence of the Ammonoosuc and Connecticut Rivers connected NH Route 135 from Bath to the north and NH Route 135 in Woodsville on the south side of the river.

In March 1827 at the town meeting, residents of Bath selected Ira Goodall, Samuel Minot, and Samuel Hutchins as a committee to meet with the selectmen of Haverhill regarding the construction and site of the bridge. September of 1828 the town of Bath allotted $300 for the purchase of stone and timber for this bridge. The bridge was completed in 1829.

The covered bridge survived many mishaps. In 1927, a severe flood caused a large tree trunk floating downstream to pierce the side of the lattice on the bridge. During that flood, a barn floating down the river rammed into the side of the bridge. In September of 1983 the bridge was the site of an unsuccessful arson attempt. Thankfully, the bridge survived.

This bridge was listed on the National Register of Historic Places on April 18, 1977.

Jefferson

Marker # 0019: Thaddeus S.C. Lowe (1823-1913)

Location: U.S. Route 2 (mile marker 5.2) & Turnpike Rd.

Sign Erected: 1964

GPS Coordinates- N 44° 26'.726″ W 71° 31'.726″

"Born nearby, this inventor and scientist gained unique distinction as a pioneer aeronaut in the United States. He organized and directed a military balloon force during the Civil War and later invented a number of important and basic devices for use in atmospheric observation and metallurgical processing."

According to *Men of Granite* (2007) by William McGee, Thaddeus S. C. Lowe was self-educated and a self-proclaimed professor. Born August 20, 1832, he was one of six children and his mother died when he was ten. He ran away at the age of 11 and traveled for two years working for food and shelter along the way until he arrived in Portland Maine. During his travels, he heard of an airship crossing the Atlantic Ocean and thus began his fascination with ballooning.

Lowe designed and built large balloons for human travel. In June 1861, Lowe's balloon design was selected by the Union Army for reconnaissance of Confederate troop movements. Lowe observed the battlefield of Fair Oaks in his balloon "Intrepid" in

1862. This moment is commemorated on the Town of Jefferson's Bicentennial postal envelope 1796-1996 (pictured below). One of Lowe's most impressive inventions was the altimeter for use during flight. Lowe also sent the first telegraph message via a balloon on June 18, 1861. This message was sent directly from Lowe at an elevation of 500 feet to the White House and War Department.

Lowe's contribution to aviation did not go unnoticed. In 1960, the US Army named the airfield at Fort Rucker Alabama the Lowe Army Airfield (McGee, 2007). Thaddeus Lowe is also credited for making the first compression ice machine in 1865. For a relatively unknown native Granite-Stater, Thaddeus S. C. Lowe has made a significant impact in history.

Jefferson

Marker # 0152: Cherry Mountain Slide

Location: NH Route 115 south of NH Route 115A at Owl's Head trailhead parking lot

Sign Erected: 1985

GPS Coordinates- N 44° 21'.613″ W 71° 29'.286″

"On July 10, 1885, at 6 a.m., a slide from Cherry Mountain's northern peak left a deep gash from Owl's Head to the valley. A million tons of boulders, trees and mud loosed by a cloudburst rolled and tumbled a tortuous two miles, destroying Oscar Stanley's new home and his cattle, barn and crops. Farm hand Don Walker, rescued from debris of the barn, died four days later; but Stanley's family was not there and was spared. Excursion trains and carriages brought people from far and wide to view the tragic sight, which has now almost disappeared through nature's healing process."

A friend who I spoke to about this marker is a descendant of Oscar Stanley's neighbor, John Boudreau. In the book, *History of Coos County New Hampshire* (1888) by Georgia Drew Merrill, Boudreau's farm was uphill from Stanley's. Boudreau's farm was spared from the mudslide because of a slight bend in contour of the land and followed the watercourse downhill. Stanley's farm was destroyed and his farmhand, Donald Walker perished. A poem was written of the tragedy which I found in Merrill's book.

"With unearthly roar and din, ripping beard from mountain chin, three thousand feet above the tide, down came the Cherry Mountain slide! Down with awful leap and bound, Down with deafening thunder sound, A million tons in a writhing heap, Tearing its' way through forest steep, rending the mountain deep and wide, Two miles down its throbbing side!". (p. 103).

The Cherry Mountain Slide was dedicated on July 10, 1985 on the centennial of this historic event. However, the current marker was not put into place until December 18, 1985. The town of Jefferson was named for author of the Declaration of Independence, Founding Father of our fledgling country, and president of the United States; Thomas Jefferson. Notably, the town was incorporated as Jefferson in 1796, four years before Thomas Jefferson was sworn in as the 3rd president of the United States.

Jefferson

Marker # 0229: Granny Stalbird, 1755-1845

Location: NH Route 115A ½ mile south from US Route 2 (110 Meadows Rd)

Sign Erected: 2011

GPS Coordinates- N 44° 24'.703″ W 71° 28'.407″

"Known as Granny Stalbird, Deborah Vicker came through Crawford Notch c.1796 as cook for Col. Joseph Whipple. It is said she brought the first bible to the north country. She married Richard Stalbird and settled on land deeded to her by Whipple in payment for her service. She became the region's "doctress," a traveling herbalist who learned native wisdom about plants and healing. Stories of her knowledge, bravery, and dedication to settlers of this new frontier are part of the history of White Mountain settlement."

The property where this marker is located had been in the Stalbird family for more than four generations. Colonel Joseph Whipple, son of William Whipple a signer of the Declaration of Independence, was the first deeded land grant holder for what is now Jefferson. Prior to 1796, the land grant was known as Dartmouth. Colonel Whipple was a successful businessman, harbormaster and customs agent from Portsmouth.

Deborah "Granny Stalbird" Vicker was born in the Portsmouth area May 21, 1755. While living in Portsmouth, she met and agreed to work for Colonel Whipple and was the second woman to settle in the town. Whipple attempted to pay Stalbird with Continental currency which was nearly worthless. She argued sternly for compensation, where Whipple agreed and deeded to her fifty acres. Research suggests that this current property was the second parcel of land she received from Whipple since the first parcel was bog land and not worthy for farming.

Granny Stalbird traveled the north country on horseback providing medical care to all. As a caregiver in the north country, Granny Stalbird is believed to have traveled as far west as the Connecticut river and east to the Maine border. Granny Stalbird is believed to have been the first female doctor in New Hampshire.

From this vantage point, it is evident of the splendid beauty of this region. A drive through the town provides excellent scenic vistas. Continue south on NH 115A and you will enjoy a vantage point of Mount Waumbek to the north and the Presidential Range of the White Mountains.

Lincoln

Marker # 0224: Betty and Barney Hill Incident

Location: US Route 3 North Lincoln next to Indian Head Resort

Sign Erected: 2011

GPS Coordinates- N 44° 05'.129″ W 71° 41'.058″

"On the night of September 19-20, 1961, Portsmouth, NH couple Betty and Barney Hill experienced a close encounter with an unidentified flying object and two hours of "lost" time while driving south on Rte 3 near Lincoln. They filed an official Air Force Project Blue Book report of a brightly-lit cigar-shaped craft the next day, but were not public with their story until it was leaked in the Boston Traveler in 1965. This was the first widely-reported UFO abduction report in the United States."

The story of the abduction of the Hill's is a vivid memory of my childhood. While I was not born yet in 1961, the investigation into the depiction made by the Hill's had captured the attention of the country in the late 1960's and early 1970's. I remember watching a television movie entitled, *The UFO Incident* in 1975. Knowing the story occurred in my backyard of New Hampshire made it even more fascinating; even at the age of ten, I loved New Hampshire's history!

A book that I had recently read detailing the recollection made by the Hill's is, *Captured! The Betty and Barney Hill UFO Experience (2007).* An interesting tidbit I learned in researching this topic, was the Hill's alien abduction incident was a focal point in an episode of the television series *X-Files.*

Prior to the construction of Interstate 93, travelers used US Route 3 to points north. This segment of US route 3 was a busy highway. One can imagine how much of a destination North Lincoln and North Woodstock were during its' heyday. Now with the extension of I-93, it is not necessary to travel this segment of highway. But, traveling this highway north to Franconia Notch is worthy because it is here where you can view the Indian Head rock formation from this marker. For a small entrance fee, you can pay to climb the observation tower owned by the Indian Head Resort. The views from here not only allow impeccable views of Indian Head, but the views of Mount Liberty, Mount Flume and views into Franconia Notch are postcard worthy. You will not regret it.

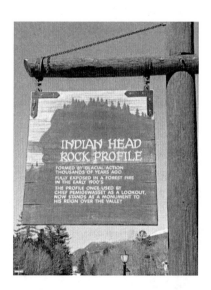

Lisbon

Marker # 0070: Old Coal Kiln

Location: US Route 302 1.8 miles north of NH Route 117 (mile marker 14.7)

Sign Erected: 1970 in cooperation with the Lisbon Historical Society

GPS Coordinates-N 44° 14'.937″ W 71° 51'.330″

"A reminder of bygone days, this stone structure was used to make wood into charcoal for the nearby iron smelters. Pine knots, a waste material from the adjacent lumber mill, were a prime source for charcoal. Charcoal production through this kiln, built in the 1860s, was necessary to the iron mining industry."

During the 19th century, timber was the major industry of the north country. As communities were established, industry such as the mining of iron-ore was found to be lucrative in nearby mines. On Iron Ore road in Sugar Hill, mines were established to fuel two smelters in Franconia (see marker #0009-Stone Iron Furnace). The logging community of Zealand had numerous coal kilns to make charcoal. The charcoal was used to fire furnaces for blacksmiths and other furnaces requiring a hot, steady heat source. The Lisbon coal kiln located near the Ammonoosuc River was convenient for the pine knots harvested from the local clear cuts and the shipping of charcoal to the Connecticut River which was the major transportation route for industry.

The ruins of the Old Coal Kiln can be viewed directly across Route 302 from this marker. While the remnants of the old kiln are still there, the base of the kiln is overgrown with vegetation. As you can see from the photo of the Old Coal Kiln, not much remains; but what is left is sadly not cared for.

Littleton

Marker # 0071: Kilburn Brothers Stereoscopic View Factory

Location: Cottage St & Kilburn St.

Sign Erected: 1970

GPS Coordinates- N 44° 18'.195″ W 71° 46'.187″

"Here, from 1867 to 1909, the world-famous Kilburn brothers, Benjamin and Edward, produced and distributed thousands of stereoscopic views. Their collection, largest in the world and collector's items today, provided popular parlor entertainment for generations."

The building at this marker is the third factory that Benjamin Kilburn had in operation. The first two were located on Main street and quickly lacked the space to keep up with the growing business. The factory located on this site was built in 1872. If you look down Cottage street from this location, you will notice how close this site is to the railroad depot. This became an integral means to transport the popular stereoscopic images to all points south. The Littleton Historical Museum has original stereoscopic photos on display. Littleton NH was the #1 producer of stereoscopic photos in the world; imagine that! In my reading of Benjamin Kilburn, it states that he was an avid mountaineer and involved in search and rescue missions on Mount Washington.

If you are to travel west on Main Street and notice a rock ledge to the west of town, that is named the Kilburn Crags. This 1.4-mile hike was rated #1 in the NH Magazine "Best Local Only Hiking Trail" in 2015. The views from this vantage point overlooks the town of Littleton with the Presidential Range of the White Mountains in the background.

While in Littleton, take the time to visit Main street. This is a quintessential New England Main street with shops for everyone's taste. Notable stops include the NH League of Craftsmen store, Chutters, a Guinness World Record store for the longest candy counter which was established in the late 1800's, and the Pollyanna statue on the front lawn of the public library. Behind Main street is the River district with popular stops including Schillings brewery. Littleton New Hampshire was rated the #6 Best Small-Town Downtown in the United States. Plan to spend some time in Littleton, it is a great break during your historic marker touring adventure.

Stereoscopic Photo of the Flume with balancing rock manufactured by the Kilburn Brothers.

Littleton

Marker # 0185: Willowdale Settlement

Location: US Route 302 1.2 miles west of Lowe's (mile marker 17.8)

Sign Erected: 2003

GPS Coordinates- N 44° 16'.738″ W 71° 48'.682″

"Willowdale was established around a sawmill that was built in 1812. The village thrived because sawmills, gristmills, and a factory producing sawmill machinery were powered by the Ammonoosuc River. After the Littleton Lumber Company opened in 1870, the village grew rapidly to include stores, a post office, a school, railroad siding, and a hall. The company employed as many as 60 workers and produced 3 to 6 million board feet yearly until fire destroyed it in 1898. The village never recovered and slowly dwindled away until it disappeared altogether, a fate suffered by other 19th century mill villages."

Much like other logging ghost towns in New Hampshire, Willowdale was a prosperous village in its time. As the marker states, the settlement was centered on the sawmill along the Ammonoosuc River. This sawmill community existed for nearly fifty years. In 1870, three Littleton lumbermen, Isaac Calhoun, Charles Easton and Charles Tarbell formed a partnership and built a sawmill on the east side of the river. This was the start of the Littleton Lumber Company.

The settlement consisted of two sawmills, a school, post office, three stores, four boarding houses and a dance hall. Lumber was shipped in by horses from around the region. In 1889, the railroad hauled logs to this sawmill from as far as Kilkenny (north of Jefferson). A railroad station was built in nearby Lisbon and was named Barrett's Station.

The demise of this settlement was the result of a massive fire in May 1898. Many buildings were destroyed as well as one of the sawmills. Over time, other fires brought the end to the Willowdale settlement. The only remnants that remain is the granite abutment of a bridge that crossed the river in sight of this marker.

Madison

Marker # 0207: Granville Homestead

Location: NH 113 (Village Rd) & East Madison Rd in front of Madison Historical Society

Sign Erected: 2007

GPS Coordinates- N 43° 53'.951″ W 71° 08'.733″

"Nearby is the birthplace of the Granville brothers: Zantford (Granny), Thomas, Robert, Mark and Edward and sisters Pearle and Gladys. With Madison natives Hiram Jones, Harry Jones, and Elson Ward, they formed the Granville Brothers Aircraft Co. in Springfield, Massachusetts, and designed, manufactured and flew notable racing aircraft of the Golden Age of Aviation. In 1932 the Gee Bee Model R-1 set a new world speed record of 296 mph. Their high performance designs represented the cutting edge of technology and dramatically influenced military and civilian aviation."

The Granville brothers grew up in a nearby home on Maple Grove Road. The Granville brothers and fellow residents of Madison formed the Granville Brothers Aircraft manufacturing in 1929. Located in Springfield Massachusetts, the aircraft were considered the fastest planes of their time. Major James (Jimmy) Doolittle set a new world speed record of 296 mph at the National Air Race in Cleveland Ohio in 1931 flying the Gee Bee

Model R-1 plane. In their short time in production, the company designed and manufactured three models of the Gee Bee airframe. Their fame was short-lived, the Granville Brothers Aircraft manufacturing company closed in 1934 due to bankruptcy. The Madison Historical Society is onsite, and their sign informs visitors that hours are 2-4pm on Tuesdays.

Not far this marker is a unique New Hampshire State Park. The Madison Boulder Natural Area is located at 473 Boulder Rd. off NH Route 113 in Madison. It is the largest glacial erratic rock in the United States. Its' dimensions are 23 feet in height, 37 feet wide, and 85 feet wide; and 10 ft of this boulder is under ground level.

 The brochure at the trailhead claims this boulder weighs 5,963 tons. Some literature that I found suggests that this glacial erratic may have come from the cliffs of Mount Willard nearly 25 miles away. The walk from the parking lot to the boulder only takes a few minutes. Madison was incorporated in 1852 and named in honor of President James Madison.

Pinkham's Grant

Marker # 0011: First Ascent of Mount Washington

Location: NH 16 near mile marker 99.6 (east side of road)

Sign Erected: 1963

GPS Coordinates- N 44° 15'.683″ W 71° 14'.829″

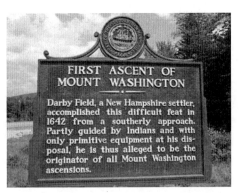

"Darby Field, a New Hampshire settler, accomplished the difficult feat in 1642 from a southerly approach. Partly guided by Indians and with only primitive equipment at his disposal, he is thus alleged to be the originator of all Mount Washington ascensions."

Early history accounts do not express the true intent of Darby Field's ascent of Mount Washington. Some claims were the reflection of the mica at the summit led explorers to believe there was treasure in minerals at the summit. No proof has been made to support this folklore. Other claims are that he climbed it "because it was there"; no one truly knows. What we do know is that Mount Washington is a formidable mountain with great risks. The first recorded death on the mountain was Frederick Strickland in 1851.

The White Mountains, specifically Mount Washington is known for its high alpine terrain as well as world class adventure. With the highest peak in the northeast, many visitors come to summit Mount Washington. The weather experienced in Crawford and Pinkham notches is no reflection of what may be at the summit.

Pinkham's Notch was originally recorded by Jeremy Belknap in 1784. Belknap is credited with authoring the first book of the history of New Hampshire. As you travel north on NH Route 16, the Presidential Range of the White Mountains is to the left including the famous Mount Washington (elevation 6,288) and the Wildcat Mountain range to the east (hence Wildcat Ski Resort). This notch is popular with adventure seekers in every season. Pinkham Notch is the trailhead to many famous locations to include Tuckerman and Huntington ravines. Travel further north and the daring driver may choose to reach the summit via the Mount Washington auto road. You will see hikers year-round as they navigate the Appalachian Trail, skiers enjoying the challenging terrain of Wildcat Mountain, photographers and artist's rendering images of the scenery, and others enjoying the beauty of this notch. A favorite stop for me is Glen Ellis Falls. This short walk on the east side of Route 16 (park on the west side) takes you to the photogenic sixty-four-foot waterfall.

Randolph

Marker # 0220: The Ravine House 1877-1963

Location: Durand Rd (off US Route 2) 1 mile from Durand Rd East

Sign Erected: 2010

GPS Coordinates- N 44° 22'.462″ W 71° 17'.424″

"In 1876 Abel Watson and his son Laban converted their farm on this site, facing King Ravine on Mt. Adams, into a summer boarding house. Enlarged in 1884 and subsequently, the Ravine House became a key institution in opening the northern Presidential Range to trail builders and hikers. At its zenith between the two World Wars, the hotel accommodated some 100 guests, offering tennis courts, a bowling alley, trout fishing, a swimming pond, and hiking. It closed in 1960 and was razed in 1963."

Randolph was first incorporated as a land grant to John Durand in 1772 from colonial Governor John Wentworth. It was originally settled as the township of Durand. In 1824, Governor Levi Woodbury (see historical marker #0043-Francestown) renamed the town Randolph in honor of his longtime friend John Randolph of Virginia. John Randolph was a fervent advocate for state's rights and a descendant of Pocahontas.

Randolph is a community that encompasses the northern Presidential range of the White Mountains. Many hikers begin their hikes of Mount Adams, Mount Madison, and Mount Jefferson from Randolph. The Randolph Mountain Club is a major caretaker of trails along the northern Presidentials. The club has four high alpine shelters which are popular for hikers. The club also maintains an extensive trail system of more than 100 miles throughout their community.

One of my more favorite destinations (speaking as a New Hampshire history fan) is the Pond of Safety and Four Soldiers path. The history states during the Revolutionary War, four Continental soldiers who were captured by the British were paroled to return to their homes and families and not return to fight. Fearing the chance of being arrested as deserters, the four soldiers hid at Pond of Safety until the end of the war. Then it was safe to return home. Randolph is generally a drive through community via US Route 2, but the visitor may be surprised how much this small community has to offer.

309—The Ravine House, Randolph, N. H.

Postcard courtesy of William Jones

Rumney

Marker # 0055: Baker River

Location: 2926 NH Route 25 at the former Rest Area parking lot (mile marker 31.6)

Sign Erected: 1968

GPS Coordinates-N 43° 48'.190″ W 71° 51'.374″

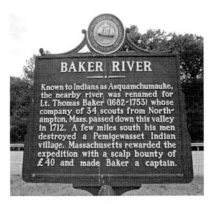

"Known to Indians as Asquamchumauke, the nearby river was renamed for Lt. Thomas Baker (1682-1753) whose company of 34 scouts from Northampton, Mass. passed down this valley in 1712. A few miles south his men destroyed a Pemigewasset Indian village. Massachusetts rewarded the expedition with a scalp bounty of £ 40 and made Baker a captain."

New Hampshire geographical data states that the Baker River is 36.4 miles long and begins at Mount Moosilauke and flows to the Pemigewasset River in Plymouth. During the colonial era, rivers were the most efficient means of travel. The Baker river was a common waterway used by Indians for fishing, travel, and encampments. The river is named after Lieutenant Thomas Baker who led a raiding party of scouts against a local Pemigewasset Indian tribe in 1712.

In early Rumney history, the first white travelers to set foot on this land was on April 28, 1752. The hunting party of Captain John Stark and his brother William were accompanied by

Lieutenant Amos Eastman (son of Jonathan Eastman of Eastman Company fame of Indian Stream Republic) and David Stinson (namesake for Stinson Lake) were captured by Abenaki Indians along the Baker River. David Stinson was killed and scalped, Captain John Stark and Amos Eastman were captured, and William Stark escaped. Stark and Eastman were taken to Quebec, Canada to be ransomed. The ransom was paid the following year and both Stark and Eastman returned to New Hampshire.

Additional details of John Stark's captivity claim Stark not only began to learn the language of his captors but was also respected by his captors. Stark and Eastman were forced to run a gauntlet of Indians with weapons. Stark took a stick from a warrior and challenged to use it against the warrior. The tribe chief was taken by Stark's action and saw him as a brave warrior. Another incident suggests that Stark was told to harvest corn from a local field and he told his captors that he refused because warriors do not do that type of work which is typically relegated to women and children.

Rumney

Marker # 0174: Loveland Bridge

Location: Stinson Lake Rd 3.1 miles from NH Route 25

Sign Erected: 1999

GPS Coordinates-N 43° 50'.314″   W 71° 48'.870″

"The crutch mill of Lewis H. Loveland, Jr., once located below this bridge, operated from 1890 into the early 20th century, when some thirty industries drew water power from the four-mile length of Stinson Brook. Loveland, known as "King of Crutches," sent exports as far away as Africa and Australia. During the World War I period his company manufactured more than 3,000 pairs weekly. Loveland's productivity and that of other local mills gave Rumney distinction as the "Crutch Capital of the World."

In the 1999 Town of Rumney Annual Report, it details the significance of the Loveland Crutch mill and its impact as the "Crutch Capital of the World". The factory was in operation from 1890 into the 1920's. Lewis Loveland Jr. was born in Lincoln New Hampshire and began work in the factory as a young man. He eventually purchased the factory along with his brother, George Loveland.

The drop of elevation from Stinson Lake along Stinson Brook to the Baker River is about 550 feet. This became a major focal point for water- power. In the early twentieth century, more than thirty industries were located along Stinson Brook for the hydro power. While Rumney is now a quiet bedroom community, it is intriguing imagining the industriousness of this town about 100 years ago.

Today, Stinson Lake is a popular destination for locals to go swimming and fishing. Not too far, is Rumney Rocks which is a popular destination for rock climbing enthusiasts of varied levels of experience. While Rumney is no longer an industrial center, those who seek adventure and solitude find Rumney the perfect destination for sport and relaxation.

Sugar Hill

Marker # 0073: First Ski School in America

Location: NH Route 117 and Lover's Lane Road

Sign Erected: 1971

GPS Coordinates- N 44° 13'.531″ W 71° 46'.131″

"In 1929., on the slopes of the hill to the east, Austrian-born Sig Buchmayr established the first organized ski school in the United States. Sponsored by Peckett's~on~Sugar Hill, one of the earliest resorts to promote the joys of winter vacationing in the snow, the school provided an initial impetus to the ski sport America knows today."

So much history of the American ski industry can be attributed to their beginnings here in the White Mountains. Not too long ago, I had read *History of Cannon Mountain: Trails, Tales, and Ski Legends* (2011) by Meghan McPhaul. Chapter one is all about Kate Peckett (daughter of the proprietors Robert and Katherine) and the creation of the first ski school in America. Within view of the iconic Cannon mountain, the Peckett's decided to keep the inn open during the winter months. They provided winter activities that many visitors would enjoy including "tobogganing, snowshoeing, ice-skating and horse-drawn sleigh rides, as well as meals cooked and served outdoors" (p. 13). When Kate Peckett expanded to include ski lessons, she hired Austrian skier

Sig Buchmayr to be the lead instructor. This ski school taught the new form of skiing known as the "Arlberg technique", created in Arlberg, Austria.

The Peckett's~on~Sugar Hill Inn closed in 1967 and was razed in 1969. The ski slope is now covered with trees. So many famous people stayed at this inn during its' heyday, that the list is extensive. I would highly encourage those interested in the birth of the ski industry in the United States to read this fantastic book. The author Meghan McPhaul is a Sugar Hill native who grew up near this marker. Also, at the parking lot of the Cannon Mountain tramway, the New England Ski Museum is free to the public and has some incredible displays from the Tenth Mountain Division to local U.S. Olympian and World Cup Champion Bode Miller. A visit to the New England Ski Museum has an extensive display of the sport of skiing, its origin in the United States and New Hampshire's influence on the sport.

Thornton

Marker # N/A: Andrew C. Robertson Memorial Bridge (1892-1980)

Location: NH Route 49 and Chickenboro Road

Sign Erected: 1981

GPS Coordinates- N 43° 52'.549″ W 71° 35'.400″

"Andy worked the Lincoln Woods and log drives on the Mad, Connecticut, and Androscoggin Rivers; served many years as a U.S. Forest Fire warden receiving a commendation from U.S.D.A. He contributed information for the Farm and Forest Museum. He and Mary raised five children and were foster parents to 21 children. Andy earned the love and respect of all who met him."

Here is my disclaimer. This is not an official New Hampshire roadside marker sponsored by the New Hampshire Department of Historical Resources. In speaking to the NHDHR representative, I was informed that select signs are sponsored solely by municipalities. This sign appears to have been cast at the same Ohio manufacturer used by the NHDHR and using the New Hampshire official marker template.

Andrew C. Robertson lived here in Goose Hollow as early as 1940. Much of the land north of the Lakes Region was prime timberland in the 19th and early 20th century. Lincoln Woods along NH Route 112 was a major logging operation under the management of James Henry. The East Branch and Lincoln railroad extended deep into the Pemigewasset Wilderness area. Today, all that remains is a walking trail that was formerly the railbed and railroad ties still in place along the deep woods trail.

Log drives were the primary means of transporting logs down river to nearby sawmills. The Connecticut and Androscoggin Rivers were the two primary rivers used in log drives in New Hampshire. The only information that I could gather about the Farm and Forest Museum is that it is an interpretative museum for children where visitors can learn of the agricultural heritage of the Connecticut River Valley region.

Warren

Marker # 0231: Norris Cotton, Statesman (1900-1989)

Location: NH Route 25 and NH Route 118 intersection (Warren Village Center)

Sign Erected: 2012

GPS Coordinates- N 43° 55'.505″ W 71° 53'.479″

"In 1973 Norris Cotton celebrated 50 years of elected public service, having served in both the state legislature and Congress. Born in Warren in 1900, Cotton worked his way through Phillips Exeter Academy and Wesleyan University before being elected to the State House in 1922. In 1947 he began writing weekly reports from Congress to his constituents, published in local newspapers. His humble beginnings, rise to power, and consistent connection to New Hampshire's people embodied an American way of life."

Warren is a quaint community in the White Mountains that does not get a lot of attention. Just north on NH Route 25, the Appalachian Trail crosses the highway with a hostel nearby. Warren is also the home of one of the White Mountains 4,000-foot peaks, Mount Moosilauke. Standing in front of this marker you cannot miss the Redstone rocket on display. Not taking anything away from the importance of Senator Cotton, but the story behind this rocket is worth sharing.

The Redstone rocket was purchased in 1971 by local resident Henry Asselin. He purchased it at the Redstone arsenal in Alabama from the United States government. The catch, buyer must pay for transportation. The rocket was donated to Warren in honor of Senator Norris Cotton.

Senator Norris Cotton is remembered for his commitment to his constituents in New Hampshire. A notable point of Senator Cotton's career in politics was that he was the only dissenting vote against the Civil Rights Act of 1964. However, Cotton supported other civil rights acts during his tenure.

Chapter Three

Lakes Region

The Lakes Region is the jewel of central New Hampshire. The namesake is due to the more than 270 lakes and ponds that make up this region. Lake Winnipesaukee is the crown jewel of them all. Lake Winnipesaukee, "The Smile of the Great Spirit" spans more than 72 square miles, has more than 250 islands with its boundaries within Carroll and Belknap counties. From the shores of the "oldest summer resort in America" in Wolfeboro, to the iconic Weirs Beach in Laconia this tourist destination has something for everyone. For history buffs, at the shore of the Weirs Channel at Weirs beach is a monument known as Endicott Rock. Here you will find a granite monument with a rock with inscriptions dated August 1, 1652. This point was believed to be the headwaters of the Merrimack River and northernmost boundary of the Massachusetts Bay Colony under the governorship of John Endicott.

The Lakes Region is a year-round destination. Summer is a major draw for vacationers enjoying the multitude of lakes, ponds, and streams. Fall is popular with visitors enjoying the foliage from shorelines, and peaks in the Sandwich, Ossipee, and Belknap mountain ranges. Winter draws skiers for downhill and Nordic trails, as well as hundreds of ice fishermen in search of the trophy lake trout.

Historically, this region has many sites to remind us of our past from native Indian tribes, to early settlers. There are several estates (and a few castles) that also reminds us of the emphasis made by wealthy summer residents. Properties such as Castle in the Clouds in Moultonborough, Kimball Castle in Gilford, and the Wentworth Estate in Wolfeboro are just a sample of properties that were built for their wealthy owners to enjoy the solitude of the Lakes Region.

It is arguable that the Lakes Region's influence by industrialists and others of wealth are still prevalent. Mansions are still in existence along shorelines. A drive through Wolfeboro to Tuftonboro will reveal beautiful stately homes. A visit to downtown Tilton, a passerby may notice the replica of the Arch of Titus on a hill on the south side of the Winnipesaukee River. The Tilton Arch built by Charles E. Tilton was a symbol to unite Tilton and Northfield into a single town. Mr. Tilton's property (to include the mansion) is now part of the Tilton School, a private college preparatory school. The Lakes Region has four prestigious private schools (Tilton, New Hampton, Holderness, and Brewster).

Enjoy your time in the Lakes Region, an area of pristine lakes surrounded by mountain ranges to the north. Your time here will convince you of why this region has been a year-round destination for travelers for more than two centuries.

Lakes Region

Alton- Marker #0164: Alton Bay Transportation Center

Ashland- Marker #0100: George Hoyt Whipple

Ashland- Marker #0163: Boston, Concord & Montreal Railroad

Barnstead- Marker #0201: Jonathan Chesley

Belmont- Marker #0235: Belmont Mills

Center Harbor- Marker #0007: Dudley Leavitt (1772-1851)

Effingham- Marker #0083: First Normal School in New Hampshire

Farmington- Marker #0098: Henry Wilson- Vice President of the United States

Franklin- Marker #0091: Birthplace of Daniel Webster

Franklin- Marker #0129: Indian Mortar Lot

Gilford- Marker #0118: Gilford Commemorating a Revolutionary War Battle

Gilford- Marker #0239: Gilford Outing Club

Gilmanton- Marker #0017: Old Province Road

Hebron- Marker #0223: Home Site of Nathaniel Berry, Governor

Hill- Marker #0162: New Hill Village

Holderness- Marker #0039: Samuel Livermore (1732-1803)

Laconia- Marker #0135: The Belknap Mill- The Busiel Mill

Laconia- Marker #0172: New Hampshire Veterans Association

New Durham- Marker #0222: New Durham Meetinghouse

Ossipee- Marker #0020: Captain Lovewell's War

Plymouth- Marker #0179: Smith Bridge

Plymouth- Marker #0189: Stream Gaging in New Hampshire

Rochester- Marker #0042: The Spaulding Brothers

Rochester- Marker #0191: Arched Bridge

Sandwich- Marker #0082: Durgin Bridge

Sandwich- Marker #0248: Wentworth Hill

Tamworth- Marker #0031: The Chocorua Legend

Tamworth- Marker #0090: First Summer Playhouse

Tamworth- Marker #0155: Chinook Kennels

Tilton- Marker #0149: Lochmere Archaeological District

Wakefield- Marker #0005: George A. Wentworth (1835-1906)

Wakefield- Marker #0123: The Governor's Road

Wolfeboro- Marker #0053: Wentworth Estate

Wolfeboro- Marker #0116: College Road

Wolfeboro- Marker #0242: Crescent Lake Ice Harvest

Alton

Marker # 0164: Alton Bay Transportation Center

Location: NH Route 11 at Railroad Depot

Sign Erected: 1991

GPS Coordinates- N 43° 28'.416″ W 71° 14'.275″

"This location became a transportation center on August 30, 1851, upon completion of the Cocheco Railroad from Dover to Alton Bay. The first "Mount Washington" steamboat was built here in 1872. For forty years a railroad terminus, here northbound travelers switched to a stage coach or steamboat. On June 17, 1890 the Lake Shore Railroad opened its line from Alton Bay to Lakeport, only to shut down in 1935. On June 17, 1990 this spot regained its historic name, "Railroad Square," to mark the centennial of the Lake Shore Railroad. At that time, seven of the line's ten original stations still stood."

Alton is on the southeast section of Lake Winnipesaukee. The town has a little more than 19 miles of shoreline of the big lake. Originally named New Durham Gore due to the rocky terrain of Mount Major, the town was first settled in 1770 and incorporated in 1796 as Alton. Interestingly, it took the settlers eight petition attempts to get the General Court to incorporate the town. The newly incorporated town was named for the local Alton family. By 1797, the town had constructed a meetinghouse.

As depicted in the historical marker, Alton is the birthplace of the original Mount Washington steamboat in 1872. The geography of this town lends to its popularity as a railroad community. As trains traveled north from the seacoast and other points south, visitors could stop in Alton Bay and transfer to steamboats to access other sections of the lake that were less accessible. In 1847, the first rail lines were installed. The transportation center opened in 1851 and this terminal remained an active rail center until 1935.

Today, Alton is a favored destination for lake visitors. The MS Mount Washington makes daily stops in Alton Bay from ice out in the Spring to late Fall. A perfect launching point for those who want to experience the Big Lake firsthand. In the winter, Alton Bay has the only active ice runway for airplanes.

Ashland

Marker # 0100: George Hoyt Whipple

Location: NH Route 132 & US Route 3 (Riverside Dr. and Highland St.)

Sign Erected: 1975

GPS Coordinates- N 43° 41'.738″ W 71° 37'.854″

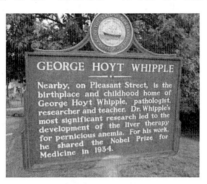

"Nearby, on Pleasant Street, is the birthplace and childhood home of George Hoyt Whipple, pathologist, researcher, and teacher. Dr. Whipple's most significant research led to the development of the liver therapy for pernicious anemia. For his work, he shared the Nobel Prize for Medicine in 1934."

Dr. Whipple was born August 28, 1878. His father and grandfather were both physicians. In researching Dr. Whipple's achievement, I found that the study consisted of drawing blood from dogs and studying the red blood cells. Then feeding the dogs red meats such as liver, kidney and apricots increased the production of red blood cells. Thereby improving patients of anemia with increased amounts of liver in their diets.

 Dr. Whipple and his colleagues Dr. s' George Minot and William Murphy were awarded the Nobel Prize for medicine in 1934. To this day, Dr. George Whipple is the only New Hampshire native to earn this achievement. Dr. Whipple passed on February 1, 1976 at the age of 98. His family bequeathed the family home to the town of Ashland to become a museum.

The Whipple House is located at 14 Pleasant Street and was bequeathed to the town of Ashland 1970. The home is now a museum that is operated by the Ashland Historical Society. The home is a short walk from this marker. Facing south of this sign, the street next to the gas station is Pleasant St.

Ashland also has a notable building that some may recognize. From this marker, travel south (only a few buildings) on NH Route 132 as you get to the small bridge, you will notice a red grist mill with waterwheel. This building known as the Ashland Grist Mill is private property so please be considerate of the owners. This building was featured as a jigsaw puzzle for Milton Bradley. Another notable structure in town is the Squam River covered bridge (NH Covered bridge #65). This 61-foot bridge spans the Squam river at the outlet of Little Squam lake on River street.

Ashland

Marker # 0163: Boston, Concord, & Montreal Railroad

Location: NH Route 132 (69 Depot St) & Winter St.

Sign Erected: 1991

GPS Coordinates-N 43° 41'.407″ W 71° 38'.008″

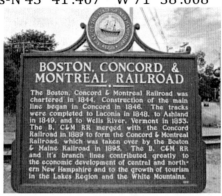

"The Boston, Concord & Montreal Railroad was chartered in 1844. Construction of the main line began in Concord in 1846. The tracks were completed to Laconia in 1848, to Ashland in 1849, and to Wells River, Vermont in 1853. The B, C&M RR merged with the Concord Railroad in 1889 to form the Concord & Montreal Railroad, which was taken over by the Boston & Maine Railroad in 1895. The B, C&M RR and it's branch lines contributed greatly to the economic development of central and northern New Hampshire and to the growth of tourism in the Lakes Region and the White Mountains."

The Ashland Railroad Station museum is located inside this Victorian-era railroad depot. This depot was built in 1869 as a passenger station for the Boston, Concord & Montreal railroad. In 1890 this rail line merged with the Concord Railroad to form the Concord & Montreal Railroad. In 1891, the depot was relocated to its current site and remained in service as a passenger depot until 1959. In 1960, the property was donated to the Ashland Historical Society.

This building was listed on the National Register of Historic Places in 1982. The railroad depot building received significant renovations in 1997-1998 for the conversion to the Ashland Railroad Museum. This building was dedicated as the Ashland Railroad Station museum on June 26, 1999.

Formerly a village of Holderness, Ashland was incorporated in 1868. The town was named in honor of the birthplace and Kentucky estate of US Secretary of State Henry Clay. Ashland is considered the geographic center for the State of New Hampshire.

Barnstead

Marker # 0201: Jonathan Chesley 1736-1826

Location: NH Route 126 (268 South Barnstead Rd) 1.2 miles from NH Route 28

Sign Erected: 2006

GPS Coordinates- N 43° 19'.781″ W 71° 15'.360″

"This patriot and civic leader rests in a nearby grave on land he once farmed. In 1764 he contracted to build Barnstead's portion of the Province Road. On December 14-15, 1774 he participated in raids on the British Fort William and Mary in New Castle capturing needed munitions for the Patriot Militia at the Battle of Bunker Hill. During the Revolution he was an army quartermaster providing critical logistical support to feed, clothe and equip the Continental Army. Following the war, Chesley served as selectman, state representative and delegate to the 1784 state convention that ratified the U.S. Constitution."

The colonial Province road was the main travel route from the seacoast in Durham to the settlements in the northern parts of Grafton and Coos counties. Other historical markers reference this vital route (Gilmanton- *Province Road* marker #0017, and Haverhill- *Haverhill Corner Historic District* marker #0160). These earliest roads were essential to provide goods from the shipping centers to outlying towns. This route also provided the means to transport much needed goods from outlying settlements to the population centers of the seacoast and shipping centers. Many of the roads commissioned by State of New Hampshire after 1780 were turnpikes which relied on the collection of tolls from those who passed through towns.

The raid of Fort William and Mary in New Castle (marker # 0004) was a critical event that led up to the infamous Battle of Bunker Hill in June of 1775 and the Battle of Lexington & Concord in April of 1775. Ralph Waldo Emerson's "Concord Hymn" phrase *the shot heard around the world* is considered the start of the American Revolution. However, much of these engagements would not have been possible without the raid of Fort William & Mary in Newcastle that occurred in December of 1774. Jonathan Chesley's participation in events such as the raid of Fort William & Mary provided the much-needed munitions to support the colonists against the professional and well-trained British army at Bunker Hill.

Belmont

Marker # 0235: Belmont Mills/Saving the Belmont Mill

Location: NH Route 140 west of Belmont Village (parking lot and walking covered bridge onsite)

Sign Erected: 2013

GPS Coordinates- N 43° 26'.640″ W 71° 28'.966″

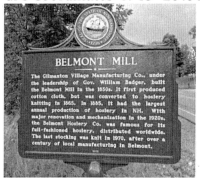 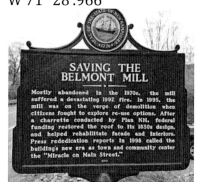

"The Gilmanton Village Manufacturing Co., under the leadership of Gov. William Badger, built the Belmont Mill in the 1830s. It first produced cotton cloth, but was converted to hosiery knitting in 1865. In 1885, it had the largest annual production of hosiery in NH. With major renovation and mechanization in the 1920s, the Belmont Hosiery Co. was famous for its full-fashioned hosiery, distributed worldwide. The last stocking was knit in 1970, after over a century of local manufacturing in Belmont."

"Mostly abandoned in the 1970's, the mill suffered a devastating 1992 fire. In 1995, the mill was on the verge of demolition when citizens fought to explore re-use options. After a charrette conducted by Plan NH, federal funding restored the roof to its 1830s design, and helped rehabilitate facade and interiors. Press rededication reports in 1998 called the building's new era as town and community center the "Miracle on Main Street."

There is a parking area at this location that also has a quaint covered walking bridge that spans the brook to the historic mill building. This walk is less than a few minutes. The renovated mill building is a beautiful four-story brick structure with the white steeple/cupola. The mill stack was demolished in 2001 due to safety concerns. In front of the mill are markers with additional information of the life of 19th century mill workers and the focal point of the mill on this community. This restored historic building now houses medical offices and the Belmont Senior center. The mill was listed on the New Hampshire State Register for Historic Places in 2015. Additional information about the history of Belmont Mill can be viewed at http://belmontnh.homestead.com.

Center Harbor

Marker # 0007: Dudley Leavitt 1772-1851

Location: NH Route 25 (mile marker 62.7) at Meredith/Center Harbor town line

Sign Erected: 1962

GPS Coordinates- N 43° 41'.223″ W 71° 27'.492″

"Author and publisher of almanacs first appearing in 1797. Best known was "Leavitt's Farmers' Almanac and Miscellaneous Year Book" which was continued after his death for about 45 years. This publication provided information vital to domestic and agricultural life of the period. He lived in house 200 yards east."

Belknap College 1963-1974- "Founders Dr. Royal M. Frye and Dr. Virginia M. Brigham were visionaries, educators, and mentors who brought together faculty, administrators and students for an outstanding education. While Degrees were earned, all who attended gained lifelong skills, enduring friendships and a fondness for Center Harbor and its residents who welcomed them. In its short 11-years, Belknap College created special memories and a bond of loyalty that lives today."

Dudley Leavitt was born in Exeter, New Hampshire in 1772. He attended Phillips Exeter Academy. As a young man, he moved to Gilmanton, New Hampshire where his wife Judith was from. Dudley Leavitt pursued his passion for mathematics and astronomy. While Leavitt was considered a scholar in this field, he was self-educated and contributed many scholarly works. He was a teacher at Gilmanton Academy which was considered one of the most prestigious schools in New Hampshire. In 1800, he established a local newspaper. Leavitt also started his popular publication, Leavitt's Farmer's Almanac in 1797 while living in Gilmanton. Leavitt moved to the farm depicted in this marker in 1819. He continued his work as a teacher, as well as publishing his almanac. Dudley died on September 20, 1851 at his farm. The almanac remained in publication until 1896.

The town of Center Harbor is a picturesque community in the heart of the Lakes Region. The town is located between Lake Winnipesaukee and Squam Lakes. Center Harbor derived its name not from its' location, but from the original family that settled and received the land grant; the Joseph Senter family. Joseph Senter was a surveyor who was commissioned by Governor John Wentworth to survey the College Road from Wentworth's Estate to Dartmouth College. Center Harbor is a bustling community in the summer and fall with tourists. With the astounding beauty of the lakes in contrast with the fall foliage, this community is worth the visit.

Effingham

Marker # 0083: First Normal School in New Hampshire

Location: NH Route 153(Province Lake Road) and Hobbs Road (Building at 38 Hobbs Road)

Sign Erected: 1972

GPS Coordinates- N 43° 45'.748″ W 70° 59'.911″

"On the rise of the ground just west of here, on the 2nd floor of the old Effingham Union Academy building (1819), was the First Normal School in New Hampshire. It was in this Academy in 1830 that James W. Bradbury, later United States Senator from Maine, took the school only on condition that it should be for the "Instruction and training of teachers." This idea was his own and at that time entirely novel."

As depicted on this marker, the concept of a school with the purpose of training future teachers was new. The first "normal school in the United States was established in Concord, Vermont in 1823. While this site may not have been the first in the country, the idea of establishing the first Normal School in New Hampshire in this town was pioneering. Effingham was not along any major thoroughfare and relatively a rural community. Established communities such as Portsmouth, Concord, and Manchester may have been the preferred location for such a school. Yet, Effingham's unprecedented establishment of the first school for training of teachers began what we now know as teacher colleges.

The area surrounding this marker encompassing NH Route 153, Hobbs Road, and Plantation Road is known as Lord's Hill Historic District. This district includes twenty-one properties with sixteen main buildings built in the 18th and 19th century. These Federal-style buildings include fourteen homes, one meetinghouse, and the Union Academy building. This district was listed on the National Register of Historic Places in 1985. Except for the Union Academy building which now houses a museum, all buildings are still used for their original purpose. The district also includes five 19th century cemeteries. The Lord's Hill historic district is a classic example of a traditional 19th century New England village.

Farmington

Marker # 0098: Henry Wilson- Vice President of the United States

Location: NH Route 153 at Farmington Country Club entrance (181 Main Street)

Sign Erected: 1975

GPS Coordinates-N 43° 22'.863″   W 71° 02'.978″

"Born in Farmington February 16, 1812, Jeremiah Jones Colbath, this self-proclaimed farm boy changed his name when of age to Henry Wilson. He became a teacher, member of Congress, United States Senator and took office as Vice President under President Ulysses S. Grant March 4, 1873. He suffered a stroke and died in the Vice President's chambers in the Capitol, November 22, 1875."

Many New Hampshire residents know of Franklin Pierce who was our 14th President of the United States. But I would wager that the majority of Granite-Staters have never heard of Henry Wilson, Vice President of the United States. Alright, Henry Wilson, was known as Jeremiah Colbath. While born and raised as a young boy in New Hampshire, he claimed Massachusetts as his home state where he served as a Congressman and Senator. Wilson's life story can be summed up as a rag to riches story. His childhood in New Hampshire was a difficult one. His father apprenticed him to a local farmer at age ten for the money. It is hard to imagine that a parent would practically sell their child to another for money, but that was a different era. When Jeremiah was 21 years old, he left the farmer who raised him and New Hampshire; changed his name to Henry Wilson in 1833 and moved to Natick, Massachusetts.

As a young man, he apprenticed as a shoemaker but aspired for politics. He had a genuine ability to listen to his constituents. Wilson started his political career in the state legislature and moved up to be a member of Congress, US Senator, and in 1873 he became Vice-President of the United States under President Ulysses S. Grant.

Henry Wilson's was a man of the people. His contempt for the aristocratic class and the desire to help blue collar workers made him a popular politician. Vice President Wilson died in office on November 22, 1875 having only served two years. The United States Senate webpage provides an excellent biography of the life of Vice President Henry Wilson.

Franklin

Marker # 0091: Birthplace of Daniel Webster

Location: North Road 7/10 mile from NH Route 127 (signage at NH Route 127)

Sign Erected: 1975

GPS Coordinates-N 43° 24'.832″ W 71° 41'.804″

"Daniel Webster was born here January 18, 1782. Statesman and lawyer, he served as U.S. Congressman from New Hampshire and Massachusetts. Senator from Massachusetts and Secretary of State under Presidents Harrison, Tyler and Fillmore. A noted orator, he achieved national recognition in the landmark Dartmouth College case. He died in Marshfield, Massachusetts October 24, 1852 and is buried there. He was one of the first men elected to the U.S. Senate Hall of Fame in 1957."

Daniel Webster served as a New Hampshire delegate in the U.S. House of Representatives from 1813-1817. He later served as a Massachusetts representative in Congress from 1823-1827. He served as a U.S. Senator for Massachusetts in 1827-1841 and 1845-1850. He is only the second person to serve as Secretary of State for three presidents. Webster also ran for president in 1836, 1840 and 1852 as a Whig party candidate. While Webster has many notable achievements, I appreciated his negotiation of the Webster-Ashburton Treaty of 1842 with Great Britain. This treaty was the establishment of the international border with Canada and the United States to include the region of the Indian Stream Republic (see Pittsburg- marker #0001). Webster lived in Portsmouth, New Hampshire until 1813 when his house was destroyed in a major fire. He moved to Massachusetts where he lived until his death on October 12, 1852.

Franklin, New Hampshire was incorporated in 1828 and was named in honor of Benjamin Franklin. Franklin is the location of where the Pemigewasset River from the north and the Winnipesaukee River from the east meet. This confluence forms the Merrimack River which flows south through the heart of Concord, Manchester, Nashua and Massachusetts to the Atlantic Ocean. With the major waterways, Franklin has always relied on its industry as a mill community. While Franklin now lays claim to the birthplace of Daniel Webster, it was originally part of Salisbury, New Hampshire.

Franklin

Marker # 0129: Indian Mortar Lot

Location: U.S. Route 3 and Dearborn St.

Sign Erected: 1979

GPS Coordinates- N 43° 26'.815″ W 71° 37'.921″

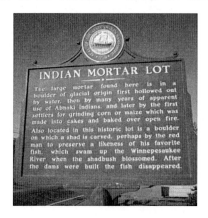

"The large mortar found here is in a boulder of glacial origin first hollowed out by water, then by many years of apparent use of Abnaki Indians, and later by the first settlers for grinding corn or maize which was made into cakes and baked over open fire. Also located in this historic lot is a boulder on which a shad is carved, perhaps by the red man to preserve a likeness of his favorite fish, which swam up the Winnepesaukee River when the shadbush blossomed. After the dams were built the fish disappeared."

I consider this marker the birth of my interest in New Hampshire history as well as the first New Hampshire historical marker that I stopped to read as a child. Having grown up in neighboring Tilton, this marker intrigued me. I found learning of the Abenaki tribes that lived in this region fascinating. Most likely, history of the local indigenous tribes can be found along the waterways throughout the state and region. While the marker makes claims of the "Abnaki Indians", further research shows this Indian language "family" were part of the Algonquins. The Algonquins and Iroquois were the two major Indian language families that settled the eastern United States. Abenaki can be interpreted to mean "people of the east".

The Algonquin Nation with local tribes known as Abenaki made their livelihood from hunting, trapping and fishing. Research also suggests that the Abenaki built walled forts in the Ft. Eddy plains (now Concord) and along the east side of the Merrimack River in Boscawen.

Gilford

Marker # 0118: Gilford Commemorating a Revolutionary War Battle

Location: NH Route 11A (near Gilford Village) at the Gilford Fire Department parking lot

Sign Erected: 1977

GPS Coordinates-N 43° 32'.986″ W 71° 24'.365″

"Gilford, the center of which is opposite this location, is the only New Hampshire town named for a Revolutionary War battle, the 1781 Battle of Guilford Court House in North Carolina. After the war, Lt. Lemuel B. Mason, a New Hampshire officer who served in that battle, retired to Gilmanton. In 1812, when the town was divided, as its oldest and most famous citizen, he was accorded the honor of choosing a name for the new town."

This area was once part of Gilmanton and known as Gunstock Parish. The Battle of Guilford Courthouse was instrumental in the surrender of General Cornwallis to the Continental Army at Yorktown, Virginia in 1781. The Battle of Guilford Courthouse was a victory for the British forces on March 15, 1781. However, Cornwallis' army suffered major losses at this battle and decidedly opted to not continue his march to the Carolina's. With nearly a quarter of his forces killed or injured, Cornwallis marched to Virginia where he ultimately surrendered to General

George Washington of the Continental Army in Yorktown, Virginia on October 19, 1781.

Lieutenant Lemuel Mason of Newington returned to New Hampshire after the war and settled here in Gunstock Parish. He loved to tell his tale of the Great Battle of Guilford Courthouse. Mason was one of the founders of this area and was given the honor to rename his new town. In honor of the Battle at Guilford Courthouse, he named his new town Guilford. This town is the only New Hampshire town named after a battle of the Revolutionary War.

The town of Gilford was incorporated in 1812. The spelling from Guilford to Gilford was due to a clerical error. A lakefront community, it has many notable points of interest. For example, located on Lockes Hill is Kimball Castle. This stone building was built by railroad baron Benjamin Kimball. The castle sits on 20 acres of picturesque land overlooking Lake Winnipesaukee. Once part of a 300-acre estate, the remaining parcel of land is now a nature preserve with hiking and ski trails encompassing more than 200 acres for public recreation.

Gilford

Marker # 0239: The Gilford Outing Club 1946-1992

Location: NH Route 11A/ NH Route 11B intersection (next to Outing Club building)

Sign Erected: 2013

GPS Coordinates-N 43° 33'.345″ W 71° 23'.901″

"Established by local families, the Gilford Outing Club provided all-seasons outdoor recreation for local children through parent volunteering. Particularly well-known for ski instruction, the Club trained hundreds of children including three Olympic athletes: Marty Hall, Dick Taylor, and medalist Penny Pitou. The Club operated from this site from 1950 until it disbanded in 1992. Donated to the town in 1994 by Gary and Lucille Allen's family, the land and buildings still serve to provide outdoor recreation for the town."

The Gilford Outing Club was a favorite ski slope for residents to learn to ski. According to the website, "Lost New Hampshire Ski Areas", the Gilford Outing Club was an operational ski slope in 1940. An earlier location near School House Hill had one rope tow in the late 1940's. In 1950, the location was moved to the current site which included an 800 ft and 650 ft rope tow as well as a warming hut.

Today, most local skiers travel the short distance up the road to neighboring Gunstock Mountain Resort. Gunstock has evolved from a winter location for skiing to a four-season destination. Some of the activities include Nordic and downhill skiing, zip-line course, a mountain coaster, hiking trails, and an event center popular for weddings and other large gatherings. I remember as a young skier, night skiing at Gunstock. Back in the 1970's, the mountain also had Nordic ski jumping competitions.

Gilford is an all-season tourist destination. Summer tourists flock to the pristine Lake Winnipesaukee shores. Here you will find large yachts and sailboats to small watercraft skirting the big lake. Another major summer attraction is the Bank of NH Pavilion (formerly Meadowbrook). This 9,000-seat amphitheater is the venue to see the biggest names in the music industry. There is nothing like an outdoor music concert to watch your most favorite artist perform. In the Fall, the vibrant foliage creates the contrast of color with the lake's deep-blue background. Gilford is the heart of the Lakes Region.

Gilmanton

Marker # 0017: Old Province Road

Location: NH Route 107- 3.6 miles south of NH Route 140 (1287 Province Rd)

Sign Erected: 1963

GPS Coordinates- N 43° 23'.501″ W 71° 21'.770″

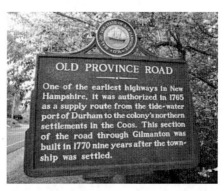

"One of the earliest highways in New Hampshire, it was authorized in 1765 as a supply route from the tide-water port of Durham to the colony's northern settlements in the Coos. This section of the road through Gilmanton was built in 1770 nine years after the township was settled."

In the 18th and 19th centuries, the Town of Gilmanton was a bustling community. Incorporated in 1727 and settled in 1761, it was once the second largest community in the state. At its peak, the town also included the areas of Alton, Barnstead, Belmont, Gilford, Northfield, and part of Laconia. Gilmanton has many notable persons associated with the town. From U.S. congress members, world-renowned musicians, diplomats, innovators of medicine, and authors. The most recent was author Grace Metalious who wrote *Peyton Place*. This novel written in 1956 depicts the unsavory life of living in a small community. The book was considered scandalous for depicting less than wholesome small-town happenings.

Gilmanton has two distinct villages Four Corners (NH Routes 107 & 140) and Gilmanton Iron Works (east on NH Route 140). Gilmanton Iron Works was originally known as Averytown Parish. In 1778, iron ore was mined from this section of town. The boon was short-lived and closed after only a few years due to the scarcity of ore.

The Four Corners village is complete with picturesque New England architecture and manicured stone walls. At the northeast corner of the intersection of NH Route 140 and NH Route 107 is the original Gilmanton Academy building. Chartered on June 20, 1794 this private school was one of the most prestigious institutions (Phillips Exeter Academy was the other) that wealthy citizens sent their children for a quality education. There is also the original Town Pound (where stray animals were penned) is 4/10 mile south from the Four Corners.

Hebron

Marker # 0223: Home Site of Nathaniel Berry Governor, 1861-1863

Location: Northshore Rd at Hebron Village. 2.3 miles west of NH Route 3A

Sign Erected: 2010

GPS Coordinates- N 43° 41'.654″ W 71° 48'.421″

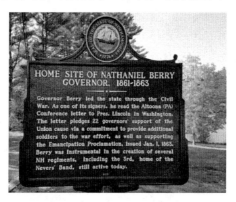

"Governor Berry led the state through the Civil War. As one of its signers, he read the Altoona (PA) Conference letter to Pres. Lincoln in Washington. The letter pledges 22 governors' support of the Union cause via a commitment to provide additional soldiers to the war effort, as well as supporting the Emancipation Proclamation, issued Jan.1, 1863. Berry was instrumental in the creation of several NH regiments, including the 3rd, home of the Nevers' Band, still active today."

The two-term New Hampshire governor served from 1861-1863. Nathaniel Berry had apprenticed in leather goods and manufacturing. He purchased a tannery in nearby Bristol, New Hampshire and later relocated his business here in Hebron. The factory was destroyed by fire in 1857. Berry was also an active member of the New Hampshire militia serving in several regiments and attained the rank of Colonel.

Nathaniel Berry served in the New Hampshire legislature as a democrat. With his opposition to the Democratic Party platform in support of slavery, he changed parties at the inception of the Republican party in the 1850's. He served as New Hampshire governor as a Republican. Governor Berry died in 1894 at the age of 97. He is buried at the Homeland Cemetery in Bristol, New Hampshire.

Hebron is a small, quaint community along the northern shores of Newfound Lake. Formed in 1791, it was formerly known as Cockermouth. If you travel from west from NH Route 3A you will experience the beautiful scenery of this community. A town of approximately 600 citizens, Hebron is a quiet, quintessential New England village.

Hill

Marker # 0162: New Hill Village

Location: NH Route 3A (Hill village) in front of Town Hall & Fire Station

Sign Erected: 1991

GPS Coordinates- N 43° 31'.177″ W 71° 42'.137″

"In February 1937, Hill residents learned that their village, near the Pemigewasset River, was to become a flood control reservoir for the Franklin Falls dam project. By January of 1940, the citizens of Hill formed an association, purchased land, and began planning a new model village with the help of the N.H. State Planning and Development Commission. Construction started in 1940, and by June of 1941 the new town hall and school were completed, along with the streets, water system, and 30 houses. The 1941 town meeting was called to order in the old town hall, recessed, and reconvened in the new village."

The town of Hill was incorporated in 1778 as New Chester and included lands currently the towns of Hill, Bristol and Bridgewater. Earlier in 1754, the grant for New Chester also included thirty-thousand acres of land that are now parts of Danbury and Wilmot. In 1837, the town changed its name to Hill in honor of New Hampshire Governor Isaac Hill.

The notoriety of the history of Hill lies with its location along the Pemigewasset River. In 1938, with the Army Corps of Engineers development of flood control plains and dams, the village of Hill fell within the floodplain of the Franklin Falls dam. Working collaboratively, the town and state government constructed a resettlement plan to design a new community. By 1940, New Hill Village was completed. The town meeting of 1941 opened in Old Hill Village, recessed and reconvened in the New Hill Village.

To this day, visitors can view the "old village" by traveling north on NH Route 3A to Old Town Road (appropriate namesake). Visitors can walk to the old village to see the remnants of the abandoned streets, cellar holes, and sidewalks. You can visit the ghost towns website (www.ghosttowns.com/states/nh/hill) for photos.

Holderness

Marker # 0039: Samuel Livermore (1732-1803)

Location: NH Route 175 & NH Route 175A in front of Holderness School athletic field

Sign Erected: 1966

GPS Coordinates- N 43° 45'.657″ W 71° 40'.298″

"Proprietor of more than half the Town of Holderness, this jurist, congressman and senator was New Hampshire's first attorney general and second chief justice. In 1788 he spurred the State's approval of the proposed Federal Constitution, thus insuring its ratification and the formation of the present Government of the United States."

As mentioned on this marker, Samuel Livermore was instrumental in the founding of our government after the Revolutionary War. Some interesting points I found in my research of Samuel Livermore is that he was a close friend of New Hampshire royal Governors John and Benning Wentworth. Livermore received his large land grant from royal Governor Benning Wentworth. When the outbreak of the Revolutionary War commenced, Livermore disassociated himself from the Royal Governor. After the Revolutionary War, Livermore became an instrumental part of the formation of both the state and federal government.

An interesting incident occurred in 1794. President George Washington sought help from U.S. Senators Samuel Livermore and John Jay of New York to construct a trade treaty with Great Britain. It was presented to the senate for ratification with no details made public. A newspaper in Philadelphia published the details of the treaty which highly favored Great Britain. Outrage ensued, particularly in Portsmouth NH. According to the New England Historical Society, *"A group of 300 furious protesters marched the figures, accompanied by fife and drum, to one of the city's wharves. There they held a trial and execution, during which they burned the two senators."* The figures were ship figureheads carved in the likeness of Jay and Livermore. Actual charges were presented to a Portsmouth court which the judge would not hear the case. The Congress ratified the treaty in 1795.

Laconia

Marker # 0135: The Belknap Mill- The Busiel Mill

Location: Beacon Street (One Mill Plaza)

Sign Erected: 1980

GPS Coordinates-N 43° 31'.677″ W 71° 28'.135″

"Constructed in 1823, the Belknap Mill is the oldest unaltered brick textile mill in the U.S. Once a hosiery mill, it houses an intact hydraulic power plant and a bell cast by George Holbrook, apprentice to Paul Revere. The Busiel Mill, built in 1853 as a hosiery mill, was later used for the manufacture of clocks, electronic relays and organs."

An earlier wooden structure mill was constructed on this site in 1811 and was owned by Caniel Avery and Stephen Perley. This mill was destroyed in a fire. In 1823, investors from Lowell, Massachusetts who owned mills in that city built a newer structure of a more modern design which was a post and beam construction and brick. This mill, known as Belknap Mill is a replica of a design which was built earlier in Waltham, Massachusetts. The new design was considered contemporary in that it contained the entire manufacturing process in one building. This design provided natural light with larger windows, a water wheel was the original power source for weaving the cloth. This building design was common in New England during the industrial revolution. However, this is the only one that still exists.

The Busiel Mill was originally founded in 1846 by John W. Busiel. The Busiel Mill was a hosiery manufacturer. The original building burned in 1853 along with several buildings and mills along the Winnipesaukee River. John Busiel purchased land and water rights and constructed the five-story building on this site. As the business grew, the footprint of the mill grew to include a four-story building and bell tower. The mill continued operation manufacturing a variety of products. Manufacturing ended in 1969. In 1971, the buildings were renovated into office space and renamed One Mill Plaza. Both buildings were listed on the National Register of Historic Places in 1971. One is listed as Belknap-Sulloway Mill and the other as Busiel-Seeburg Mill.

Laconia (Weirs Beach)

Marker # 0172: New Hampshire Veterans' Association

Location: Lakeside Avenue & New Hampshire Avenue

Sign Erected: 1998

GPS Coordinates-N 43° 36'.445″ W 71° 27'.568″

"This "campus" mostly built in the 1880's is home to the NH Veterans' Association. Formed in 1875 and chartered in 1881, it is the oldest organization of its kind in the U.S. Initially a summer retreat for Civil War veterans, the NHVA now admits all honorably discharged NH veterans. Its purpose is to guard and protect the colors under which its members fought and all that those colors represent. Listed in the National Register of Historic Places since 1980, this site was leased to the NHVA by the B&M Railroad until 1924, when it was bought by the NHVA with state funds."

The New Hampshire Veterans Association formed in Manchester New Hampshire in 1875 and held its first encampment here at Weirs Beach in 1878. Construction of the row of buildings began in the 1880's into the early 1900's. In 1924, one of the buildings was destroyed by fire as well as other structures. The Hurricane of 1938 damaged many of the buildings including trees, a pavilion and other smaller buildings. Other buildings and barracks were destroyed by fire from the 1940's through the 1980's. The 1990's brought efforts to renovate these historical buildings. While many of the other features such as the pavilion and smaller encampment barracks were lost from fires and neglect, the regimental buildings you now see on Weirs Boulevard are still in use by members of the NHVA.

Weirs Beach is a famous destination in the Lakes Region. The boardwalk and boulevard offer nostalgic activities for families. The M/S Mount Washington docks directly across the street as well as the US Mail Boat Sophie C. and M/V Doris E. At the beach on Weirs Boulevard is the Endicott Rock. This rock marks the northernmost point of the Massachusetts Bay Colony and was engraved by the surveyors in 1652.

New Durham

Marker # 0222: New Durham Meetinghouse

Location: NH Route 11 (mile marker 94.4) and Davis Crossing Road

Sign Erected: 2010

GPS Coordinates- N 43° 24'.794″ W 71° 08'.271"

"The New Durham Meetinghouse was built by settlers from Durham and nearby towns in 1770 as their house of worship and seat of government until 1819 when the town's first church was built. This area was the town center until the 1850's when the arrival of the railroad favored development in "The Plains." The Meetinghouse was reduced to 1 story in 1838, vacated in 1908. The town had it listed in the National Registry in 1980. It can be found by following Davis Crossing Rd and turning left on Old Bay."

According to the New Durham Historical Society, the town was granted in 1749 as Cocheco Township as part of the Masonian Grant. The land was settled as early as 1750 by settlers from Durham. On December 7, 1752, the town was incorporated as New Durham. The town remained small and prospered with sawmills along the Merrymeeting and Cocheco Rivers. In 1850, the Cocheco Railroad was completed and connected the seacoast from Durham to the lakes in Alton. The change also meant a shift of the town center to "The Plains".

The meetinghouse is easy to find from the location of the marker. Travel north and turn right onto Davis Crossing Road and turn left onto Old Bay Road. The property surrounding the meetinghouse includes a nature trail and the town pound. The property was sold to a local farmer who used the building for storage. The heirs returned the building to the town in 1979. However, the building needed major restoration. Major fundraising was made to improve this historic structure. The Meetinghouse park nature trail is short but relaxing through the local woods and includes the pauper's cemetery. There is an information sheet box at the trailhead that provides visitors information of the local property.

Ossipee

Marker # 0020: Captain Lovewell's War

Location: NH Route 16 & NH Route 16B (mile marker 56.5) adjacent to Indian Mound Golf course

Sign Erected: 1964

GPS Coordinates- N 43° 46'.536″ W 71° 09'.784″

"Was fought between 1722 and 1725 against several tribes of eastern Indians. The principal campaigns took place in the Ossipee region and led to the eventual withdrawal of the Indians to the north. Commemorated in Colonial literature by the "The Ballad of Lovewell's Fight."

The Abenaki Indians were allied with the French who convinced the tribes to raid English settlements. The French considered the territory of Maine and parts of New Hampshire their own. While the Abenaki tribes raided English settlements, the retaliation by the English was inevitable. Here lies the premise of the French and Indian War of 1723-1726, also known as Dummer's War. The English were embattled with the Wabanaki Confederacy over settlements. The English settlers were imposing on lands that the Indians had lived on and the French wanted. The French used Catholic missionaries to convert Indians and claim the English (non-Catholic) were evil for taking Indian lands.

In 1724, Indians had captured two men from Dunstable (now Nashua). A search party set off to retrieve the captives. In their search, the Indians ambushed the search party and killed nearly a dozen men. The provincial government put out a bounty on Indian scalps. Captain John Lovewell gathered thirty men to raid the Indians as retribution. In 1725, Lovewell's 3rd expedition built a garrison in the Ossipee area and set out with more than 30 men to raid the Abenaki settlement of Pequawket (now Fryeburg, ME).

On May 9, 1725, along the route to Pequawket, a tribe of Abenaki Indians led by Chief Paugus ambushed Lovewell and his men. Captain Lovewell was killed as well as seven other men. One of Lovewell's rangers did kill Chief Paugus. Without their chief, the Indians retreated and vacated their settlement of Pequawket and fled to Canada.

Songs, poetry, and stories were written about Captain Lovewell and his defeat of the Abenaki Indians. Famous writers such as Nathaniel Hawthorne and Henry Wadsworth-Longfellow depict the bravery of Lovewell and his men.

Plymouth

Marker # 0179: Smith Bridge

Location: Smith Bridge Road ½ mile from NH Route 25

Sign Erected: 2002

GPS Coordinates-N 43° 46'.531″ W 71° 44'.388″

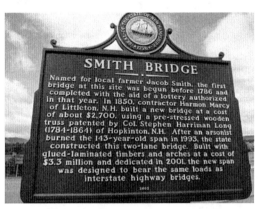

"Named for local farmer Jacob Smith, the first bridge at this site was begun before 1786 and completed with the aid of a lottery authorized in that year. In 1850, contractor Harmon Marcy of Littleton, N.H. built a new bridge at a cost of about $2,700, using a pre-stressed wooden truss patented by Col. Stephen Harriman Long (1784-1864) of Hopkinton, N.H. After an arsonist burned the 143-year-old span in 1993, the state constructed this two-lane bridge. Built with glued-laminated timbers and arches at a cost of $3.3 million and dedicated in 2001, the new span was designed to bear the same loads as interstate highway bridges."

An earlier bridge spanned this section of the Baker River. Captain Charles Richardson built a bridge at this site in the early 1800's. The Smith Bridge constructed in 1850 was designed as a replica style to the Fayette bridge that was constructed in 1804 and spanned the Pemigewasset river between Plymouth and Holderness at Pont Fayette until 1934. The current Smith Bridge is 149' long with a clear span of 140'6". The Smith Bridge had repairs conducted in 1940, 1949 and 1958. The bridge received a major rehabilitation in 1971.

Plymouth is home to Plymouth State University founded in 1871 with a campus of more than 4,100 undergraduate and 3,000 graduate students. The town of Plymouth is considered the gateway between the Lakes Region and the White Mountains. The town of Plymouth was incorporated in 1763 and was named after Plymouth Massachusetts. The town is situated at the convergence of the Baker and Pemigewasset rivers. An interesting tidbit of history is that Plymouth is the home of three lost ski areas. Frontenac was west of I-93 southbound along the Pemigewasset river (remnants of the trails can be viewed near mile marker 79.6 looking west). Locals could also ski at the Holderness Hill slopes near the Holderness school campus. This slope closed in late 1970's. The third ski hill was Huckins Hill located on the east side of I-93 north near exit 26.

Plymouth

Marker # 0189: Stream Gaging in New Hampshire

Location: NH Route 175A (Holderness Rd) and US Route 3 next to bridge

Sign Erected: 2005

GPS Coordinates- N 43° 45'.573″ W 71° 41'.199″

"This is the site of the longest continuous stream gaging in New Hampshire. Daily measurement of the level of the Pemigewasset River was begun here in 1886 by the Locks and Canals Company of Lowell, Massachusetts, which controlled flowage in the Merrimack River and its headwaters. In 1903, with funding from the State of New Hampshire, the U.S. Geological Survey began to measure the discharge of the river to determine available waterpower and the effects of White Mountain deforestation. The original gage was on the abutment of a covered bridge at this site. The concrete gaging station, just downstream, dates from 1926."

Stream gaging is the measurement of water surface elevation. The Pemigewasset River is notorious for frequent flooding. With the shallow and winding river, flooding is common from winter ice jams to spring floods. While the purpose of stream gaging in the late 1800's and early 1900's provided notice of levels of water upstream. This was critical in the manufacturing centers such as Manchester and Lowell, Massachusetts which relied on hydropower of their dams. Today, stream gaging provides observers downstream along the Merrimack River, which are heavily populated areas, providing notice of rising water levels and potential flooding.

Looking east from this location you will notice two convenience stores and the Plymouth State Field House. A simple stop at the convenience store across from the Field House will reveal the water levels from previous years flooding. Some of the water level markings reveal depths more than 7 feet. A recent search of the National Weather Service Advanced Hydrologic Prediction Service reveals many floods as recent as 2011 has flood crest levels more than 21 feet.

Rochester

Marker # 0042: The Spaulding Brothers

Location: 78 Wakefield Road (in front of The Governor's Inn)

Sign Erected: 1966

GPS Coordinates-N 43° 18'.459″ W 70° 58'.609″

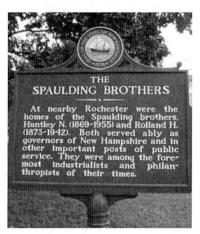

"At nearby Rochester were the homes of the Spaulding brothers, Huntley N. (1869-1955) and Rolland H. (1873-1942). Both served ably as governors of New Hampshire and in other important posts of public service. They were among the foremost industrialists and philanthropists of their times."

This marker was formerly located at the Rochester Toll Plaza on NH Route 16 (Spaulding Turnpike). It was relocated to its present site which were the homes of brothers Huntley and Rolland Spaulding. Today, the properties are part of Governors Inn & Restaurant. The Governors Inn building built in 1920 was the home of Huntley Spaulding. The adjacent building was the home of Rolland Spaulding.

The Spaulding brothers began their entrepreneurship following in their father's footsteps. Jonas Spaulding had a fiberboard manufacturing company in Massachusetts. Jonas later founded the Rochester Fiberboard Company. Sons Rolland and Huntley joined the family business and renamed the company J. Spaulding & Sons. The brothers eventually took over the family business.

Younger brother, Rolland H. Spaulding went on to pursue a career in politics. He was elected governor of New Hampshire in 1914. However, he declined to run again in 1916. Older brother, Huntley N. Spaulding followed Rolland's political interests and served as New Hampshire governor from 1927-1929. Huntley also served in federal positions during World War I. He also served as head of the State Board of Education from 1921-1926.

Both Spaulding brothers were important philanthropists. Huntley and his sister established the Spaulding charitable trust which divested their wealth following the death of the last Spaulding sibling in 1957. Both Rolland and Huntley died here in Rochester. Huntley is buried in Cambridge, Massachusetts.

Rochester

Marker # 0191: Arched Bridge

Location: NH 202 A: 103 North Main Street (in public parking lot)

Sign Erected: 2005

GPS Coordinates-N 43° 18'.301″ W 70° 58'.775"

"Designed and built between 1881 and 1883 by Silas Hussey, Jr. (1828-1913), this bridge is unique in New Hampshire in having heavy brick arches faced with split granite. Its fifty-foot width was exceptional for the time. Hussey was a local quarryman and stonecutter who also designed Rochester's Civil War monument. He built the three-arched bridge for a contract price of $13,800, subcontracting the bricklaying to Henry J. Wilkinson (1848-1899) of Rochester, a British born mason."

This bridge is also known as the North Main Street Bridge. It spans 133 feet over the Cocheco River. Each of the three parabolic granite arches spans 36 feet 8 inches. This bridge was built in 1883 and rehabilitated in 2010. At the ceremony re-opening of the bridge after the rehabilitation project in 2010, a man dressed in 19th century attire as stonemason Silas Hussey, Jr. read a proclamation and informed the 21st century audience that in 1883, he received much backlash over the construction of the bridge with stone. His neighbors believed it should have been constructed of timber. If his neighbors had won out, we can agree that this historic bridge would not have been the original and most likely not one as pleasing to the eye. While I found this bridge graceful in its design, I was unable to capture a picture worthy to show the beauty of the design due to overgrowth of vegetation along the shore.

Rochester was incorporated as a town on May 10, 1722. Rochester was the tenth town in New Hampshire to receive its charter. The major industry for the area was manufacturing, powered by the Cocheco and Salmon Falls rivers. The Rochester Historical Society has published an interesting self-guided walking tour of the city. The descriptions of the architecture, history, and notable achievement of the town's citizens is interesting. The historical society is located at 58 Hanson Street. The National Register of Historic Places include the Rochester Industrial and Commercial Historic District which includes the North Main Street Bridge. The listing was approved on February 25, 1983.

Sandwich

Marker # 0082: Durgin Bridge

Location: Foss Flats Rd & Durgin Bridge Rd (1.5 miles north of NH Route 113)

Sign Erected: 1972

GPS Coordinates- N 43° 51'.323″ W 71° 21'.867″

"Built by Jacob Berry of North Conway, this bridge is the fourth to span Swift River here since 1820. Freshets in 1844, 1865 and 1869 destroyed the first three. The bridge is named for James Holmes Durgin (1815-73) who ran a grist mill near it; drove stage from Sandwich to Farmington; and was a link in the underground slave railroad, Sandwich to Conway."

The current bridge was built in 1869 and is 96 feet long with a clear span of 72 feet. The original bridge was constructed in 1820 as a replacement for the Ford bridge that was located about a quarter mile upstream. That bridge was destroyed and the Durgin bridge was constructed. The historical records claim the freshet of 1869 was so strong that the river current bent and twisted the 2-inch bolts secured to the rocks below holding the bridge in place. The bridge was also used as a passageway in the underground slave railroad from Sandwich to North Conway. The Durgin Bridge was listed on the National Register of Historic Places in 1983.

The town of Sandwich is a charming New Hampshire village settled in 1763. It is situated between the Lakes Region and the White Mountains Region. Known for its exceptional beauty, many visitors come to view the scenery of the town village. I always enjoy a motorcycle ride to Sandwich village, particularly during peak foliage. The colonial era white buildings, stone walls and colorful foliage makes this a bucket list stop for those who appreciate Norman Rockwell-type village scenery.

The town also has a unique historical area known as Sandwich Notch. Once the only passageway for commerce from the Pemigewasset River valley to the seacoast, this route was built in 1801. During its heyday, nearly 40 families settled here. Fifty years later, all settlers living in the notch have moved away. Today, there is only one remaining farmhouse on the Sandwich Notch road. Other points of interest on this road are Pulpit rock, Beede Falls, and Cow cave. Traveling this road is not for the faint of heart (or at least a low suspension).

Sandwich

Marker # 0248: First House Site in Sandwich

Location: NH Route 109 (253 Wentworth Hill Rd)

Sign Erected: 2015

GPS Coordinates- N 43° 47'.576" W 71° 24'.845"

"The first house in town was built on this hill. Daniel Beede and 15 men built a log house in Nov. 1767. Beede was a dominant character in the early history of Sandwich, a surveyor, a businessman, the first town clerk and on the first Board of Selectmen. He was Sandwich's delegate in 1775 to the 5th Provincial Congress; Col. John Wentworth was president of the first three. John's grandson, Paul, later owned the Beede farm. Beede died in 1799; he is buried in the cemetery next to the house site."

While the first house built in Sandwich is no longer standing, there is some interesting history associated with Wentworth Hill and an eccentric citizen. Across the street from this marker is a property known as the former Isaac Adams estate. Folklore suggests that in 1824 Isaac Adams (then 22 years old) was not a well-liked young man, nor successful as a printer apprentice. He decided to move to Boston and build his fortune, but he had no money for the stagecoach ride. He had asked his neighbors to lend him money for the trip. Everyone turned him away. Adams went to Boston despite the lack of help from his Sandwich neighbors and did eventually become successful, inventing a steam printing press in 1828. He vowed to return to his home town with a vengeance.

He returned in 1861 and began buying up all his neighbor's property and tore their homes down. He built a giant wall of granite from the foundations of the destroyed homes. The wall can be viewed by traveling down Little Pond Rd (2/10 mile from this marker). Atop the wall is a marble statue of the figure Niobe. Greek mythology claims that Niobe was punished by the god Apollo for excessive pride in her children. A trip down Little Pond road is worthwhile to view the Great Wall of Sandwich. The wall and stairs to the statue are private property. Please do not trespass.

Tamworth

Marker # 0031: The Chocorua Legend

Location: NH Route 16 (mile marker 67.0) 3.5 mile north of NH Route 113

Sign Erected: 1965

GPS Coordinates- N 43° 54'.530″ W 71° 14'.070"

"In several versions, the legend's sequence relates the mysterious death of Chocorua's son while in the care of a settler named Campbell. Suspicious of the cause, the Pequawket chieftain took revenge on the settler's family. Then, in retaliation, Campbell killed Chocorua on the peak of the mountain now bearing the Indian's name."

Mount Chocorua and the Chocorua Legend are easily one of my favorites stories and roadside stops in New Hampshire. Mount Chocorua is the easternmost peak within the Sandwich Mountain range. It is also one of the most identifiable peaks in New Hampshire.

The Chocorua legend claims that Chief Chocorua remained in the area even after many of his people had fled to St. Francis, Canada after Lovewell's War in 1725. Chocorua was a friend of settler Cornelius Campbell. Chocorua's son, Tuamba was entrusted to the care of the Campbell's while the chieftain was away. Upon his return, Chocorua learned that Tuamba had died.; possibly of poisoning.

One story suggests that the Indian boy ingested some poison liquid, possibly arsenic, prepared as bait for a fox. Learning of his son's death, Chocorua sought revenge by killing Cornelius Campbell's wife and children.

After the death of his family, Campbell and other settlers pursued Chocorua to the summit of this mountain. Some stories claim that Campbell and his men shot and killed Chocorua. Another legend claims that Chocorua jumped off the peak rather than be taken by the settlers. The legend claims Chocorua placed a curse on his pursuers. Stating, "*May the Great Spirit curse you when he speaks in the clouds and his words are fire! May lightning blast your crops! Wind and fire destroy your homes! The Evil One breathe death on your cattle! May panthers howl and the wolves fatten on your bones!*" Whichever legend is factual, the truth is that families were lost in this tragedy and a legend was born.

Tamworth

Marker # 0090: First Summer Playhouse

Location: Intersection of NH Route 113/ NH Route 113A/Main Street

Sign Erected: 1973

GPS Coordinates- N 43° 51'.578″ W 71° 15'.753″

"Nearby stands "The Barnstormers" summer playhouse, the oldest in New Hampshire and one of the first in the nation. Opened in 1931, at one time the cast covered a weekly 80-mile circuit. Currently its performances are limited to this community. Founder of the theater was Francis Grover Cleveland, son of the 22nd President."

Founded by Francis and Alice Cleveland and Ed Goodnow, "The Barnstormers" began in this town where the Cleveland's had a summer home. Francis Cleveland was the youngest child of President Grover Cleveland. According to the theater webpage (www.barnstormerstheatre.org), most of the original troupe were recent graduates of Harvard, Wellesley, and Amherst colleges. The name "Barnstormers" was derived from their barnstorming of communities in New Hampshire and Maine with their show. The theater is now located in the village. From 1931 to 1934, the troupe performed at the Tamworth Gardens. The Barnstormers Theatre purchased the former Kimball general store building in 1935. Summer theater shows have been open to the public in this location since and it has been the longest continuous summer theatre organization in New Hampshire. While President Grover Cleveland died in 1908, and did not visit the theater, his widow former First Lady Frances Cleveland did attend shows.

Tamworth was incorporated in 1766. The original land grant was made in 1765 to John Webster by Governor Benning Wentworth and named in honor of a British admiral. The town of Tamworth is comprised of five villages, Tamworth, Chocorua, South Tamworth, Whittier and Wonalancet. The town is another community that can take pride in their locale between the Lake Region and White Mountains. The most popular tourist stops in town (in my opinion) would be the scenic point of Mt. Chocorua overlooking Chocorua Lake from the Narrows bridge. While this may be my favorite stop in Tamworth, many of the backroads particularly during the foliage season are simply stunning.

Tamworth

Marker # 0155: Chinook Kennels

Location: NH Route 113A (2865 Chinook Trail Rd, Wonalancet)

Sign Erected: 1988

GPS Coordinates-N 43° 54'.514″ W 71° 19'.665"

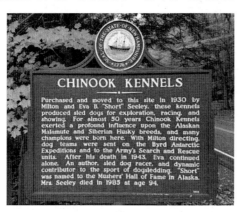

"Purchased and moved to this site in 1930 by Milton and Eva B. "Short" Seeley, these kennels produced sled dogs for exploration, racing, and showing. For almost 50 years Chinook Kennels exerted a profound influence upon the Alaskan Malamute and Siberian Husky breeds, and many champions were born here. With Milton directing, dog teams were sent on the Byrd Antarctic Expeditions and to the Army's Search and Rescue units. After his death in 1943, Eva continued alone. An author, sled dog racer, and dynamic contributor to the sport of dogsledding, "Short" was named to the Musher's Hall of Fame in Alaska. Mrs. Seeley died in 1985 at age 94."

I can only imagine how vibrant this kennel was during its heyday. I was keenly interested in the importance of this kennel in Admiral Byrd's Antarctica expeditions with New Hampshire's state dog. According to an article in the Laconia Daily Sun in December 2016, written by Roger Amsden, the Chinook breed originated with a male dog born in 1917 named "Chinook". The breed is derived from breeds of mastiff, Belgian sheepdog,

German shepherd and Canadian Eskimo dog. Sadly, the patriarch "Chinook" was lost during Byrd's 1929 Antarctic expedition.

The Chinook breed is famous for its playful temperament, strength as a working dog and sociability. Chinooks were also widely used in the US Army for search and rescue operations. The Chinook breed was accepted into the American Kennel Club as a registered breed in 2001 in the working dog class. The Chinook became the New Hampshire state dog breed in 2009 after a petition was introduced by seventh graders from Bedford, New Hampshire.

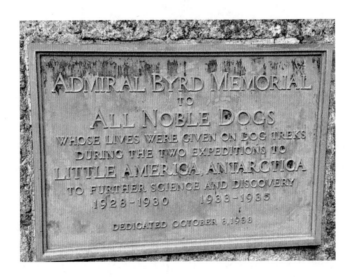

Tilton

Marker # 0149: Lochmere Archaeological District

Location: NH Route 3 to River Rd & Silver Lake Rd

Sign Erected: 1984

GPS Coordinates- N 43° 28'.320″ W 71° 32'.013″

"The history of Lochmere, in the broadest sense, is the history of human use of the Winnipesaukee River. Navigable by canoe, the river served as a major transportation and communications route and, with falls and rapids, it served as a source of food and water power. Thirteen archeological sites record nine millennia of prehistory by native Americans, and eighteen sites relate directly to the domestic and industrial life of early mill owners and the early industrial period of the Village of Lochmere."

This historical marker is in East Tilton, in the village of Lochmere. This is the community where I grew up and spent many days fishing and swimming here. The state identifies this site as the Brennick Lochmere Archaeological Site. The area is believed to have been inhabited from the Middle Archaic through the Late Woodland periods. Upstream from this marker, just past the trestle observers paying close attention may locate the fishing weirs built by native Americans to channel and capture fish.

In the following photo, the stone weirs were visible due to the abnormally low level of the river. A weir is a fish trap in the shape of a "W" made of stones where fish were trapped as they swam upstream. The Indians could easily net or spear the fish in these pools. The Winnipesaukee River begins south of this point and flows to Franklin where the Winnipesaukee and Pemigewasset rivers form the Merrimack River.

This region was predominantly inhabited by the Algonquin tribe which settled in the region of both the Winnipesaukee and Pemigewasset rivers. North of this point on what is now Weirs channel at Weirs beach was a major gathering place of area tribes. Researchers believe that tribes gathered along these weir traps during the salmon, alewives, and shad runs. White settlers were believed to have settled here in the 1770's for fish, farming, and notably water powered mills. This area was listed in the National Register of Historic Places in 1982.

Wakefield

Marker # 0005: George A. Wentworth (1835-1906)

Location: NH Route 16 (mile marker 44.6 - ½ mile south of Ossipee town line)

Sign Erected: 1962

GPS Coordinates-N 43° 38'.000″ W 71° 03'.005″

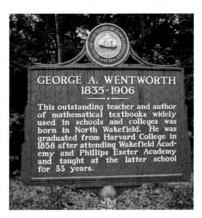

"This outstanding teacher and author of mathematical textbooks widely used in schools and colleges was born in North Wakefield. He was graduated from Harvard College in 1858 after attending Wakefield Academy and Phillips Exeter Academy and taught at the latter for 33 years."

Finding information about George Albert Wentworth was a bit difficult. However, when I researched what mathematical textbooks he authored, I found that it was more than forty. A biography written by Dr. B.F. Finkel (1907) states that George Wentworth was the youngest of eight children. After graduating from Harvard College with high honors in 1858, he taught locally at Phillips Exeter Academy where he was appointed Professor of Mathematics on March 23, 1858.

The town of Wakefield was granted to settlers from Somersworth and Dover in 1749. The area which comprises Wakefield was part of the battlefield for Captain Lovewell's War (also known as Father Rale's War). The first settlers arrived in 1766 and built their first assembly house in 1771. Wakefield's historic district was once known as Wakefield Corner. As the town center, it flourished until the 1870's with the arrival trains to the area now known as Sanbornville. With access to local rivers and streams, early industry relied heavily on water-powered mills. Today, the area is more reliant on tourism seeking to enjoy the eleven local lakes.

Wakefield

Marker # 0123: The Governor's Road

Location: NH Route 16 (mile marker 36.9- south of the junction of NH Route 109)

Sign Erected: 1978 & 1998

GPS Coordinates- N 43° 31'.640″ W 71° 01'.586"

"This name was given to the highway from Portsmouth to Governor John Wentworth's summer estate in Wolfeborough. Passing through Newington, it crossed the Piscataqua River at Knight's Ferry to Dover. From Rochester it skirted Teneriffe Mountain to Middleton Four Corners. Rounding Moose Mountain to Union Meadows it passed through Brookfield, arriving at Wentworth House. The fifty mile highway was completed in 1769."

The Governor's Road is also referred to as the King's Highway through and north of Middleton. The Governor Wentworth estate on Lake Wentworth was the first summer residence built in the Lakes Region and was commonly known as Kingswood Estate. There is a marker "Wentworth Estate" (#0053) that goes into detail about this summer home of the last royal governor. While most of the New Hampshire colony resided near the seacoast, Governor John Wentworth constructed the road to his summer residence in the Lakes Region. This project allowed him a relatively easy "commute" from the state capital in Portsmouth to his Kingswood residence along the shores of Lake Wentworth.

According to the book, *John Wentworth- Governor of New Hampshire 1767-1775* by Lawrence Shaw May (1921), Wentworth preferred to reside most of his time at Wentworth Estate and return to Portsmouth only when government business needed him to be there. The road was paid for by quitrents. This was the payments of rent by landowners to the colonial government. Landowners could also charge citizens for use of these byways. The book also suggests that the Governors Road from Portsmouth to Middleton was relatively smooth in the summer and fall months. The Middleton land grant was not fulfilled; therefore, citizens of the community were unable to complete their section of road from their village to Wolfeboro. Governor Wentworth hired men to complete the road and billed the proprietors in Middleton the cost of the road improvements.

Wolfeboro

Marker # 0053: Wentworth Estate

Location: NH Route 109 at Wentworth State Park (297 Gov. John Wentworth Highway)

Sign Erected: 1968

GPS Coordinates- N 43° 36'.759″ W 71° 08'.872"

"This marker stands on the north-westerly part of a 4,000-acre tract which comprised the elegant country estate of John Wentworth, last royal governor of New Hampshire (1767-1775). The manor house, erected in 1769 on the northeast shore of this lake, was the earliest summer home in the Lakes Region. It was destroyed by fire in 1820."

According to archive records, the Wentworth Estate was commonly known as "Kingswood". My belief is that this name was derived from the area having an abundance of tall pines that were the property of the King of England for making masts for ships. Governor John Wentworth succeeded his uncle as royal Governor Benning Wentworth in 1766. While the property was deeded and reserved for the governor, it was John Wentworth who built this summer retreat. The lake was then known as "Smith Pond". Archeological digs on the property has revealed artifacts that detail what life was like for the privileged elite class of the late 18th century. A unique fact I found as I researched this marker. The largest island on Lake Wentworth is notably named "Stamp Act Island".

The marker is located at the entrance of the 50-acre Wentworth State Park. On the shore of Lake Wentworth, the Governor Wentworth Historic site is a short drive east of this marker on Wentworth Farm Rd. This site is a 96-acre historic property that is open to the public. Onsite, I found a simple stone wall with a plaque commemorating the location of where the Wentworth House once stood. You can walk around and check out the area. The estate well is also visible and has a plaque. The Wentworth estate consisted of the mansion which was 104 feet long and 42 feet wide, two stables, coach house, dairy barn, and a blacksmith shop. Other outbuildings existed onsite as well, but these were the major structures. The estate was known to be one of the finest in New England. While John Wentworth cherished him time on the Kingswood Estate, Lady Frances Wentworth preferred the city-life of Portsmouth. Does this remind anyone of the television series of the 1970's "Green Acres"?

Wolfeboro

Marker # 0116: College Road

Location: NH Route 109 and Lang Pond Road

Sign Erected: 1977

GPS Coordinates- N 43° 36'.855" W 71° 15'.476"

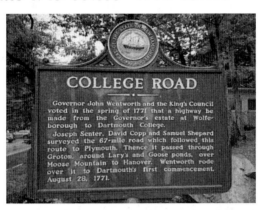

"Governor John Wentworth and the King's Council voted in the spring of 1771 that a highway be made from the Governor's estate at Wolfeborough to Dartmouth College.

Joseph Senter, David Copp and Samuel Shepard surveyed the 67-mile road which followed this route to Plymouth. Thence it passed through Groton, around Lary's and Goose ponds, over Moose Mountain to Hanover. Wentworth rode over it to Dartmouth's first commencement, August 28, 1771."

Reading about the origin of Dartmouth College is fascinating. As the first college in colonial New Hampshire, it was originally proposed under Governor Benning Wentworth as an Episcopal College (Church of England). However, that was unfavorable to the citizens of the colony. When nephew John Wentworth became governor, he worked with Reverend Eleazar Wheelock to start a school to educate the native Indians. In 1769, Dartmouth College was granted by Governor John Wentworth. An interesting fact was that Dartmouth College was first considered to be built in Landaff New Hampshire. The town near Littleton was the favored location for Governor Wentworth but was ultimately decided to be built in Hanover for its accessibility. The site in Hanover was selected on July 5, 1770.

The College Road was one of four major roads built during the era of Governor John Wentworth. This road built in 1771 allowed for the governor to travel from his estate in Wolfeboro to Dartmouth College situated along the banks of the Connecticut River. The first commencement of Dartmouth College was on August 28, 1771. The governor and his party left in celebration from Portsmouth through Wolfeboro on the Governor's Road to Hanover via the College Road to witness the first commencement of four Dartmouth graduates.

Wolfeboro

Marker # 0242: Crescent Lake Ice Harvest

Location: NH Route 28 (mile marker 76) and Birch Rd. (.4 mile north of NH Route 109A)

Sign Erected: 2014

GPS Coordinates- N 43° 35'.791″ W 71° 11'.995″

"Natural ice was harvested in the Lakes Region. Goodwin Basin and Crescent Lake, visible across the road, and Lake Wentworth were local sources. In 1895, Alonzo Avery set up an ice house near Crescent Lake. In 1913 a warm winter caused an ice shortage in Boston, and ice was shipped from NH by rail. Locally, ice was delivered to family ice chests, businesses, camps, and lake cruisers. Refrigeration technology in the 1930s decreased the need for natural ice. The last family ice business, Moody's closed in 1965."

Ice harvesting was an integral commodity in this area. Ice was harvested from Goodwin basin on Crescent Lake (across the street), and Fernald basin just north of this location on Lake Wentworth. In 1956, E.V. Moody Company delivered more than 1,600 tons of ice to residents during the summer months.

Typically, ice was harvested in blocks and stored in cold storage buildings packed in sawdust. The local ice storage building was located off Center Street. According to the Wolfeboro Chronicle

(February 2010), there is a granite bench with a bronze plaque located near the ice harvest area on Bridge Falls Path which was donated by the Moody family. Each February, the Remick Country Doctor Museum and Farm hold an ice harvesting event in Tamworth Village.

A short distance from this marker is the Wright's Museum of World War II. You cannot miss the tank crashing through the side of the building! While the museum is closed from November through April, it is worthwhile to plan a trip to the Lakes Region in the late spring or early Fall. Make sure to plan a visit to this attraction. It is a museum that has exhibits interesting for the entire family.

Chapter Four

Dartmouth/Lake Sunapee Region

The Dartmouth/Lake Sunapee region is another spectacular four-season destination. From the shores of Lake Sunapee for summer fun, Mount Sunapee ski resort for all-inclusive winter activities, foliage, hiking, and so much more. This region of the state is comprised of two distinct areas; the Upper Valley and Lake Sunapee. This region is also home to eight New Hampshire State Parks and to the U.S. Park Service National Historic Site of Saint-Gaudens in Cornish.

The Upper Valley segment of the region is framed with the Connecticut River forming its' western border. The cities of Claremont and Lebanon are situated along the shores of the Connecticut River. To the north, the idyllic farming community of Orford. Here you will find the historic seven Ridge houses. The town of Groton is the home to the Sculptured Rocks State Park. Travel south to the town of Hanover and home to the Ivy League's Dartmouth College founded in 1769. Brick, ivy-covered buildings and quaint niche stores make up a walkable downtown.

Central to the Upper Valley region is the city of Lebanon. Further south is the communities of Newport and Claremont. Here you will find rejuvenated early 20th-century manufacturing communities. Further south along NH Route 12 is the community of Charlestown. Along the main street of Charlestown, you will find three historic markers all within walking distance to each other. Other picturesque communities include Canaan and Enfield.

To the east is the Lake Sunapee segment of the Dartmouth/Lake Sunapee region. Quaint villages along country roads make this drive especially pleasing during the foliage season. Traveling from Bradford, Warner, Sutton and Washington promises nice country communities with beautiful early 19th century architecture.

The town of Newbury will take you along the shore of Lake Sunapee. Here, you can visit the Town Hall that has plenty of local information for visitors. The Town Hall is also located next to the historical marker for the Center Meeting House. The town is also home to the John Hay National Wildlife Refuge which includes the summer home of former U.S. Secretary of State John Hay. This grand summer home is known as the "Fells" and is located on NH Route 103. Newbury is also the home of Lake Sunapee State Park and the four-season destination of the Mount Sunapee Ski resort.

To the north and east of Lake Sunapee are the towns of New London and Warner. These two towns have quaint downtown shopping. Warner is home to the New Hampshire Telephone Museum, located at 1 Depot Street. Here you will see the era of the telephone. Yes kids, phones were not always portable! Their website is www.nhtelephonemuseum.com

 A favorite stop of mine is the Homestead restaurant on Main street in Warner. Griddle-size pancakes, homemade ingredients and a homestyle feel makes this a must stop. Enjoy coffee on the front porch while relaxing in the rocking chairs.

Dartmouth/Lake Sunapee Region

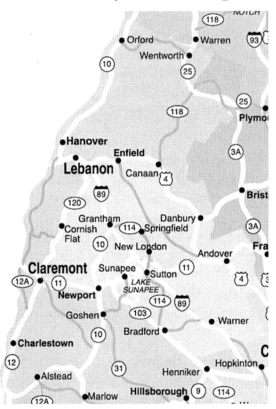

Andover- Marker #0054: Potter Place

Bradford- Marker #0108: Bradford Center

Canaan- Marker #0021: Canaan Street

Canaan- Marker #0246: Noyes Academy

Charlestown- Marker #0002: Fort at Number 4

Charlestown- Marker #0117: General John Stark's Expedition to Bennington, August 1777

Charlestown- Marker #0177: Charlestown, Home of Carlton E. "Pudge" Fisk

Claremont- Marker #0041: First Roman Catholic Church

Claremont- Marker #0057: Union Church

Claremont- Marker #0188: Historic Handshake

Cornish- Marker #0016: Winston Churchill

Cornish- Marker #0076: Salmon Portland Chase

Cornish- Marker #0134: The Cornish Colony

Cornish- Marker #0158: Cornish-Windsor Bridge

Enfield- Marker #0202: Enfield Shakers

Enfield- Marker #0241: Downtown Enfield Village

Goshen- Marker #0140: Captain John W. Gunnison

Grafton- Marker #0251: Dr. Jennie Sarah Barney (1861-1956)

Grafton- Marker #0252: Bungtown

Lempster- Marker #0182: Lighting Up Rural New Hampshire

Newbury- Marker #0081: Center Meeting House

Newport- Marker #0006: Sarah Josepha Buell Hale (1788-1879)

Newport- Marker #0106: Joel McGregor-Last Surviving Soldier of the Revolutionary War

Orford- Marker #0033: The Ridge

Plainfield- Marker #0077: Kimball Union Academy

Sutton- Marker #0044: John Sargent Pillsbury (1828-1901)

Warner- Marker #0243: Mount Kearsarge and the U.S.S. Kearsarge

Washington- Marker #0094: Birthplace of Seventh Day Adventist Church

Wilmot- Marker #0040: Mason's Patent

Andover

Marker # 0054: Potter Place

Location: NH Route 11 (mile marker 43) near Potter Place village

Sign Erected: 1968

GPS Coordinates- N 43° 26'.307" W 71° 51'.245"

"The community takes its name from Richard Potter, noted magician, ventriloquist and showman. This 19th century master of the Black Arts was known throughout America. He died here in 1835 in his mansion, a showplace in the town. He is buried in a small plot on his once extensive estate."

Richard Potter (1783-1835) was the first African-American born magician to gain his fame in the United States. Born the son of a slave and a minister, Potter perfected his skills as a ventriloquist, hypnotist and magician in Europe under the tutorship of Scottish entertainer John Rannie. Potter returned to the United States and was an assistant to John Rannie.

In 1811, after Rannie's retirement, Potter continued entertaining on his own. In 1814, he purchased 175 acres in this community and built his estate. Potter died September 20, 1835. He was buried in front of his estate alongside his wife Sally. The graves were moved in 1849 to their current location (adjacent to the

Potter Place Station) after the mansion burned down and the introduction of the railroad line through the property.

The Potter Place Railroad Station and Museum building was built in 1874. This building replaced an earlier depot built in 1847. This building was registered on the National Register of Historic Places in 1989. It is considered one of the finest architecturally concise railroad stations of the 19th century in New Hampshire.

The town of Andover was originally settled in 1761, then known as Emerisstown. The name was changed in 1779 to Andover. The private secondary school, Proctor Academy was founded in 1848 which is in the heart of the village center on NH Route 11. The town is comprised of the villages of East and West Andover, Cilleyville, and Potter Place.

Bradford

Marker # 0108: Bradford Center

Location: 15 Rowe Mountain Rd. 0.1 mile east of Center Rd

Sign Erected: 1976

GPS Coordinates- N 43° 14'.222" W 71° 58'.237"

"This Common, designated the geographic center of the town in 1791, at one time was bordered by the Town Pound, constructed in 1789, the existing District One School, built in 1793, and the still-standing Congregational Society Meeting House, dedicated in 1838. This also marks the site of the first Meeting House in the Town of Bradford. Erected in 1797, it was dismantled in 1863, moved to Bradford Village and re-erected as the Town Hall."

The original Bradford Center meetinghouse built in 1796 was used for both civic and religious service gatherings. The Congregational Society Meetinghouse now known as the Bradford Center Meetinghouse was built in 1838 after state legislation mandated the separation of church and state. The building is Greek Revival-style architecture and is maintained by the Union Congregational Society that is devoted to the preservation of the building. The building was listed on the National Register of Historic Places in 2013. The original meetinghouse built in 1797 was dismantled and the timbers were used in the construction of the town hall building. Onsite is the Bradford Center burial ground.

The town of Bradford was settled in 1772 and is believed to be named after Bradford Massachusetts where many of the settlers came from. The town was incorporated in 1787, nine days after the ratification of the Constitution. Not far from this site on Center road is the Bement covered bridge. Built in 1854, the long-truss bridge spans 53 feet over the Warner river. The Bement covered bridge was listed on the National Register of Historic Places in 1976.

Canaan

Marker # 0021: Canaan Street

Location: US Route 4 and Canaan Street (alongside building)

Sign Erected: 1964

GPS Coordinates- N 43° 38'.799" W 72° 00'.710"

"First known as 'Broad Street,' this early venture in town planning was laid out in 1788. About a mile in length and beautifully situated, starting about two miles in on next northerly road, the plan provided for an orderly arrangement of attractive homesteads."

I frequently traveled this road in the 1980's when I lived in Enfield. I recall as a young boy this marker when the adjacent building was an active grocery store and I visited with my father. It is interesting to look down Canaan Street and imagine what it was like during its heyday. Canaan village was the heart of the community and in 1884 had more than 30 businesses.

An interesting fact is that this community of Canaan village was destroyed in a fire on June 2, 1923. The fire destroyed 48 homes and businesses. The only structure to remain was the veteran's monument. The townspeople quickly banded together to rebuild their community. A visit to the Canaan Historical Society museum, visitors can view the extensive photos of the tragic fire and of the infamous train wreck that occurred on September 15, 1907. The accident claimed the lives of 25 passengers. The Canaan Street Historic District was listed on the National Register of Historic Places in 1973.

Canaan was chartered in 1761 and named after the community of Canaan Connecticut which was named for the biblical land of Canaan. The town was not settled until 1766. Once a bustling community centered around the railroad and mills along the Indian River, Canaan maintains its small-town charm and intimacy of neighbors helping neighbors to preserve their heritage. While US Route 4 is the main thoroughfare through the town village, a turn onto Canaan Street and travel northwest to Canaan Lake will offer visitors a surprising change in architecture and a stunning view of what this town resembled in the late 19th century.

Canaan

Marker # 0246: Noyes Academy

Location: 570 Canaan Street in front of the Canaan Historical Society building

Sign Erected: 2015

GPS Coordinates- N 43° 39'.916″ W 72° 02'.546″

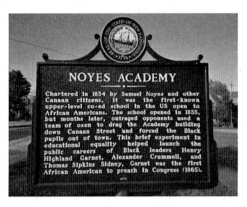

"Chartered in 1834 by Samuel Noyes and other Canaan citizens, it was the first-known upper-level co-ed school in the US open to African Americans. The school opened in 1835, but months later, outraged opponents used a team of oxen to drag the Academy building down Canaan Street and forced the Black pupils out of town. This brief experiment in educational equality helped launch the public careers of Black leaders Henry Highland Garnet, Alexander Crummell, and Thomas Sipkins Sidney. Garnet was the first African American to preach in Congress (1865)."

When I visited this marker, it was during the peak of foliage season. The colors were so vibrant and spectacular. I was fortunate to have visited when the Historical Society and museum was open. I took the picture of the Noyes Academy building on this visit and was treated to a wonderful presentation of the history of this event by one of the volunteers.

The Noyes Academy which opened in 1835 began with twenty-eight white and fourteen black students. The charter for the school was focused on an equal education regardless of the student's race. According to research conducted by a Dartmouth professor, Noyes Academy's opportunity for black students was such a draw that many African-American families moved here from as far as New York City to attend the school. While the black students were from states across the Northeast, the white students were local.

Many of the residents were angry of the inclusion of black students in their school as well as living in their community. In August of 1835, enraged residents with 90 oxen moved the school building down Canaan street and the building was destroyed. The residents built a new school known as Canaan Union Academy and it was open to white students only.

Currently, the Cardigan Mountain School resides at the end of Canaan Street. This private all-boys school was chartered in 1945 on the site of the original Noyes Academy. The Canaan Union Academy building is now the Canaan Museum.

Charlestown

Marker # 0002: Fort at No. 4

Location: NH Route 12 on Main Street (west side of road)

Sign Erected: 1964

GPS Coordinates- N 43° 13'.990″ W 72° 25'.427"

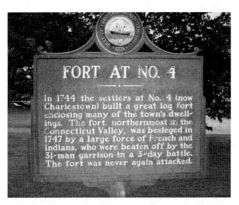

"In 1744 the settlers at No. 4 (now Charlestown) built a great log fort enclosing many of the town's dwellings. The fort, northernmost in the Connecticut Valley, was besieged in 1747 by a large force of French and Indians, who were beaten off by the 31-man garrison in a 3-day battle. The fort was never again attacked."

In 1744, the settlement known as Fort Number 4 was the northernmost settlement and trading post of the colony made in a land grant by the Massachusetts General Court. The "plantation" land grant was made in 1735 with the original settlers arriving in 1740. Original families settling on this plantation land were three Farnsworth brothers. Their efforts to establish a settlement drew additional families. The remoteness of this location truly made it a wilderness experience.

The closest colonial settlement was Fort Dummer which was 40 miles south. To the west of the Connecticut River, land was claimed by both New Hampshire and New York and inhabited by the Abenaki Indians. The land west of the Saint Lawrence river and to the north was also claimed by the French as New France and by the English. With the French claiming land and using the St. Lawrence waterway as an expeditious means of travel, the Fort at No. 4 was on the edge of disputed territory. With the Abenaki Indians allied with the French, the English settlers at Fort No. 4 were in constant fear of attack.

In 1753, the settlement was re-chartered as part of New Hampshire. Colonial Governor Benning Wentworth granted the name change to Charlestown in honor of Sir Charles Knowles an admiral in the British navy. Today, the Fort No. 4 is a living history museum. Visitors can walk through the settlement and observe reenactors living life as a pioneer of the 18th century. The Fort No. 4 is located at 267 Springfield Rd. (NH Route 11) in Charlestown. Their website is www.fortat4.org.

Charlestown

Marker # 0117: General John Stark's Expedition to Bennington, August 1777

Location: NH Route 12 on Main Street (west side of road)

Sign Erected: 1977

GPS Coordinates- N 43° 14'.019″ W 72° 25'.438"

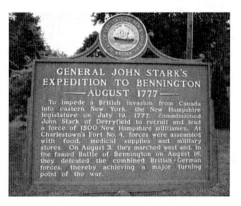

"To impede a British invasion from Canada into eastern New York, the New Hampshire legislature on July 19, 1777, commissioned John Stark of Derryfield to recruit and lead a force of 1500 New Hampshire militiamen. At Charlestown's Fort No. 4, forces were assembled with food, medical supplies and military stores. On August 3, they marched west and, in the famed Battle of Bennington on August 16, they defeated the combined British-German forces, thereby achieving a major turning point of the war."

General John Stark is prevalent in much of New Hampshire's history. At least four historical markers have reference to John Stark. Brigadier General Stark along with Colonel Seth Warner of the Green Mountain boys were victorious against British General Burgoyne at the Battle of Bennington. During this battle, General Stark is believed to have led his men to assault the British with the claim, "They are ours, or this night Molly Stark sleeps a widow".

General John Stark had retired from militia service. He had commanded forces at the Battles of Bunker Hill, and Trenton and Princeton with General Washington. Being passed over for promotion, Colonel Stark retired. When New Hampshire needed a competent commander of the militia, they petitioned the retired John Stark to return to service. Stark was promoted to Brigadier General.

The Battle of Bennington took place from August 14-16, 1777. British General Burgoyne made progress south along Lake Champlain and the Hudson River towards Albany, New York sacking English forts and outposts. His mission was to separate New England from the rest of the colonies. With provisions running low, General Burgoyne sent a force of two detachments to Bennington to capture needed supplies. He was met with strong resistance from Brigadier General John Stark and Colonel Seth Warner. This tactical victory provided the colonial militias time to resupply and regroup. This American victory over a dominant British army was an impetus in the defeat of Burgoyne's army at the Battle of Saratoga.

Charlestown

Marker # 0177: Charlestown, New Hampshire Home Town of Carlton E. "Pudge" Fisk

Location: NH Route 12 on Main Street in front of Charlestown School (east side of road)

Sign Erected: 2001

GPS Coordinates- N 43° 13'.934″ W 72° 25'.407"

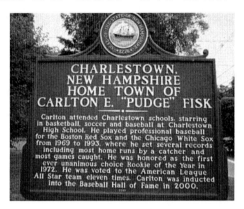

"Carlton attended Charlestown schools, starring in basketball, soccer and baseball at Charlestown High School. He played professional baseball for the Boston Red Sox and the Chicago White Sox from 1969 to 1993, where he set several records including most home runs by a catcher and most games caught. He was honored as the first ever unanimous choice Rookie of the Year in 1972. He was voted to the American League All Star team eleven times. Carlton was inducted into the Baseball Hall of Fame in 2000."

Carlton "Pudge" Fisk was a childhood hero of mine. As a loyal Red Sox fan and catcher, I wanted to emulate Pudge Fisk. Carlton Fisk's famous moment in the 1975 World Series against the Cincinnati Reds is a moment locked in Red Sox history. It was during game 6 of the World Series. The game was at Fenway Park. I stayed up to watch my team, even though it was a school night. In the top of the 12th inning, Fisk hit a flyball down along the left field line. As Fisk trotted down the baseline, it appeared as if he was willing the ball to stay in fair territory. It bounced off the pole above the Green Monster and stayed a fair ball. The Red Sox won 7-6 and forced a game 7. The foul pole in left field is now known as Fisk Pole. This moment caught on film is classic footage of baseball legacy.

Fisk holds numerous Major League Baseball records and is a Hall of Fame inductee. Many folks outside of New Hampshire do not know that Carlton Fisk still holds a New Hampshire Interscholastic Athletic Association tournament record in basketball from a championship game in 1965.

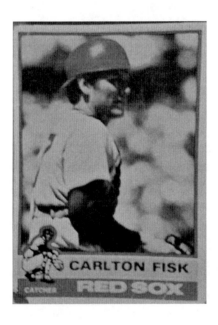

Claremont

Marker # 0041: First Roman Catholic Church

Location: NH Route 12/ NH Route 103/Plains Road (West Claremont)

Sign Erected: 1966 & 2002

GPS Coordinates- N 43° 23'.525″ W 72° 22'.578"

"Southerly on Old Church Road is located the first Roman Catholic edifice in New Hampshire. It was erected in 1823 under the direction of the Reverend Virgil Horace Barber, S.J. The building serves St. Mary's parish and contained the first Roman Catholic school in the State."

Old St. Mary's parish built in 1823 is the oldest Catholic building in the state. According to the Old St. Mary's Church history, Reverend Barber was the son of Reverend Daniel Barber who was the Episcopal rector at the Union Church (see marker #0057). Reverend Daniel Barber resigned as rector of the Episcopal Union Church and converted to Roman Catholicism in 1818.

Daniel Barber's son, Reverend Virgil Horace Barber was responsible for the construction of this building in 1823.The first floor of this building was used as a chapel and the second floor was a high school. I could not find what the third floor was used for. According to the church history, there is evidence along the south wall that the brickwork shows where the rectory was attached. Father, Reverend Daniel Barber resided in the home attached to the south side of the church.

This building was used for nearly fifty years and was put up for sale in 1876. The St. Mary's parish built a church more central to city center in 1870. The current building fell into disrepair and in 1965, restorations were completed for approximately $30,000. The building can be found near 128 Old Church Rd. The Union Church (marker #0057) is just across the street.

Claremont

Marker # 0057: Union Church

Location: NH Route 12 North and Half Mile Road

Sign Erected: 1968

GPS Coordinates- N 43° 23'.188" W 72° 23'.339"

"Located easterly on Old Church Road, this wood-framed structure, built 1771-1773, is the oldest standing Episcopal Church in the State, serving the second oldest parish. The parish began in 1768 as a mission of the Society for the Propagation of the Gospel in Foreign Parts. The first rector was Reverend Ranna Cossitt (1773-1785)."

The church was built by master carpenter Ebenezer Rice and is believed to have been built to resemble Queen's Chapel in Portsmouth, NH. According to church history, the New Hampshire legislature incorporated the Union Church in 1794 as a union of Episcopal and Congregational parishioners under the leadership of one minister. While Reverend Daniel Barber became the rector in 1795, he was trained as a Congregationalist.

The record claims the union of the two faiths did not come to fruition. Reverend Daniel Barber converted to Catholicism in 1818. The church history openly mentions how the Union

Church was instrumental in its efforts to combine episcopal and congregational faiths, as well as being part of the birth of the Roman Catholic church in New Hampshire. The church was listed on the National Register of Historic Places in 1980 located at 133 Old Church Rd.

To visit both the Union and Old St. Mary's churches, take Half Mile Road which is directly across the street from this marker. Follow to the end and cross Plains Road and continue straight on Half Mile Road. This short dirt road will take you to Old Church Road. Turn right onto Old Church Road. The Union Church is ahead on the left and the Old St. Mary's Church is on the right adjacent to the cemetery.

Claremont

Marker # 0041: Historic Handshake

Location: Intersection of Maple Avenue and Buena Vista Road (67 Maple Ave.)

Sign Erected: 2003

GPS Coordinates-N 43° 21'.791″ W 72° 21'.152″

"On June 11, 1995, President William Jefferson Clinton and Speaker of the U.S. House of Representatives Newt Gingrich met at the invitation of the Congress of Claremont Senior Citizens, Inc. to debate issues affecting senior citizens. During the debate, the political foes shook hands and pledged to create a bi-partisan commission to study federal limits on lobbying and the financing of election campaigns. This famous "handshake" on campaign finance reform was carried live on television and received widespread media coverage including front page attention in newspapers nationwide."

New Hampshire loves the political spotlight. The First in the National primaries is a sacred rite for Granite-Staters. The historic handshake between President Clinton and Speaker Newt Gingrich came about due to the concern and behest of New Hampshire senior citizens in Claremont concerned about the excessive money in campaigns. The idea of inviting the two most powerful men in government at the time and having them accept is impressive. Having the two men debate on national television in the community of Claremont was historic. The notion of bipartisan efforts on behalf of the citizens seems like a distant fantasy in today's political climate. With the determination of a small group of Claremont seniors, it is refreshing to know the impact of a local effort.

While the promise with a handshake was commendable, it can be argued that not enough was accomplished. Campaign influence is still concerning more than three decades later. Yet, kudos to the Congress of Claremont Senior Citizens to influence Washington D.C. power players to sit at the table to talk to each other. My guess is the senior citizens of Claremont using their parenting experience is just what our politicians needed!

Cornish

Marker # 0016: Winston Churchill

Location: NH 12A south of Plainfield/Cornish town line

Sign Erected: 1963

GPS Coordinates- N 43° 31'.020″ W 72° 23'.145"

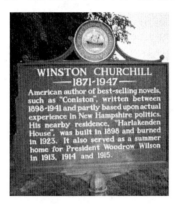

"American author of best-selling novels, such as 'Coniston', written between 1898-1941 and partly based upon actual experience in New Hampshire politics. His nearby residence, 'Harlakenden House', was built in 1898 and burned in 1923. It also served as a summer home for President Woodrow Wilson in 1913, 1914, and 1915."

Winston Churchill who this sign is dedicated to is the less famous of the namesake. Most Americans think of the British Prime Minister during World War II. Frankly, I had not heard of the American author who bears the famous name until I visited this historical marker. Born in St. Louis, Missouri on November 10, 1871, Churchill attended the U.S. Naval Academy and graduated in 1894. He resigned from the navy in 1895 to pursue his career as a writer.

Churchill's residence, "Harlakenden House" was named after his wife Mabel Harlakenden Hall who he was married to for fifty years. Once Churchill moved to Cornish in 1899, he was an active participant with the nearby Cornish Colony. As an author, two of his more notable books are *The Celebrity* and *Richard Carvel.* An interesting point of history is that the Harlakenden House was the summer "White House" for President Woodrow Wilson from 1913 to 1915. The house offered President Wilson and his wife a relief from the Washington D.C. heat of summer.

Churchill also pursued politics. He was elected to the New Hampshire General Court in 1903 and 1905. He also ran an unsuccessful campaign for governor in 1906 on the Bull Moose ticket. The novel, "Coniston" was written in 1906 and was based upon the story of New Hampshire politician Ruel Durkee. From what I could gather, this fictional character Jethro Bass was a corrupt New Hampshire political figure.

American Winston Churchill had known the British Churchill. It is believed that the Brit, suggested his signature would include his middle surname of Winston Spencer-Churchill in his novels. The American Churchill stated he would do the same if he had a middle name.

Cornish

Marker # 0076: Salmon Portland Chase (1808-1873)

Location: NH 12A 2 miles north of Claremont/Cornish town line

Sign Erected: 1971

GPS Coordinates- N 43° 27'.327" W 72° 23'.250"

"In this house was born Salmon P. Chase, U.S. Senator from Ohio (1849-55), Governor of Ohio (1855-59), a founder of the Republican Party and leader in the anti-slavery movement. After serving as Secretary of the Treasury in Lincoln's Cabinet, he was appointed Chief Justice of the United States. The Chase Manhattan Bank in New York was named in his honor."

While Salmon P. Chase was born in this house on January 13, 1808, he only resided here until the death of his father in 1817. He then moved to Ohio to live with his uncle. Salmon Chase attended school in Ohio and returned to the Upper Valley to attend Dartmouth College where he graduated in 1826.

After serving the State of Ohio as both U.S. Senator and Governor, Chase was unsuccessful in a bid for the Republican nomination for U.S. president in 1860. The nomination went to a former congressman from Illinois named Abraham Lincoln. Lincoln beat out both challengers Salmon P. Chase and William H. Seward.

Chase was appointed to the position of Secretary of the Treasury under Lincoln in 1861. He was instrumental in the development of the national banking system and the issuance of paper currency, which had been solely coins. I read that Salmon Chase was also responsible for getting "In God We Trust" on U.S. currency. In 1864, Chase left the position at the Treasury and was appointed Chief Justice of the Supreme Court by President Lincoln. He remained Chief Justice until his death in 1873.

The Chase homestead at this site was originally located across the road. It was moved around 1848 to make way for the railroad. The home was listed on the National Register of Historic Places and designated a National Historic Landmark in 1975.

Cornish

Marker # 0134: The Cornish Colony

Location: NH 12A just north of Saint Gaudens National Historic Site

Sign Erected: 1979 and 1990

GPS Coordinates- N 43° 29'.758" W 72° 22'.560"

"The Cornish Colony (1885-1935) was a group of artists, sculptors, writers, journalists, poets, and musicians who joined the sculptor Augustus Saint-Gaudens in Cornish and found the area a delightful place to live and work. Some prominent members were sculptor Herbert Adams, poet Percy MacKaye, architect Charles A. Platt artist Kenyon Cox, Stephen Parrish and his son Maxfield, and landscape architects Rose Nichols and Ellen Shipman."

The Cornish Colony, also known as the Cornish Artists' Colony began after Augustus Saint-Gaudens moved to the property in 1885. Saint-Gaudens was considered the most renowned American sculptor of his time. Some of his more famous works of art include the Standing Lincoln in Washington D.C. and the Shaw Memorial here at Saint-Gaudens property.

The draw to the colony was the natural beauty of the region. Some believe the scenery and landscape of the area resembled Italian landscapes. Even after Saint-Gaudens death in 1907, many artists, writers, poets and painters who summered at the Cornish Artist Colony, moved here permanently.

Adjacent to the site of this marker is the Blow Me Down mill built in 1891. Originally, part of the Blow Me Down farm, this mill was named for the stream that flows through it. The property was purchased by New York attorney Charles Beaman in 1882, who introduced Augustus Saint-Gaudens to the area. The mill produced grain and electricity to the Cornish Colony and the Blow Me Down farm. The mill closed in 1910. In 1984, the Blow Me Down property was included in the Saint-Gaudens National Historic Site. The estate was declared a National Historic Landmark in 1962 and placed on the National Register of Historic Places in 1966. The Saint Gaudens National Historic Site is the only New Hampshire property that is part of the National Park System.

Cornish

Marker # 0134: Cornish-Windsor Bridge

Location: NH 12A at Cornish-Windsor Bridge

Sign Erected: 1989

GPS Coordinates- N 43° 28'.379″ W 72° 23'.004"

"Built in 1866 at a cost of $9,000, this is the longest wooden bridge in the United States and the longest two-span covered bridge in the world. The fourth bridge at this site, the 460-foot structure was built by Bela J. Fletcher (1811-1877) of Claremont and James F. Tasker (1826-1903) of Cornish, using a lattice truss patented by architect Ithiel Town in 1820 and 1835. Built as a toll bridge by a private corporation, the span was purchased by the State of New Hampshire in 1936 and made toll-free in 1943."

The Cornish-Windsor bridge that is currently in place is the fourth bridge at this site. The previously three were built in 1796, 1824, and 1828 were all destroyed by floods. During the construction of the current bridge, the framing was completed in a meadow northwest of this site and moved into place. The State of New Hampshire made renovations to this bridge in 1954 but was again damaged by flooding and ice jams in 1977 and additional renovations had to be made.

The entire structure is in New Hampshire due to the state boundary being the western mean low water mark of the river.

The American Society of Civil Engineers designated the bridge as a National Historic Civil Engineering Landmark in 1970. The Cornish-Windsor Bridge was listed on the National Register of Historic Places in 1976. The bridge is 449 feet long with spans of 203 feet and 204 feet respectively.

The Town of Cornish was granted in 1763 and incorporated in 1765 by colonial Governor Benning Wentworth. Agriculture and shipping via the Connecticut River made this area a desired place to settle. The Connecticut River Scenic Byway travels along NH Route 12 through this community. Possibly the most notable resident was J.D. Salinger, author of *"The Catcher in the Rye"*. Salinger moved to Cornish and led a reclusive life. He died January 27, 2010 at the age of 91.

Enfield

Marker # 0202: Enfield Shakers

Location: 460 NH 4A at Lower Shaker Village

Sign Erected: 2006

GPS Coordinates- N 43° 37'.207″ W 72° 08'.831"

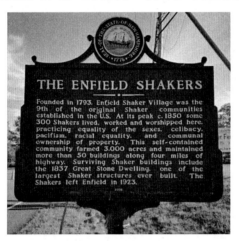

"Founded in 1793, Enfield Shaker Village was the 9th of the original Shaker communities established in the U.S. At its peak c. 1850 some 300 Shakers lived, worked and worshipped here, practicing equality of the sexes, celibacy, pacifism, racial equality, and communal ownership of property. This self-contained community farmed 3,000 acres and maintained more than 50 buildings along four miles of highway. Surviving Shaker buildings include the 1837 Great Stone Dwelling, one of the largest Shaker structures ever built. The Shakers left Enfield in 1923."

The United Society of Believers in Christ's Second Coming, or more commonly known as Shakers was established in England during the mid-18th century. They derived the name "Shaker" or "Shaking Quakers" because of the movements they made as they worshiped in dance. The mother of the Shaker religion was Mother Ann Lee who moved to the United States and founded the religion in 1774. As stated on this marker, the Shakers were celibate, pacifists, believed in communal ownership and gender and race equality. The Shaker community would raise orphans in their communities and these children could decide to stay or leave when they reached adulthood. The Shakers communities peaked in the United States with approximately 6,000 members throughout the eastern United States. The Shakers were the first group to receive conscientious objector status. A Shaker elder traveled to Washington D.C. to meet with President Abraham Lincoln and plead for exclusion from the Draft Act of 1863 during the Civil War.

Today, Shaker communities are chapters into the past. The Shaker museum is in the Great Stone Dwelling building across the street. The first floor was dedicated to the preparation and eating of the meals. The second story was primarily a meeting room and some "dwelling rooms". The third and fourth floors were dwelling rooms, and the fifth and sixth floors were storage. The Shaker Village was listed with the National Register of Historic Places in 1979.

Enfield

Marker # 0241: Downtown Enfield Village

Location: 51 Main Street West of Shaker Hill Road (Municipal Rail Trail parking lot)

Sign Erected: 2014

GPS Coordinates- N 43° 38'.481″ W 72° 08'.760″

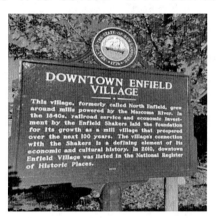

"This village, formerly called North Enfield, grew around mills powered by the Mascoma River. In the 1840's, railroad service and economic investment by the Enfield Shakers laid the foundation for its growth as a mill village that prospered over the next 100 years. The village's connection with the Shakers is a defining element of its economic and cultural history. In 2010, downtown Enfield Village was listed in the National Register of Historic Places."

The Town of Enfield was incorporated in 1761 by colonial Governor Benning Wentworth. The name was derived from the number of settlers who came from Enfield, Connecticut. The influence of industry along the Mascoma River as far back as 1800, was instrumental in creating the village district. According to the National Register of Historic Places, in 1800 the area was used for industry.

In 1804, the construction of the Grafton Turnpike which ran from Orford, NH south through Enfield to Danbury where it linked with the Fourth New Hampshire Turnpike. In addition, the Croydon Turnpike ran through this area connecting travel from Lebanon through Enfield to Newport connecting to the Second New Hampshire Turnpike. In 1840, the addition of rail service only increased the vitality of the region for industry. With the Shaker population as a skilled workforce, the region was a vibrant industrial center of the 19th century.

The town is comprised of four distinct villages. Upper and Lower Shaker Village are along the western shore of Mascoma Lake on NH Route 4A. Eastman Village is located along the southwest corner on Eastman Pond which is accessible via Interstate 89. Enfield Center is at the southern end of Mascoma Lake along NH Route 4A. Today, Enfield draws visitors for its beauty and recreational activities. The Shrine of our Lady La Salette located next to the Shaker Village property is a major draw for visitors. During the Christmas season, the grounds are beautifully decorated with lights and nativity scenes.

Goshen

Marker # 0140: Capt. John W. Gunnison

Location: NH Route 10 North (mile marker 48.3)

Sign Erected: 1981

GPS Coordinates- N 43° 18'.124″ W 72° 08'.959″

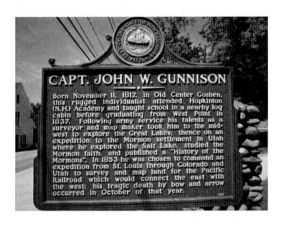

"Born November 11, 1812, in Old Center Goshen, this rugged individualist attended Hopkinton (N.H.) Academy and taught school in a nearby log cabin before graduating from West Point in 1837. Following army service his talents as a surveyor and map maker took him to the midwest to explore the Great lakes; thence on an expedition to the Mormon settlement in Utah where he explored the Salt Lake, studied the Mormon faith, and published a "History of the Mormons". In 1853 he was chosen to command an expedition from St. Louis through Colorado and Utah to survey and map land for the Pacific Railroad which would connect the east with the west; his tragic death by bow and arrow occurred in October of that year."

Second in his West Point class of fifty cadets, John Williams Gunnison earned his notoriety as an Army officer in the Corps of Topographical Engineers. Gunnison led several survey expeditions throughout the Great Lakes area as well into the Utah Territory. In 1849, Gunnison was the deputy commander of an expedition to the Great Salt Lake area. During the expedition, he befriended Mormon settlers and studied the Latter-Day Saints religion.

On May 3, 1853, Captain Gunnison was ordered to lead a survey expedition to the Utah Territory between the 38th and 39th parallel for a route for the Pacific railroad. On the morning of October 26, 1853, near Sevier Lake in the Colorado Territory (now Utah), Captain Gunnison and seven of his survey crew were killed by warriors of the Ute Indian tribe. Only four of Gunnison's men escaped. The massacre site was listed in the National Register of Historic Places in 1976.

The town of Goshen was first settled in 1768 by three families. The community was incorporated in 1791 after the residents petitioned New Hampshire Governor Josiah Bartlett. The Captain John W. Gunnison homestead is located on Goshen Center Road and was listed on the National Register of Historic Places December 19, 1979. The major lake in Goshen is named Gunnison Lake in honor of the town's famous son.

Grafton

Marker # 0251: Dr. Jennie Sarah Barney (1861-1956)

Location: US Route 4 and Prescott Hill Road (in front of Town Offices)

Sign Erected: 2016

GPS Coordinates- N 43° 33'.680″ W 71° 56'.981”

"Born to a prominent family in Grafton, J. Sarah Barney graduated valedictorian from Boston University with degrees in medicine and surgery in 1896. A founding doctor at Franklin Hospital, where she practiced from 1910 to her retirement, Dr. Barney was remembered for her grit, humor, and involvement with women's suffrage. Upon her death, newspapers called her a pioneer and urged young readers to "gather a little inspiration from the life of Dr. Barney to face up to the problem of the hour."

Dr. Jennie Sarah Barney was born June 8, 1861, the daughter of Jesse and Elvira Barney in Grafton New Hampshire. Dr. Barney joined the Women's Christian Temperance Union in 1906. This organization's mission was to protest social injustices of women during the early 20th century. One of their movements was the promotion of the prohibition of alcohol through non-violent protests in bars. Dr. Barney never married, nor had any children.

She died February 24, 1956 and is buried in Franklin New Hampshire.

Grafton was incorporated in 1778 and is believed to be named after the 3rd Duke of Grafton who was the cousin of colonial Governor Benning Wentworth. This quiet town is home to Ruggles Mine. Ruggles Mine began in the early 19th century as a mica quarry. Today, the property is privately-owned and closed to the public in 2016. For decades, it was an attraction for families to search and quarry for some gems and stones. Who knows, maybe someday this family attraction will re-open for those who seek to find a rare gem.

Photo Courtesy of Grafton NH Historical Society

Grafton

Marker # 0252: Bungtown

Location: 32 Turnpike Road 1/10 mile from US Route 4 (Grafton Town Hall)

Sign Erected: 2016

GPS Coordinates- N 43° 34'.061″ W 71° 55'.565″

"In the 19th century this industrial village developed between the Grafton Turnpike and the banks of Mill Brook. East Grafton was once known as Bungtown, a name derived from an accident involving an overturned cart of failed barrel stoppers or "bungs." At peak production, one could find shingles, clapboards, cider, harnesses, axes, paint, woolens, bobbins, carriages, and coffins made here, powered by several mill ponds. Today, the carding mill, axe factory, and harness shop still stand."

According to the *Gazetteer of Grafton County, N.H., 1709-1886* by Hamilton Child (1886), the town of Grafton was comprised of three villages; Grafton, Grafton Center, and East Grafton. The village of East Grafton was situated between the area known as Whittier and Mill brooks. East Grafton village (also known as Bungtown), powered much of the area manufacturing and industry off the hydro power of Mill Brook. Today, much of what remains is located on Mill Brook along the Grafton Turnpike which is about ¾ mile from U.S. Route 4. The buildings that remain include Hinkson's Carding Mill, the former Lang axe manufacturing building, the harness shop (red house), Folsom's store, Town Hall (a former schoolhouse) and the Union Church which was built in 1883.

The Grafton Turnpike was incorporated in 1804 as a bi-way from Orford New Hampshire to Andover where it connected with the Fourth New Hampshire Turnpike. This travel way was approximately 35 miles in length. This main travel route helped to establish East Grafton as a vital community in conjunction with the railway route through Grafton Center.

Lempster

Marker # 0182: Lighting Up Rural New Hampshire

Location: 112 Lempster Street & Allen Road (in front of Silver Mountain Grange Hall)

Sign Erected: 2002

GPS Coordinates- N 43° 14'.327" W 72° 12'.606"

"On nearby Allen Road on December 4, 1939, the New Hampshire Electric Cooperative set its first utility pole, an important event in bringing electric service to the farms, mills, and homes of the New Hampshire countryside. A group of citizens formed the Cooperative and, with funding from the federal Rural Electrification Administration (REA), built and maintained its own power lines. By 2001, the member-owned Cooperative served more than 70,000 members and remained the state's only electric cooperative."

It is difficult to fathom that electrical power service in rural parts of New Hampshire is relatively new. Less than a century ago, many rural citizens still worked by the light of oil lamps and wood stoves. The establishment of electrical power to rural segments of the state, would also lead to telephone service, greater efficiency in manufacturing, and an improved quality of life.

During the early 20th century, most electrical lines could only carry adequate usable power for about seventy-line miles. That severely limited extending electrical power to rural areas. The New Hampshire State Grange Association was instrumental in obtaining the electrical cooperative to bring rural power. The original construction of electrical lines in Sullivan County totaled one hundred eleven miles of rural power for approximately $400,000. I found it intriguing how the quiet village of Lempster was the birth of rural electrical service in the Granite State.

Lempster was incorporated in 1772 yet had been settled as early as 1735 as a fort established to guard against Indian attacks. The historical marker is located on the property of the Lempster Meetinghouse. The meetinghouse was built in 1794. The original building was located at the intersection of the Charlestown Turnpike and the 2nd New Hampshire Turnpike which is one mile southeast of this location. The building was moved to this current site in 1822 and the bell tower was added. Today, the meetinghouse is used as the town hall and the Silver Mountain Grange. This building is a part of Lempster history where the citizens are working tirelessly to maintain it to its original elegance.

Newbury

Marker # 0081: Center Meeting House

Location: NH Route 103 and NH Route 103A in front of the Meeting House

Sign Erected: 1971

GPS Coordinates- N 43° 19'.253″ W 72° 02'.168″

"This edifice of Bulfinch design was rebuilt here about 1832 with old timbers from the Meeting House on Bly Hill. Its age, name and denomination remain uncertain. The building has become known as a museum piece of the 1820 decade. Its beautiful high colonial pulpit, with pews facing the vestibule, renders it unique among New Hampshire churches."

This Federal-style building is one of the few remaining original intact buildings of its kind. The building was rebuilt from an earlier structure that was located about one-mile north from its current location. As stated in the narrative, the uniqueness of the building is the pews facing the vestibule. During my visit, the building was closed, and I was unable to go inside to see this. The building is currently owned by a local non-profit organization and used as a community center. The major restoration of the structure was completed in 2011. The building was listed on the National Register of Historic Places in 1979.

The town of Newbury was incorporated in 1772 as Fisherfield in honor of John Fisher, brother-in-law of colonial Governor John Wentworth. The name was changed to Newbury in 1837. Newbury is a four-season resort community. In the summer, Lake Sunapee draws thousands to its shore. In the fall, visitors come to view the colors of foliage. Winter brings skiers who are drawn to the recreation on Mount Sunapee. Even with such a large influx of tourists, the town retains its quaint charm. One of the must visit destinations for visitors to the area is to the Fells Historic Site. The Fells is on the John Hays estate. John W. Hays was an accomplished statesman, having served as a journalist, diplomat, and Secretary of State in the Lincoln Administration. The Fells Estate was listed on the National Register of Historic Places in 2000. The Fells Historic site is located at 465 NH Route 103A, 2.2 miles north of this marker.

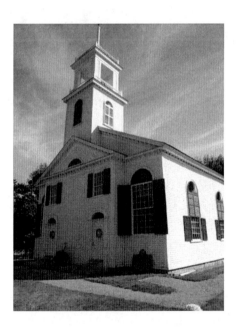

Newport

Marker # 0006: Sarah Josepha Buell Hale (1788-1879)

Location: NH Route 103 and 8 Hale Street near the Guild Post Office (16 Hale St)

Sign Erected: 1962

GPS Coordinates- N 43° 22'.672″ W 72° 08'.402"

"Prominent humanitarian, poet and author was born and taught school in Guild section of Newport. Widowed mother of five, she edited "Godey's Lady's Book," 1837-1877; composed poem now called "Mary Had a Little Lamb"; advocated proclamation of Thanksgiving Day as national festival; and appealed constantly for higher education for women."

Sarah Josepha Hale was born here in Guild and was home schooled by her mother and older brother. Sara became a school teacher and married her husband David Hale in 1813 and they had five children. David died in 1822. Notably, after his death Sarah wore black for the remainder of her life as a sign of mourning his passing. In 1823, she published a collection of her poems. A second publishing of her literary poems to include the now famous "Mary Had a Little Lamb" was published in 1830. Her first novel was published in 1827 entitled, *Northwood: Life North and South* and was about anti-slavery and emancipation.

A distinguished teacher, poet, and author Sarah Josepha Buell Hale added the title of editor to her list of accomplishments. In 1837, Sarah became the editor of the *Godey's Lady's Book* in Philadelphia, Pennsylvania. She held the position of editor until 1877 at nearly 90 years of age.

Hale's other notable achievements include the founder of the Seamen's Aid Society in 1833 to assist families of Boston families who lost loved ones at sea. Arguably her most influential accomplishment is her effort to make Thanksgiving a national holiday. Sarah worked tirelessly for nearly two decades and five U.S. presidents to formalize a National Day of Thanksgiving. It was not until a letter she wrote to president Abraham Lincoln in 1863 did her dream come to fruition. Whether it was the suffering felt from the Civil War, it seemed worthwhile to establish a national day to give thanks. Sarah Josepha Buell Hale died April 30, 1879 in Philadelphia, Pennsylvania.

Newport

Marker # 0106: Joel McGregor- Last Surviving Soldier of the Revolution

Location: NH Route 10 (North Main Street) and Corbin Rd. (mile marker 54.8)

Sign Erected: 1976 & 2000

GPS Coordinates- N 43° 23'.367" W 72° 10'.951"

"Born in Enfield, Connecticut in 1760, McGregor enlisted in 1777 and served five years. Taken prisoner by the British, he was confined eight months in the famous Old Sugar House in New York City. He settled in Newport in 1789 and was resident for 72 years, dying October 31, 1861 at the age of 101. He is believed to have been New Hampshire's last surviving soldier of the Revolution."

Joel McGregor fought at the battle of Fort Washington on November 16, 1776 in the northern part of Manhattan New York along the Hudson River. The colonial garrison at Fort Washington was lost to the British. In this defeat, 2,837 patriots were captured. With such large numbers of prisoners, the British had to locate the prisoners on a prisoner ship and three sugar houses in New York.

The sugar houses were ideal due to their construction with small windows and thick walls. McGregor was held in the Livingston Old Sugar House. Conditions were ruthless and only 800 prisoners survived in captivity from this battle. The British released the survivors on New Year's Day in 1779. McGregor returned to Newport, New Hampshire and worked as a blacksmith in this section of town. An interesting note regarding Newport and Antrim New Hampshire. Both towns claim to have the last known survivor of the Revolutionary War. Antrim claims that Samuel Downing is the last known survivor (marker #0178).

The Town of Newport was incorporated in 1761. Early settlers were drawn to the area for the excellent soils in this valley as well as the hydro power potential from the Sugar River. Conflicting documents claim the origin of the name Newport. One source claims the name is derived from an English soldier and statesman. Another source claims the name originated from the number of settlers who came from Newport, Rhode Island.

Orford

Marker # 0033: The Ridge

Location: NH Route 10 (.3 mile north of NH Route 25A)

Sign Erected: 1965

GPS Coordinates- N 43° 54'.323″ W 72° 08'.213”

"Orford's seven Ridge houses were built over a period of time from 1773 to 1839 by professional and business men of the town. The Bulfinch-style house of John B. Wheeler, built in 1814-1816, southernmost in the row, was designed by a Boston architect, probably Asher Benjamin who was then an associate of Charles Bulfinch. Other Ridge houses also display Asher Benjamin influence."

The seven Federal-style homes along this ridge represent a style that was not typically found in rural settings during the 18th century or early 19th century. According to the National Register of Historic Records archives, a Dartmouth professor claimed The Ridge as "the finest group of Federal-style houses in the United States". The village district that encompasses The Ridge homes has approximately thirty-eight buildings including an academy building, church, post office, private residences and barns. These dwellings are located on both sides of NH Route 10.

In 2017, the John Rogers House, built in 1817 was sold by the town to a family who intend to return the home to its original splendor. The seven homes on the ridge include the Samuel Morey House built in 1773, the Wilcox House built in 1832, the John B. Wheeler House built in 1814, the John Rogers House built in 1817, the Dyar T. Hinckley House built in 1822, the William Howard House built in 1829, and Stedman Willard House built in 1840. The Ridge houses were listed on the National Register of Historic Places in 1977.

Orford was incorporated in 1761. The settlement was originally Fort #7 along the Connecticut River. While Orford is a small rural community, it has been the home for a couple of notable residents. Inventor of the marine steam engine Samuel Morey and former three-term New Hampshire Governor Meldrim Thomson Jr.

Plainfield

Marker # 0077: Kimball Union Academy

Location: NH Route 120 (Meriden Village) South of Main Street

Sign Erected: 1971

GPS Coordinates-N 43° 32'.618″ W 72° 15'.206"

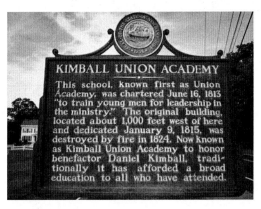

"This school, known first as Union Academy, was chartered June 16, 1813 "to train young men for leadership in the ministry." The original building, located about 1,000 feet west of here and dedicated January 9, 1815, was destroyed by fire in 1824. Now known as Kimball Union Academy to honor benefactor Daniel Kimball, traditionally it has afforded a broad education to all who have attended."

In 1811, Piermont resident John Foord journeys to Scotland to study theology. Foord becomes intrigued by the mission of the school to provide a free education to those who choose to pursue a career in the ministry. He writes home to his friends in New Hampshire to pursue a similar form of institution.

In 1813, the Union Academy is chartered by the New Hampshire General Court as a "Union of Churches" school. A charter Trustee, Daniel Kimball donated $6,000 and much of his estate if the school would relocate to his property in Meriden after his death.

The first academy building was built onsite in 1815 where seven students were the first enrolled. Six men became the first graduates of the Union Academy in 1816. School history states that four women also completed the course requirements but did not receive the certificates of graduation. Today, the school is known as one of the oldest co-educational boarding schools in the country.

The Town of Plainfield was incorporated in 1761. The original Kimball estate was originally known as "Meriden Parish" and was the property of Massachusetts Governor (1730-1741) Jonathan Belcher.

Sutton

Marker # 0044: John Sargent Pillsbury (1828-1901)

Location: NH Route 114 and Meetinghouse Hill Rd (next to flagpole) South Sutton

Sign Erected: 1967

GPS Coordinates-N 43° 19'.153″ W 71° 56'.065″

"Born in a house bordering this common, he migrated to Minneapolis in 1855. There, he, his brother George, and his nephew Charles, established the famous Pillsbury flour milling business. Three times elected governor of Minnesota and noted benefactor of its State University, his career in industry and public service reflects great credit on his native state."

John Pillsbury was born in Sutton July 29, 1827. In his early years, he opened a general store in Warner with future New Hampshire Governor Walter Harriman in 1851. Four years later, Pillsbury moved to Minneapolis, Minnesota and succeeded as a businessman. These businesses included real estate, a lumber mill and hardware store.

John Pillsbury's notoriety was established when he co-founded the C.A. Pillsbury company with his nephew Charles Alfred Pillsbury. As noted on the sign, John Pillsbury served the State of

Minnesota as a senator and then three-time governor. While John Pillsbury was a successful businessman, politician and philanthropist, he also is claimed to have brought a "miracle" to the state.

From 1873 to 1877, the state agricultural crops were being devastated by grasshoppers. In the Spring of 1877, then Governor Pillsbury called for a day of prayer for divine intervention to rid the state of the pests. Soon after the weather turned and brought a heavy frost that killed all the grasshoppers and their eggs. The plague was destroyed and citizens of that time credit the salvation to Governor Pillsbury. John Sargent Pillsbury died on October 18, 1901 and is buried in Minneapolis.

The Town of Sutton was incorporated in 1784 after unsuccessful attempts for settlement in earlier grants. The town is named after Sutton, Massachusetts and includes four villages; North Sutton, South Sutton, East Sutton, and Sutton Mills.

Warner

Marker # 0243: Mount Kearsarge and the U.S.S. Kearsarge

Location: Kearsarge Mountain Road and Church Street (north of NH Route 103)

Sign Erected: 2014

GPS Coordinates- N 43° 16'.891″ W 71° 49'.001″

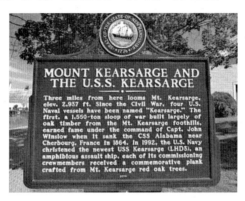

"Three miles from here looms Mt. Kearsarge, elev. 2,937 ft. Since the Civil War, four U.S. Naval vessels have been named "Kearsarge." The first, a 1,550-ton sloop of war built largely of oak timber from the Mt. Kearsarge foothills, earned fame under the command of Capt. John Winslow when it sank the CSS Alabama near Cherbourg, France in 1864. In 1992, the U.S. Navy christened the newest USS Kearsarge (LHD3), an amphibious assault ship, each of its commissioning crewmembers received a commemorative plank crafted from Mt. Kearsarge red oak trees."

According to Warner town history, the first U.S.S. Kearsarge was launched from the Portsmouth Navy Yard on September 11, 1861. As mentioned on the marker, the ship earned the fame for sinking the Confederate ship Alabama in 1864. Captain John Winslow took command of the ship on April 8, 1863.The sinking of the C.S.S. Alabama off the coast of France was instrumental in blockading European ships from providing supplies to the confederates during the Civil War.

The second U.S.S. Kearsarge (BB-5) was launched in 1898 and served the U.S. Navy in numerous capacities until she was renamed in 1941 and scrapped in 1955. The third U.S.S. Kearsarge (CV-33) aircraft carrier was launched in 1945 and served in both the Korean and Vietnam Wars. She was decommissioned in 1970.

The Winslow State Park which is located on the northwest slope of Mount Kearsarge was named for the 19th century Winslow House in 1935, which was named in honor of Admiral John Winslow. Early records believe that the expedition of the New Hampshire wilderness by Massachusetts Bay Colony Governor Endicott were the first Europeans to see this mountain. Their records identify the mountain with the Indian name "Carasaga" which means "notch-pointed mountain of pines"

Washington

Marker # 0243: Birthplace of the Seventh Day Adventist Church

Location: NH Route 31 and Valley Road

Sign Erected: 1974

GPS Coordinates- N 43° 10'.407″ W 72° 05'.583″

"In April 1842, a group of citizens in this town banded together to form "the first Christian Society." In the Adventist movement of 1842-43, they espoused the Advent hope. In January 1862, these Washington Sabbath-keepers, after meeting for many years as a Seventh Day Adventist Church. Take second left, opposite the Common, 2.3 miles on Millen Pond Road to the site of this building."

The Church of Seventh Day Adventist began with followers of the Millerite faith. William Miller was a reformed atheist who preached the Apocalypse would occur. When both proclaimed dates passed, followers disbanded. The citizens who formed the Seventh Day Adventist faith in 1842 believed in the Second Advent of Christ was imminent. They referred to themselves as the "Christian Brethren". Unlike other Christian denominations, the Adventists observes the Sabbath on Saturday. They also grew as a church when other residents worshipped in this first Adventist church and became members.

The church building is located at 153 King Street (off Faxon Hill Road). The building in known as the Mother Church of the Seventh-day Adventists. I traveled down Millen Pond Road and came to King Street via Faxon Hill Road. The church is still actively used. During my visit, the Church was hosting a Seventh Day Adventist pilgrimage and was remarkably busy.

The Town of Washington was incorporated on December 13, 1776 and named in honor of General George Washington.

Wilmot

Marker # 0040: Mason's Patent

Location: NH Route 4A westside of Springfield/Wilmot town line (6.9 miles from Route 11)

Sign Erected: 1966

GPS Coordinates- N 43° 28'.958″ W 71° 58'.520″

"New Hampshire, as granted by authority of the English Crown to Captain John Mason in 1629, was bounded on the west and north by a curved line 60 miles distant from the sea. The course of this proprietary boundary, called the "Masonian Curve", coincides with the nearby town line between Wilmot and Springfield."

According to my research, the "Masonian Curve" extended from the town line of Richmond-Fitzwilliam-Massachusetts in a sweeping arc through the center of the State and concluded in the center of Conway and the Maine border. The center point of this arc was the town line of Springfield and Wilmot where you are now standing. The Grafton-Danbury town line also follows this arc. The purpose was with endpoints of the arc defined, any point along the arc would be exactly 60 miles from the ocean. A simple geometric solution to measuring a boundary for the newly granted land which will become known as New Hampshire! The second diagram was located the on-website

Mike in New Hampshire, http://mikenh.wordpress.com. This blog was helpful in researching hard to find information.

The Town of Wilmot was incorporated in 1807 as an annexation from neighboring New London. It was named in honor of Dr. James Wilmot who was an ardent voice against the mistreatment of the colonies by England. In my research, the Wilmot Historical Society has a fascinating story of the beloved horse-drawn Wilmot hearse and the Hearse House. Take a moment to read about the town's restoration project of this bit of town history.

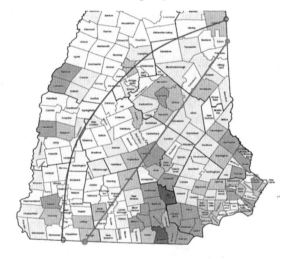

Photo courtesy of Mikenh.wordpress.com

Chapter Five

Monadnock Region

The region is named for Mount Monadnock, the highest peak in the southwest segment of the state. Mount Monadnock is claimed to be the most hiked peak in the world followed by Mount Fuji in Japan. Whether that is accurate, I am not certain on how that is measured. I do know that this 3,165-foot peak is the crown jewel of the region. This lone peak has been written about by famous authors Ralph Waldo Emerson and Henry David Thoreau.

The region is comprised of about 40 towns predominantly in Cheshire county. With Keene generally at the center, the region has four distinct segments. To the northwest are the northern hills; the northeast is known as the Hillsboroughs; the southwest is the Ashuelot Valley; and the southeast is home to the mountain section with Mount Monadnock. This region has the southern section of the Connecticut River scenic byway, the 80-mile Monadnock Region Scenic Loop, seven covered bridges, eight State Parks and plenty of outdoor recreation. The region is also home to a popular arts center. Peterborough is a hub for visitors interested in the arts and cultural exhibits. Keene, home of Keene State University is also a popular destination for those interested in theater, art performances, art festivals, and museums.

The Monadnock region is a snapshot of what life was like in the early 20th century. The country roads through scenic villages offers visitors glimpses of century-old farms, taverns, and buildings. A must visit destination in the region should include the Madame Sherri Forest in Chesterfield. This 513-acre preserve is owned by the Society for the Protection of New Hampshire Forests. What makes this property so unique is the castle ruins; more specifically the sweeping stone stairway that ends mid-air. While there, be sure to read of the colorful life of Madame Sherri.

Another find during my travels to this region is the Sweetwater Distillery in Winchester. Driving through town, I noticed this newly renovated business in the center of the village. I was offered a tour of the facility by the owner who shared about the work and vision he put forth in the renovation project. I then learned that the building he owns adjacent to the distillery is also the birthplace of Leonard Wood (October 9, 1860). General Leonard Wood (namesake for the U.S. Army post Fort Leonard Wood in Missouri) was a Commander of the infamous Rough Riders, U.S. Army Chief of Staff, Governor of Cuba, and Governor General of the Philippines.

The Monadnock region is a place to visit during any season. The rolling hills, farmlands, and scenic vistas make this area a destination for those who love history and the outdoors. I was happy to have had the opportunity to spend quality time in this region of the Granite State.

Monadnock Region

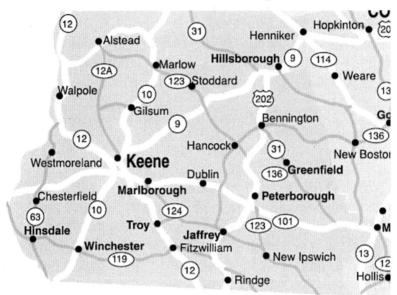

Antrim- Marker #0178: New Hampshire's Last Soldier of the Revolution (Samuel Downing)

Antrim- Marker #0228: Cork Plain Bridge, Second New Hampshire Turnpike

Bennington- Marker #0153: Factory Village

Chesterfield- Marker #0060: First Methodist Meeting Place in New Hampshire

Chesterfield- Marker #0095: Chief Justice Harlan Fiske Stone

Chesterfield- Marker #0216: Pierce Shops

Fitzwilliam- Marker #0099: Brigadier General James Reed (1722-1807)

Francestown- Marker #0023: Soapstone

Francestown- Marker #0043: Levi Woodbury (1798-1851)

Gilsum- Marker #0168: Gilsum Stone Arch Bridge

Greenfield- Marker #0130: Town Meeting House

Hillsborough- Marker #0065: Pierce Homestead

Hillsborough- Marker #0107: Colonial Grant

Hillsborough- Marker #0203: Stone Arch Bridge

Hinsdale- Marker #0112: Hinsdale Auto Pioneer

Hinsdale- Marker #0204: Newhall & Stebbins

Jaffrey- Marker #0013: Hannah Davis-Amos Fortune

Keene- Marker #0069: Keene Glass Industry

Keene- Marker #0086: Hampshire Pottery

Keene- Marker #0226: Jonathan Myrick Daniels (1939-1965)

Mason- Marker #0035: Uncle Sam's House

New Ipswich- Marker #0010: First Textile Mill

New Ipswich- Marker #0101: Site of Wilder's Chair Factory

New Ipswich- Marker #0137: Barrett House

Peterborough- Marker #0206: The MacDowell Graves

Peterborough- Marker #0210: Settler's Rock

Peterborough- Marker #0244: Revolutionary War Drummer William Diamond

Richmond- Marker #0059: Hosea Ballou (1771-1852)

Rindge- Marker #0138: Second Rindge Meeting House

Sharon- Marker #0068: Toll House and Toll Gate

Stoddard- Marker #0027: Stone Arch Bridge

Stoddard- Marker #0052: Stoddard Glass

Surry- Marker #0093: Surry Mountain Gold Mine and Lily Pond

Swanzey- Marker #0022: Denman Thompson (1833-1911)

Swanzey- Marker #0232: The Homestead Woolen Mills Dam

Temple- Marker #0012: Temple Glass Factory

Walpole- Marker #0061: First Connecticut River Bridge

Westmoreland- Marker #0074: Park Hill Meeting House

Antrim

Marker # 0178: New Hampshire's Last Soldier of the Revolution

Location: 67 Main Street (front yard of Maplehurst Inn on US Route 202)

Sign Erected: 2001

GPS Coordinates-N 43° 01'.788″ W 71° 56'.287"

"Samuel Downing, born in Newburyport MA in 1764, was enticed to Antrim while still a boy to be an apprentice of Robert Aiken, a Scots-Irish spinning wheel maker. In 1780 Samuel ran away to Hopkinton NH to enlist in the Continental Army; refused, he went to Charlestown NH where he joined the 2nd NH Regiment. He served to the end of the war, returned to Antrim and became a respected citizen. In 1794 he emigrated to Edinburg NY where he settled permanently. At his death in 1867 he was the oldest recorded pensioner of the Revolution, although two others were enrolled later."

According the book, The *Last Men of the Revolution (1860)*, Samuel Downing was interviewed about his life. Downing stated that he left home with Robert Aiken when he was about ten years old. He left while his parents were out for the day and stated "'Where are your parents?' asked he. 'They aint at home,' said I; 'but that won't make no odds; I will go.'"

Samuel Downing apprenticed for Aiken for six years before he left to enlist in Hopkinton, New Hampshire. Denied for being too young, the colonel in Hopkinton gave Downing a letter to give to the commander of the 2nd Regiment in Charlestown where he enlisted.

An interesting note, Samuel Downing believed his parents thought he may have fallen off a dock and drowned. It was nearly one year after Samuel left the home in Newburyport, Massachusetts that Robert Aiken wrote a letter to inform Downing's parents that he was alive and well. For further reading, please visit www.americanrevolution.org about the interview with Samuel Downing. I found it interesting as well as entertaining. By the way, this marker conflicts with the Joel McGregor marker in Newport New Hampshire for the last surviving soldier of the American Revolution. I say we should be proud to commemorate both men.

Antrim

Marker # 0228: Cork Plain Bridge- Second NH Turnpike

Location: US Route 202 (southbound picnic parking area) mile marker 30.3

Sign Erected: 2011

GPS Coordinates- N 43° 04'.814″ W 71° 55'.056″

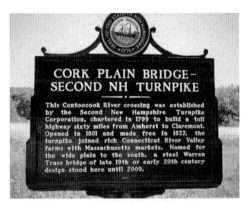

"This Contoocook River crossing was established by the Second New Hampshire Turnpike Corporation, chartered in 1799 to build a toll highway sixty miles from Amherst to Claremont. Opened in 1801 and made free in 1837, the turnpike joined rich Connecticut River Valley farms with Massachusetts markets. Named for the wide plain to the south, a steel Warren Truss bridge of late 19th or early 20th century design stood here until 2009."

The New Hampshire Turnpike system was created to connect distant communities with major cities such as Portsmouth and Boston. To pay for the construction, communities were responsible to construct their segment of the road. They were then entitled to collect a fee from travelers using the road. The term "turnpike" is believed to originate from the barrier that barred the road and was opened once the toll was collected. The Second New Hampshire Turnpike, chartered in 1799 and completed in 1801 was the primary arterial road connecting

Boston, Massachusetts to Vermont. The Second New Hampshire Turnpike began in Amherst and traveled northwest up to Claremont to the Lottery Bridge across the Connecticut River. It is stated in the book, *The Turnpikes of New England and Evolution of the Same Through England* (1919) by James Edward Wood that this Turnpike "for twenty-five years carried enormous traffic of farm products and timber to Boston, the teams returning with loads of rum and store goods" (p. 219).

The Town of Antrim was incorporated on March 22, 1777 and was named for the County Antrim in Northern Ireland. Much of the growth of the town was localized along the Contoocook River where the major industry was cutlery manufacturing, to include apple-paring machines in 1864 for more than thirty years. The Second New Hampshire Turnpike is east of this location at the intersection of Old Concord Road and Second New Hampshire Turnpike where it crosses the Contoocook River.

Bennington

Marker # 0153: Factory Village

Location: U.S. Route 202 and NH Route 31 (mile marker 24.4)

Sign Erected: 1987

GPS Coordinates- N 43° 00'.021″ W 71° 55'.691″

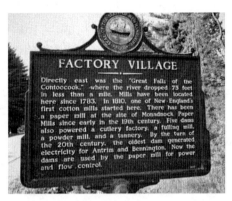

"Directly east was the "Great Falls of the Contoocook," where the river dropped 75 feet in less than a mile. Mills have been located here since 1783. In 1819, one of New England's first cotton mills started here. There has been a paper mill at the site of Monadnock Paper Mills since early in the 19th century. Five dams also powered a cutlery factory, a fulling mill, a power mill, and a tannery. By the turn of the 20th century, the oldest dam generated electricity for Antrim and Bennington. Now the dams are used by the paper mill for power and flow control."

The Town of Bennington website explains that the land on the east side of the Contoocook River was purchased by Joseph Putnam in 1782 to build a saw and grist mill at the "Great Falls". More settlers came to the area to make use of the power of the "Great Falls" in early industry. The area was originally called Society Land as early as 1753. With growing industry drawn from the power of the falls and the Contoocook River, Society

Land and a segment of Hancock became known as Factory Village.

In 1835, on the site of the current Monadnock Paper Mill the first paper making machinery was used. Moody Butler who emigrated from Ireland settled here and started the industry of making paper. He used the flax that was remaining from linen making. The flax fibers were mashed and pounded into high quality paper. While most New England paper mills have since disappeared, the Monadnock Paper Mill has survived through adapting to specialty paper products. This paper mill has the distinction of being the longest running, single family-owned paper manufacturing mill in the country. It was purchased by Gilbert Verney in 1948 and is still a family business.

Bennington was incorporated in 1842 and named for the 1777 Battle of Bennington in Walloomsac, New York near Bennington Vermont. The village of Bennington was listed on the National Register of Historic Places in 2010.

Chesterfield

Marker # 0060: First Methodist Meeting Place in New Hampshire

Location: NH Route 9 and Pond Brook Road

Sign Erected: 1970

GPS Coordinates- N 42° 54'.099" W 72° 28'.664"

"In 1772 "the people called Methodist" held their first religious meeting in this state on the James Robertson farm, 1.2 miles north of here, on Christian Street, with Philip Embury as the preacher. On June 20, 1803, Francis Asbury spoke here using as his text: "Let us run with patience the race that is set before us."

While researching this marker, I had a difficult time finding relevant information. What I did find is that the current Methodist church in Chesterfield is the Asbury United Methodist Church which is located nearby on NH Route 63. The Asbury United Methodist churches of North America are named for the first bishop of the Methodist Episcopal Church of North America. The sermon text that Francis Asbury spoke of is from Hebrews 12:1. The Asbury United Methodist Church was listed on the National Register of Historic Places in 1983. This building is known as the "Mother Church of Methodism in New Hampshire".

Chesterfield is also the home of Madame Sherri's castle ruins and forest. This unique property is part of the Society for the Protection of New Hampshire Forests. This destination is only 3.1 miles via Stage Road (across the street from this marker). Madam Sherri was an eccentric woman of theater and lived a vivacious life. The haunting sweeping stone stairway that ends mid-air is a popular photo opportunity. The remaining 500 + acre forest also offers hiking trails and remnants of an abandoned mine.

Chesterfield was incorporated in 1752 named in honor of the Fourth Earl of Chesterfield who joined William Pitt in opposition of English treatment of the colonists. Prior to being incorporated, the area was the location for Fort #1 along the Connecticut River.

Chesterfield

Marker # 0095: Chief Justice Harlan Fiske Stone

Location: NH Route 63 and Old Chesterfield Road (in front of Chesterfield Central School)

Sign Erected: 1974

GPS Coordinates- N 42° 53'.210″ W 72° 28'.246"

"Born October 11, 1872, in a modest cottage 1.7 miles southeast of here on Horseshoe Road, Stone graduated from Amherst College and Columbia Law School, returning to the latter as Dean, 1910-1924. Attorney General of the United States in President Coolidge's Cabinet, he was appointed a Justice of the Supreme Court in 1924 and Chief Justice in 1941, serving until his death April 22, 1946. A teacher, lawyer, judge and judicial craftsman of the highest order, he held the affection and respect of the lawyers of the nation."

Chief Justice Stone was raised in a modest farming family. There is a marker at the cul-de-sac on Horseshoe Road of the site of the Stone family home. After primary schooling, Harlan Stone attended Amherst College where he excelled as an athlete and scholar. He graduated in 1894.

Graduating from Columbia University Law school in 1898, Stone practiced law in New York City. From 1902-1905 he was a professor at Columbia Law School, becoming the Dean in 1910. He resigned as Dean in 1924 when he was appointed U.S. Attorney General by President Calvin Coolidge where he served to oversee a string of scandals in the Harding Administration.

Harlan Stone served as Attorney General for eleven months before his appointment to the U.S. Supreme Court on February 5, 1925. He served as Associate Justice of the Supreme Court until his appointment by President Franklin D. Roosevelt as the 12th Chief Justice on July 3, 1941. Chief Justice Stone was the shortest tenured Chief Justice, having served less than five years before his death on April 22, 1946. Chief Justice Stone was commemorated on a U.S. postage stamp in 1948.

Photo courtesy of U.S. Library of Congress

Chesterfield

Marker # 0216: Pierce Shops

Location: NH Route 9A and Joslin Road (Spofford Village)

Sign Erected: 2009

GPS Coordinates-N 42° 54'.408″ W 72° 25'.206"

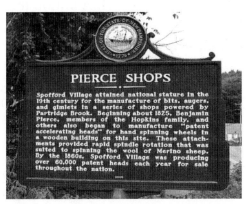

"Spofford Village attained national stature in the 19th century for the manufacture of bits, augers, and gimlets in a series of shops powered by Partridge Brook. Beginning about 1825, Benjamin Pierce, members of the Hopkins family, and others also began to manufacture "patent accelerating heads" for hand spinning wheels in a wooden building on this site. These attachments provided rapid spindle rotation that was suited to spinning the wool of Merino sheep. By the 1860's, Spofford Village was producing over 60,000 patent heads each year for sale throughout the nation."

This unincorporated village of Spofford was deemed viable due to its availability of power from Partridge Brook. This village also was the hub of commerce for Chesterfield in the 19th century. During this peak, the village included numerous homes, a hotel, two stores and a church in addition to the numerous factories and mills along the brook and Spofford Lake. A map of 1858 Spofford Village shows the outlet of the lake had a Gate House indicating the location of a dam. According to Gazetteer of

Cheshire County (c. 1886) "In 1805, Ebenezer Stearns, Moses Smith, Ebenezer Cheney and seventeen others were incorporated into a company called the Chesterfield Manufactory for the purpose of manufacturing "cotton yarn, cloth and woolens" (p. 153).

With the concentration of industry in this small area, it was locally known as "Factory Village". In addition to the manufacturing of augers, bits, and gimlets (which was a t-shaped tool with a screw that was used to bore holes). The "patent accelerating spinning wheel heads" manufactured by Pierce was a major component produced onsite and put Spofford Village on the manufacturing map.

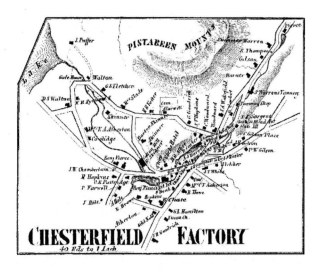

Photo courtesy of Chesterfield Historical Society

Fitzwilliam

Marker # 0216: Brigadier General James Reed (1722-1807)

Location: NH Route 119 and Templeton Turnpike Road (on north end of Town Common)

Sign Erected: 1975

GPS Coordinates- N 42° 46'.832" W 72° 08'.720"

"This veteran Captain of the French and Indian War, born in Woburn, Mass., settled here about 1765 as an original proprietor of Monadnock no 4, now Fitzwilliam. After the Battle of Lexington, he recruited several companies to form the Third New Hampshire Regiment which aided General Stark at the Battle of Bunker Hill in the Revolutionary War. He was commissioned a Brigadier-General following the siege of Boston and his engagement at the Battle of Ticonderoga."

Born in Massachusetts and claimed Fitzwilliam his home for most of his life. James Reed was one of the first proprietors in 1765 to settle in what was known as Monadnock Number Four, which is now Fitzwilliam. This land was granted by the New Hampshire colonial Governor Benning Wentworth.

Reed's military experience began during the French and Indian War where he commanded a company of soldiers. In 1758, Reed fought at Fort Ticonderoga when it fell to the British in 1759. He served in the militia until the Paris Treaty of 1763. Reed's military career excelled earning acknowledgement from General George Washington who ranked Reed's regiment as the second ranked in the entire Continental Army. In July 1776, Reed incurred a severe fever which resulted in his loss of vision. General Washington appointed James Reed the rank of Brigadier General, but he soon retired due to ill health. James Reed was a notable figure in Fitzwilliam. He built the second home in town and it was used as tavern and inn. This "public house" was also used as the first schoolhouse in Fitzwilliam. He also served as the first Town Moderator in 1769.

Fitzwilliam is a quaint village with a relaxing atmosphere. It feels like a snapshot back in time. A worthwhile stop is to the Rhododendron State Park on Rockwood Pond Road. We were fortunate to be here in July when the flowers were in peak bloom. It is also a wonderful stop on a warm day to walk an easy hiking trail with plenty of shade and beautiful flowers.

Francestown

Marker # 0023: Soapstone

Location: NH Route 136 and Potash Road

Sign Erected: 1964

GPS Coordinates- N 42° 59'.099″ W 71° 48'.259″

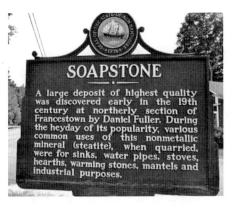

"A large deposit of highest quality was discovered early in the 19th century at northerly section of Francestown by Daniel Fuller. During the heyday of its popularity, various common uses of this nonmetallic mineral (steatite), when quarried, were for sinks, water pipes, stoves, hearths, warming stones, mantels and industrial purposes."

Steatite (soapstone), a mineral composed of talc and is a soft malleable stone. It was used by the indigenous people who lived here prior to the early settlers. Artifacts reveal that this mineral was used to create pots for cooking. Early settlers used this material to make cookstoves, steps, tombstones, and bed warmers.

When Daniel Fuller first discovered this mineral, it was by accident. Archive records suggest that he found the mineral as early as 1794 while he was tilling the rocky soil. He began quarrying the material in 1802. Fuller's quarry was considered the finest grade of steatite in the region. This would consist of material with no rusty streaks, or variation of densities.

The Civil War brought an increased demand for soapstone and at its peak, the Francestown quarry produced more than two thousand tons of soapstone per year. The quarry closed in 1912 after sparks from blasting caused two adjacent farms to burn to the ground. Legal issues relating to this fire put the company in bankruptcy and the quarry closed. Today, soapstone is still a popular material in the manufacturing of sinks, wood stoves and kitchen countertops.

Francestown was incorporated in 1772 and was named for Frances Wentworth Deering, the wife of colonial Governor John Wentworth. The Second New Hampshire Turnpike ran through town where two toll booths were staged to collect tolls from travelers until 1837. Francestown was also the home to the now defunct Francestown Academy which was in operation from 1800-1921. This prestigious high school was known for its academic rigor and had many notable graduates to include Franklin Pierce and Levi Woodbury.

Francestown

Marker # 0043: Levi Woodbury (1789-1851)

Location: Intersection of NH Route 136 and NH Route 47 (next to flagpole)

Sign Erected: 1967 & 2000

GPS Coordinates- N 42° 59'.230″ W 71° 48'.743"

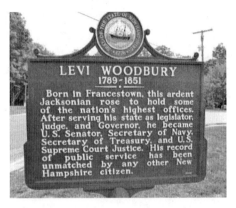

"Born in Francestown, this ardent Jacksonian rose to hold some of the nation's highest offices. After serving his state as legislator, judge, and Governor, he became U.S. Senator, Secretary of Navy, Secretary of Treasury, and U.S. Supreme Court Justice. His record of public service has been unmatched by any other New Hampshire citizen."

Levi Woodbury, a Jacksonian democrat is a man of a rather impressive credentials. Regrettably, I do not believe that Mr. Woodbury gets the acknowledgement from New Hampshire citizens as he should. Levi Woodbury served in all three branches of both state and federal government. That is quite the accomplishment! The next most notable New Hampshire native to have served in all three branches of government to include holding the office of Governor is Salmon P. Chase of Cornish. Woodbury even served as Speaker of the New Hampshire General Court in 1825, after serving as New Hampshire Governor from 1823-1824.

Prior to serving in public office, Woodbury graduated from Dartmouth College in 1809. After studying law in Connecticut and Boston, he returned to Francestown to practice law from 1813-1816. In 1816, he was appointed a judge in Superior Court. For the next 35 years, Levi Woodbury served in all three branches of the New Hampshire government as well as the federal government.

Woodbury was appointed an Associate Justice to the United States Supreme Court in 1845 and served in this capacity until his death on September 4, 1851. Levi Woodbury was the first U.S. Supreme Court Justice to have attended law school. Levi Woodbury died in Portsmouth, New Hampshire. The Levi Woodbury Homestead on Main St. in Francestown was listed on the National Register of Historic Places in 2007.

Gilsum

Marker # 0168: Gilsum Stone Arch Bridge

Location: NH Route 10 Surry Road (sign on north side of bridge off Surry Rd.)

Sign Erected: 1995

GPS Coordinates- N 43° 02'.355″ W 72° 16'.221"

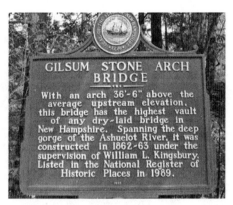

"With an arch 36-6" above the average upstream elevation, this bridge has the highest vault of any dry-laid bridge in New Hampshire. Spanning the deep gorge of the Ashuelot River, it was constructed in 1862-63 under the supervision of William L. Kingsbury. Listed in the National Register of Historic Places in 1989."

This bridge is a work of art, and a popular stop for those seeking photos. This bridge is one of the highest stone arched bridges in the state and largest mortarless spans without supports. It has a span of 47 feet 8 inches. From my research, there were four previous bridges and one was also a stone arched bridge. However, that bridge failed in 1860 due to poor construction. This bridge was built immediately after the demise of the 1860 collapse. The construction includes split-faced granite blocks with some blocks with a smooth finish and others left rough. While this bridge was constructed in 1862, it received rehabilitative work in 1951.

Gilsum was incorporated in 1763. The land was originally granted in 1752 but was not settled due to the hostilities from the French and Indian War. The re-charter of the land was made in 1763 and the town was named from the combination of two proprietors Samuel Gilbert and Thomas Sumner. The settlements of this land grant were situated mostly along the Ashuelot River using the hydropower source for manufacturing of wool, bobbins, and chairs.

Greenfield

Marker # 0130: Town Meeting House

Location: NH Route 31 and NH Route 136 (771 Forest Rd)

Sign Erected: 1979

GPS Coordinates-N 42° 57'.026" W 71° 52'.303"

"The oldest original meeting house in New Hampshire serving both church and state. The frame, built from local timber by resident Hugh Gregg, was raised by one hundred volunteers from the village and surrounding towns on September 16, 1795. This fine old structure has serve the people of Greenfield continuously since that time as a gathering place for them to worship their God, to legislate their town's civil affairs and to enjoy the good company of their neighbors."

Records indicate at the time of the original construction in 1795 this structure had a gallery instead of a full second floor. During original construction, the building had porches at both gabled ends to shelter the doorways. The bell tower was added in 1825 and the second floor was renovated to complete the second floor in 1848.

In 1867, the building underwent a major renovation project. The building was rotated ninety degrees and raised two additional feet. The new direction placed the front of the building facing Forest Road. The clock was added to the bell tower in 1895. The Town Meeting House was listed on the National Register of Historic Places in 1983.

The town of Greenfield was incorporated in 1791. The area was originally known as Lyndeborough Addition and named for the Lynde family who first settled in this area in the 1750's. When those who petitioned to have the town incorporated, they chose the name Greenfield to represent topography of fertile fields of green.

Hillsborough

Marker # 0065: Pierce Homestead

Location: On NH Route 31 north of NH Route 9 (301 2nd NH Turnpike, second home on right)

Sign Erected: 1970

GPS Coordinates- N 43° 06'.961″ W 71° 57'.020"

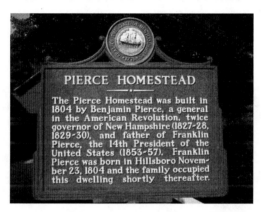

"The Pierce Homestead was built in 1804 by Benjamin Pierce, a general in the American Revolution, twice governor of New Hampshire (1827-28, 1829-30), and father of Franklin Pierce, the 14th President of the United States (1853-57). Franklin Pierce was born in Hillsboro November 23, 1804 and the family occupied this dwelling shortly thereafter."

According to the U.S. National Parks Service, Franklin Pierce lived in this home from infancy until he married in 1834. Franklin's father, Benjamin also operated a tavern in this dwelling and it was a popular gathering place in the community.

Franklin Pierce studied law at Bowdoin College and returned to this home in 1824 to practice law. While he still lived in this home, his law office was across the road. The interior of this home still retains the original elegance of what it was like when Franklin lived here. The main floor consists of four rooms that include the parlor, dining room, kitchen and master bedroom.

The second-floor front is the ballroom where the Pierce family entertained guests. The back segment of the second floor include two bedrooms. The Pierce Homestead is situated on 13 acres

The Pierce Homestead remained in the Pierce family until 1925 when ownership was transferred to the State of New Hampshire. Tours of the home are available in the summer months. Franklin Pierce has two historical markers in Concord. One is for the Pierce Manse where Franklin resided in Concord. The second marker is at the Old North Cemetery where he was laid to rest in 1869.

Hillsborough (Hillsborough Center)

Marker # 0107: Colonial Grant

Location: 27 East Washington Road and Center Road (2.8 miles from U.S. Route 202)

Sign Erected: 1976

GPS Coordinates- N 43° 08'.804″ W 71° 56'.152"

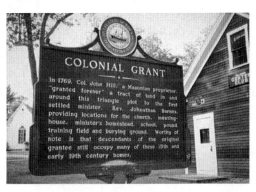

"In 1769, Col. John Hill, a Masonian proprietor, "granted forever" a tract of land in and around this triangle plot to the first settled minister. Rev. Johnathan Barnes, providing locations for the church, meetinghouse, minister's homestead, school, pound, training field and burying ground. Worthy of note is that descendants of the original grantee still occupy many of these 18th and early 19th century homes."

Colonel John Hill of Boston was granted the land by New Hampshire colonial Governor Benning Wentworth. While some records show that the land grant was named for Sir Wills Hill, Earl of Hillsborough in England; the Hillsborough Chamber of Commerce and town website claims that the namesake for the settlement is Colonel John Hill himself. Most of the early settlers were from eastern Massachusetts and the Scotch-Irish communities of southern New Hampshire.

The town was incorporated in 1772 by colonial Governor John Wentworth. The original name at incorporation was Hillborough (without the "s"). Hillsborough is comprised of four villages; Hillsborough Center, Upper Village, Lower Village, and today's downtown, Hillsborough Bridge.

Hillsborough Center was the economic center of the town of Hillsborough up to the early 20th century. Today, many of the original buildings remain except for the Meeting House which was in front of the cemetery north of this marker. This picturesque village common still maintains the charm of the 18th century. Here you will find an artist gallery of a local painter, as well as a home and barn where Gibson Pewter began (business now located in nearby Washington NH). The town pound is across the road from the First Congregational Church directly north of this marker.

Hillsborough

Marker # 0203: Stone Arch Bridges

Location: Intersection of U.S. Route 202 and N.H. Route 9

Sign Erected: 2006

GPS Coordinates- N 43° 06'.699″ W 71° 55'.115″

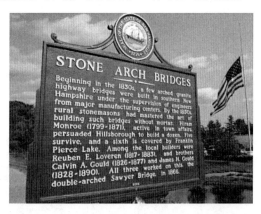

"Beginning in the 1830's, a few arched granite highway bridges were built in southern New Hampshire under the supervision of engineers from major manufacturing centers. By the 1850's, rural stonemasons had mastered the art of building such bridges without mortar. Hiram Monroe (1799-1871), active in town affairs, persuaded Hillsborough to build a dozen. Five survive, and a sixth is covered by Franklin Pierce Lake. Among the local builders were Reuben E. Loveren (1817-1883), and brothers Calvin A. Gould (1826-1877) and James H. Gould (1828-1890). All three worked on this, the double-arched Sawyer Bridge, in 1866."

The granite arched bridges were significant improvements over wooden structures. With the increased industrialization of the area, manufacturers needed bridges that were more sturdy and able to bear increased weight. At one time, Hillsborough had more than a dozen stone arched bridges. As stated on this marker, only five survive today, with one submersed under Franklin Pierce lake. The submersed bridge is the result of the reservoir built on the North Branch River in 1926. Of the five-surviving stone arched bridges, four are still actively used. This is the only surviving stone arched bridge that is no longer in use in Hillsborough.

The uniqueness of these structures is the that each stone had to be cut precisely to secure the joint and retain its strength without the use of mortar. While this bridge was completed in 1866, the construction of the dozen-plus stone arched bridges took place from 1830 to 1866. The five remaining bridges were designated National Historic Engineering Landmarks in 2002. The Cog Railroad in Bean's Grant (marker # 0045) is the only other site in New Hampshire to share this prestigious designation.

Hinsdale

Marker # 0112: Hinsdale's Auto Pioneer

Location: NH Route 118 2/10 mile east of NH Route 63 (across from 63 Canal Street)

Sign Erected: 1976

GPS Coordinates- N 42° 47'.262″ W 72° 28'.448″

"In the Holman and Merriam Machine Shop opposite this location, George A. Long of Northfield (Mass.) in 1875 built a steam-propelled four wheel automobile with a fifth wheel for steering. This vehicle, fired by hardwood charcoal, had a bicycle-type frame, ordinary wooden wheels, solid rear axle and could maintain 30 miles per hour, roads permitting. This early inventor patented and built another automobile, propelled by gasoline, now in the Smithsonian Institution."

The three-story building across the street from this marker is where George Alvin Long (1850-1952) came to apprentice in 1875. His early invention of the Long steam tricycle was the first steam-powered motorized vehicle. Long would take his invention out for test drives but heard strong negative sentiments from neighbors claiming the contraption was too loud, spit out burning cinders and scared the livestock. Long would sneak out at night and test his "horseless" carriage, but finally gave in to his unhappy neighbors and disassembled his invention. The disassembled chassis was used by the Hinsdale Fire department.

Long continued tinkering and built a gasoline powered vehicle which was patented in 1883. When you consider what comprises an automobile, the idea of steam-propelled motors does not top the list. But, while you may find untold claims of who invented the first automobile, Long's invention would certainly hold solid claim to the title self-propelled, steam-powered road vehicle.

An interesting note is that George A. Long lived in Northfield, Massachusetts and not in Hinsdale. But, he did not have an adequate space to build his invention in his hometown, so he worked in Hinsdale. George Long lived until the age 101 and died penniless.

Photo courtesy of Smithsonian

Hinsdale

Marker # 0204: Newhall & Stebbins

Location: NH Route 119 (Canal Street) east of NH Route 63 (next to Ashuelot River bridge)

Sign Erected: 2006

GPS Coordinates- N 42° 47'.238″ W 72° 28'.774″

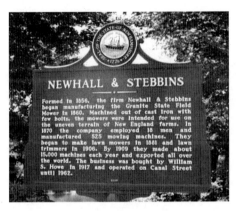

"Formed in 1856, the firm Newhall & Stebbins began manufacturing the Granite State Field Mower in 1860. Machined out of cast iron with few bolts, the mowers were intended for use on the uneven terrain of New England farms. In 1870 the company employed 18 men and manufactured 525 mowing machines. They began to make lawn mowers in 1881 and lawn trimmers in 1906. By 1909 they made about 15,000 machines each year and exported all over the world. The business was bought by William S. Howe in 1917 and operated on Canal Street until 1962."

The original machine shop was opened by Cyrus Newhall in 1830. In 1856, Lorenzo Stebbins became a partner and they formed Newhall & Stebbins. The Granite State Field Mower was widely popular, and manufacturing of the mower lasted a century. The company developed and sold four models of mowers which varied in size from a one-horse 3 ½ foot cut, to a two-horse 5-foot cut mower. In 1881, the company expanded to include hand mowers with sizes ranging from a 10-inch cut to a

20-inch cut included at least nine models. William S. Howe bought the company in 1911 and renamed it Granite State Mowers. The company gained a nationwide market for hand and power lawn mowers. The company remained in business until the 1960's.

Hinsdale was chartered in 1753 and named for Colonel Ebenezer Hinsdale. Hinsdale lays claim to the oldest continuously operating U.S. Post Office in the country which opened in 1816. Its first postmaster was Mr. Nathaniel Babbitt. This post office shared space with a local store until the post office occupied the entire space. The post office building is commemorated on the town seal. The post office is located on Main Street next to the town hall.

Jaffrey

Marker # 0013: Hannah Davis-Amos Fortune

Location: NH Route 124 2.0 miles west of US Route 202 (across from Thorndike Pond Rd)

Sign Erected: 1963

GPS Coordinates- N 42° 49'.627" W 72° 03'.266"

"Buried behind Jaffrey's colonial Meeting House nearby are "Aunt" Hannah Davis, 1784-1863, resourceful and beloved spinster who made, trademarked and sold this country's first wooden bandboxes; and Amos Fortune, 1710-1801, African-born slave who purchased his freedom, established a tannery and left funds for the Jaffrey church and schools."

According to an article in the Union Leader in April 2016, *"it's hard to connect the two people who are commemorated on this sign. A white woman, orphaned, and a freed black slave."* The connection is how both individuals while facing hardship, prospered as respected business owners of their community. The bandbox invented and built by Hannah Davis was a small round, or curved box. Davis constructed her bandboxes of wooden veneer and were nailed together. She covered the exterior with scraps of wallpaper to enhance the appearance and lined the interior with newspaper. Each box was unique in size and the wallpaper covering. They were typically used as hat boxes, or storage for small items. Today, a Hannah Davis bandbox is a highly sought-after collector item. "Aunt" Hannah Davis was a beloved member of the community. She died on November 29, 1863.

Amos Fortune was born in Africa and taken to America as a slave. He learned the trade of a tanner from his owner Ichabod Richardson. He had an agreement with Richardson to work for him for four years and he would earn his freedom. Richardson passed before the conclusion of the four-years. Amos Fortune had to negotiate an agreement and he bought his freedom at the age of 60. He then moved to Jaffrey in 1781. Amos Fortune opened his own tannery business and became a successful tradesman.

Fortune shared in his success by donating money to Jaffrey schools and the Congregational Church. Amos Fortune died on November 17, 1801. His headstone reads, "Sacred to the memory of Amos Fortune who was born free in Africa, a slave in America, he purchased liberty, professed Christianity, lived reputably, and died hopefully" Both Davis and Fortune are buried at the Old Burying Ground on Blackberry Lane Road.

Keene

Marker # 0069: Keene Glass Industry

Location: 312 Washington Street (Keene Recreation Center-Fuller Park)

Sign Erected: 1970

GPS Coordinates- N 42° 56'.582" W 72° 16'.521"

"The first of two famous Keene glass factories was established near this site in 1814 and produced window glass for the New England area until 1853. Another glass works (1815-1842), 1.5 miles southeast of here on Marlboro Street, made bottles and flasks now known as "Keene Glass" and prized today by museums and collectors."

The Keene Glass Factory manufactured primarily aqua window glass. This factory also produced free-blown bottles and other glass products. The original factory was created by local stockholders who realized the need for glass products. Having no glass making experience, the proprietors hired Lawrence Schoolcraft who was the superintendent of Mt Vernon New York Glassworks. Schoolcraft began his new job in Keene in June 1814. According to the history of the Keene Glass Factory, once the work day was complete, workers could freelance and make their own creations of glass. Collectors strive to find some of these beautiful creations made "after hours" from leftover glass.

The Monadnock Region was a successful region for glass production. Other historic markers in the region emphasis the importance of this early 19th century industry (Stoddard & Temple, NH).

Keene was granted as Upper Ashuelot in 1735 and was granted to New Hampshire in 1741 after the boundary with Massachusetts was determined. It was re-granted in 1753 by colonial Governor Benning Wentworth and named Keene in honor of English minister Sir Benjamin Keene.

Keene

Marker # 0086: Hampshire Pottery 1871-1923

Location: 580 Main Street & Manchester Street (in front of Cheshire Tire Center)

Sign Erected: 1972

GPS Coordinates- N 42° 55'.143″ W 72° 16'.485″

"About 150 feet north of here stood the famous Hampshire Pottery Works, founded by James Scolly Taft for the manufacture of earthenware. In 1878 Majolica ware was a major product, followed in 1883 by the addition of useful and decorative art objects and souvenir pieces. With the introduction in 1904 of the famous "mat glaze," Hampshire Pottery was recognized a leader in its field."

James Scolly Taft was born in nearby Nelson, New Hampshire on July 16, 1844. In 1871, Taft and his uncle purchased the former Milestone Mill, a former clothespin factory and converted it to the Hampshire Pottery Works. The site was ideal because the local grounds contained rich blue clay and silica deposits. The first items manufactured were flowerpots. Ironically, the first pottery fired caught the building on fire and a new building was constructed within six weeks.

Taft experimented in mastering the art and science of pottery ware. He tried several products for marketability including jugs, soap dishes, milk pans and pitchers. Production also included drainpipes. A nearby earthenware business went under and Taft purchased the business in 1874. This brought a focus to earthenware with the majolica ware. The matte green glaze became popular in 1883.

In 1904, Cadmon Robertson came to Hampshire Pottery Works and oversaw production. During his time with the company, Robertson created more than 900 different glazes. Robertson died in 1914 and Taft resumed production responsibilities. Taft ceased production and sold Hampshire Pottery Works the next year to George Morton. Morton continued production for a short time and eventually closed the business in 1917. He reopened and began the manufacture of white chinaware for hotels and closed the doors one final time in 1923.

Keene

Marker # 0226: Jonathan Myrick Daniels 1939-1965

Location: 44 West Street and St. James Street

Sign Erected: 2011

GPS Coordinates- N 42° 55'.992" W 72° 16'.819"

"Civil Rights activist Daniels worshiped at St. James Episcopal Church during his high school years. Born in Keene, he graduated from Virginia Military Institute before entering the Episcopal Theological School in Cambridge, MA. While studying for the priesthood, he went south to assist with voter registration. On August 20, 1965 in Haynesville, AL, Daniels was shot and killed as he stepped in front of a young African-American coworker, saving her life. His funeral was held at St. James."

Jonathan Daniels was born in Keene on March 20, 1939. He was raised in the Congregational Church and began worshiping at St. James Episcopal while in high school. After high school he attended Virginia Military Institute and graduated first in his class. Daniels attended graduate school at Harvard University and during an Easter Service at the Church of the Advent, Daniels decided to pursue the priesthood. In 1963, he attended the Episcopal Theological School in Cambridge.

In 1965, Daniels was moved by Dr. Martin Luther King's speech for all clergy to join his march from Selma to Montgomery,

Alabama. On March 7, 1965 Jonathan Daniels traveled to Selma and joined Dr. King on his march to Montgomery. After the march, Daniels returned to Cambridge to complete his exams. But he could not stay in New England knowing of the need for help in Alabama. Daniels went back and helped with tutoring and local voter registration drives.

On August 20, 1965, Jonathan Daniels, Reverend Richard Morrisroe (Catholic priest), Joyce Bailey, and Ruby Sales attempted to enter a store to purchase a drink on this hot day. In front of the store entrance, Tom Coleman blocked the door while carrying a shotgun. A confrontation broke out and Coleman pointed the shotgun at Ruby Sales. Daniels pushed her away and was shot and killed instantly. Reverend Morrisroe was shot in the back. Bailey and Sales escaped injury. Daniels' funeral was here at St. James on August 24, 1965.

Mason

Marker # 0035: Uncle Sam's House

Location: NH Route 123 ½ mile south of Mason Village and north of Cascade Road

Sign Erected: 2006

GPS Coordinates- N 42° 44'.356″ W 71° 45'.905″

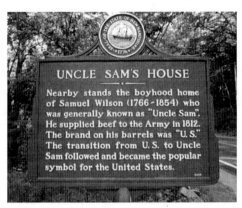

"Nearby stands the boyhood home of Samuel Wilson (1766-1854) who was generally known as "Uncle Sam". He supplied beef to the Army in 1812. The brand of his barrels was "U.S." The transition from U.S. to Uncle Sam followed and became the popular symbol for the United States."

Samuel Wilson was born in Arlington, Massachusetts and grew up here in Mason. Samuel moved here with his parents and ten siblings in 1780. At the age of 23, he married Betsy Mann who also lived here in town. The couple moved to Troy, New York, along with Samuel's brother and began their career as meatpackers. The brothers were successful and well-known in Troy.

During the War of 1812, the Eban and Samuel Wilson Packing Company was selected to provide barrels of corned beef to the U.S. Army. At that time, contractors were required to place their initials on their food products. The initials "E. and S.-U.S." was branded on the barrels. The "E and S" denoted Eban and Samuel, and U.S. (United States). The abundance of barrels branded with initials, soldiers began the association that the U.S. really referred to "Uncle Sam" Wilson.

The cartoon we recognize today was an evolution of other patriotic characters from as early as the Revolutionary War. Notably, the depiction from cartoonist Thomas Nast in 1860 of the tall, serious character with a top hat and white beard. The cartoon we know from posters with the phrase "I Want You for the U.S. Army" was created by cartoonist Jonathan Flagg at the early years of World War I. This image became the symbol of military recruiting. In 1961, the U.S. Congress passed a resolution proclaiming Uncle Sam Wilson as namesake for this national patriotic symbol. Wilson died in 1854 and is buried in Troy, NY.

New Ipswich

Marker # 0010: First Textile Mill

Location: NH Route 124 (Turnpike Road) and west of River Road

Sign Erected: 1962

GPS Coordinates- N 42° 45'.051″ W 71° 49'.766”

"Established in New Hampshire at New Ipswich in early 1800's for the carding, spinning and weaving of cotton and wool. This manufacture of fabrics spread throughout the state and contributed prominently to its economic and social growth and the development of the textile industry nationally."

Many would consider the birthplace of the wool and cotton manufacturing industry in New Hampshire to be the Amoskeag Mills and others along the mighty Merrimack River. So, it came as a surprise that New Ipswich is the "birthplace of New Hampshire textile mills". Considering that this industry brought the Granite State into the Industrial Revolution, this is significant.

The Warwick Mills along the Souhegan River is the oldest textile mill still in production in New Hampshire. The building onsite is the third mill building. The first two buildings were constructed of wood and burned. The current building was constructed in

1872 and is still in operation. Mills built in the 19th century were powered by hydro power. There was no electricity. Therefore, mills were built tall and narrow to accommodate the terrain (typically narrow and deep) and for maximum lighting with windows. The Warwick Mill building is 6-stories high to maximize floor space and allow for weaving machines to be near windows.

At the height of industry in New Ipswich, a saw mill and grist mill were located downstream from the current mill. Located upstream from the mill site were two additional mills. About ½ mile upstream from the current mill site was the state's first cotton mill in 1804, which was located at what was known as Bank Village. New Hampshire Public Radio has a short audio clip of this local history on their "Marking History" program.

New Ipswich

Marker # 0101: Site of Wilder's Chair Factory

Location: NH Route 124 (Turnpike Road) east of Nashua Road (south side of road)

Sign Erected: 1975

GPS Coordinates- N 42° 47'.216″ W 71° 55'.586″

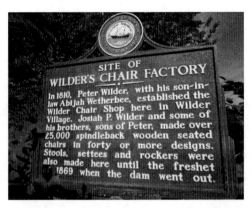

"In 1810, Peter Wilder, with his son-in-law Abijah Wetherbee, established the Wilder Chair Shop here in Wilder Village. Josiah P. Wilder and some of his brothers, sons of Peter, made over 25,000 spindleback wooden seated chairs in forty or more designs. Stools, settees and rockers were also made here until the freshet of 1869 when the dam went out."

Finding information relating to the history of Wilder's Chair Factory was not an easy task. The limited information found suggests that Peter Wilder's chair factory manufactured "pine-seated, curved-back chairs" as well as rocking chairs. The Wilder chair design was like the Boston rocker design which is believed to be from Peter Wilder and his eldest son, Joseph. Both worked as chairmakers in Boston prior to opening their factory here in New Ipswich. A notable modification of the Wilder chair from the Boston rocking chair is the more pronounced tablet top of the chair. This style of rocking chair is also commonly known as

Windsor rockers. Source: American Windsor Furniture-Specialized Forms (1997).

New Ipswich was granted in 1735 to settlers Colonel John Wainright and John Choat from Ipswich, Massachusetts. In 1762, colonial Governor Benning Wentworth incorporated the town as Ipswich, and later as New Ipswich in 1766. The focal point for industry in this community was situated along the Souhegan River. The Great Flood of October 1869 which breached the dam and destroyed the chair factory was the result of a 36-hour tropical storm that dumped 6-12 inches of rain.

The town is also home to New Ipswich Academy that was chartered in 1789. Local industrialist Samuel Appleton endowed the academy and it was renamed Appleton Academy. This school was considered on par with Phillips Exeter Academy in Exeter. It closed in 1968 as a public high school and became a college-prep private school that same year. Unfortunately, due to difficult economic hardships, the school closed in 1974.

New Ipswich

Marker # 0137: Barrett House

Location: NH Route 123A (79 Main Street) ¼ mile south of NH Route 123

Sign Erected: 1980

GPS Coordinates- N 42° 45'.203″ W 71° 51'.329″

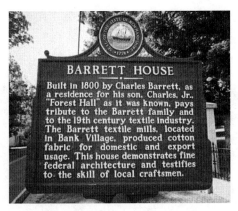

"Built in 1800 by Charles Barrett, as a residence for his son, Charles, Jr., "Forest Hall" as it was known, pays tribute to the Barrett family and to the 19th century textile industry. The Barrett textile mills, located in Bank Village, produced cotton fabric for domestic and export usage. This house demonstrates fine federal architecture and testifies to the skill of local craftsmen."

This home built by Charles Barrett was a wedding gift to his son, Charles Jr. and daughter in-law Martha Minot. Martha's father, Jonas Minot encouraged Charles Barrett to build it to the impressive scale and he would provide suitable furnishings. Charles and Martha had five children and raised them in this mansion. At the time of Martha's death in 1842, son Charles III lived in the home until 1848. At this time, the eldest son George and wife Frances lived in this home. This residence remained a Barrett home until 1916.

The home was boarded up for more than forty years. In 1948, descendant Caroline Barr Wade donated the home to the Historic New England organization who renovated the home to its original grandeur. The property was opened to the public as a museum in 1950. The Barrett House museum includes original furnishings, carriages, and the third-floor ballroom with original musical instruments. The 1979 movie *The Europeans* was filmed in the Barrett House.

The Barrett family cotton mill was located ½ mile upstream from the current Warwick Mill in Bank Village.

Peterborough

Marker # 0206: The MacDowell Graves

Location: High Street .2-mile past MacDowell Road (stay right)

Sign Erected: 2007

GPS Coordinates- N 42° 53'.180″ W 71° 57'.263"

"Buried on this site are noted composer Edward MacDowell (1860-1908) and his wife, Marian Nevins MacDowell (1857-1956). The composer often paused at this boulder to watch the sun set behind Mount Monadnock. Edward and Marian purchased a small farm and moved to Peterborough in 1896. Together they founded The MacDowell Colony in 1907, the first and leading residency program for artists in the United States. On the acres to the north and west of this site, The MacDowell Colony continues to offer talented artists ideal working conditions in which they can produce enduring works of the imagination."

Edward was born in New York City, New York in a Quaker household. At the age of 15, he moved to France with his mother to expand his musical talent. Two years later, he moved to Germany to continue his musical training. Music critics suggest that MacDowell's music education in Germany made the greatest impact on his music composition. Edward is considered one of the greatest American composers.

His wife Marian was a former student of Edward's whom he married on July 11, 1884. The MacDowell's moved to Boston in 1888 and purchased this land in 1896. The property inspired Edward's music. In a cabin on this property, Edward composed, *Woodland Sketches op.51* in 1896. In 1907, wanting to share their love for the area they created the "Peterborough Idea". The MacDowell Colony artists, sculptors, painters, and musicians used the retreat to inspire their work. While Edward lived to see the birth of the artist colony, it was under the leadership of Marian that it flourished.

This property was not only an inspiration to Edward and Marian, but to a multitude of other artists. The MacDowell Colony is still in operation and the foundation grants more than 300 fellowships each year. The colony was listed as a National Historic Place in 1962.

Peterborough

Marker # 0210: Settler's Rock

Location: U.S. Route 202 at Noone Falls Bridge (Old Sharon Road)

Sign Erected: 2007

GPS Coordinates- N 42° 51'.550" W 71° 57'.753"

"Scotch-Irish immigrant Thomas Morison and a companion camped beside this rock about 1739. The large boulder supported a temporary shelter of green poles and boughs, and its vertical face served as a fireplace. In 1749 Morison returned as the first permanent settler of Peterborough and the following year he brought his family to a log house he had built near the rock. Morison was an incorporator of the town in 1760, served on the first board of selectmen and was the town's first moderator. He resided on the farm until his death in 1797 at the age of 87."

While the original large boulder is no longer here, I found a photo of what may be the boulder on the Monadnock Center for History and Culture website. However, permission for use was not granted and therefore not included on this page. The boulder may have been destroyed during the construction of the highway; I am not certain. Thomas Morison built his lean-to against the boulder as a shelter in 1769 along the Contoocook River. He had purchased this lot as part of a land grant while it was still part of provincial Massachusetts. Not much is known of Morison's companion except his name was Mr. Russell (first name is unknown).

Morison returned to Massachusetts to gather his family and bring them back to this location in 1750. Scotch-Irish settlers began to move here and establish themselves in the 1750's. In 1761, the provincial New Hampshire legislature granted a charter to incorporate this land as Peterborough. Ironically, the namesake for the town was of another original founder of this community, Peter Prescott. I am curious why the incorporated town was not named in honor of the original founder and settler, Thomas Morison. Would the town have been named Thomasborough, or Morisonborough? By 1780, more than 120 men over the age of 21 had settled here. At the time, the town census also included one male slave and two female slaves.

Peterborough

Marker # 0244: Revolutionary War Drummer William Diamond

Location: 229 Old Street Road (1.1 miles from NH Route 123)

Sign Erected: 2014

GPS Coordinates- N 42° 52'.821" W 71° 56'.248"

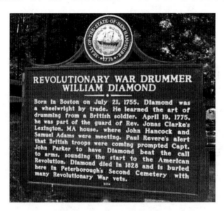

"Born in Boston on July 21, 1755, Diamond was a wheelwright by trade. He learned the art of drumming from a British soldier. April 19, 1775, he was part of the guard of Rev. Jonas Clarke's Lexington, MA house, where John Hancock and Samuel Adams were meeting. Paul Revere's alert that British troops were coming prompted Capt. John Parker to have Diamond beat the call to arms, sounding the start to the American Revolution. Diamond died in 1828 and is buried here in Peterborough's Second Cemetery with many Revolutionary War vets."

Records differ on Diamond's birth date. Some records in Boston cite that he was born in 1758, but his gravestone and military pension records indicate 1755. Diamond's military service was not limited to the infamous Battle of Lexington and Concord on April 19, 1775. Military records reveal that Diamond served numerous tours until his final tour ended on December 5, 1781. Most enlistment terms during this era were six months in duration.

An interesting fact was that not only did Diamond sound the drum alarm for the beginning of the Revolution at Lexington, Massachusetts in April 1775, but also extended his tour and served under the command of General George Washington at the Battle of Trenton on Christmas night 1776. This battle was the infamous Washington crossing the Delaware River to seize needed supplies from the British and Hessians who were encamped on the New Jersey-side of the Delaware river.

Diamond lived most of his life in Massachusetts and moved to Peterborough in 1795. He was married to Rebecca Simonds, the daughter of John Simonds, one of the wealthiest men in Lexington Massachusetts. In 1798, William Diamond purchased sixty acres of land in Peterborough where he farmed until his death in 1828 at the age of 73. On Diamond's headstone it reads, "A Revolutionary Soldier, drummer at Lexington and Bunker Hill".

Richmond

Marker # 0210: Hosea Ballou (1771-1852)

Location: NH Route 32 Old Homestead Highway & Mill Road (north of intersection)

Sign Erected: 1969

GPS Coordinates- N 42° 46'.811″ W 72° 16'.327"

"Born in an almost uncleared wilderness in an area then known as Ballou's Dell, 1.5 miles east of here, on Fish Hatchery Road, this farm boy, reared in the Baptist faith, became known as the Father of Universalism. In the 19th century, as an author and preacher, he expounded religious liberalism from pulpits in Portsmouth, N.H., Salem and Boston, Mass."

Hosea Ballou was born April 30, 1771 of Maturin and Lydia Ballou. Hosea's father, Maturin was a Calvinist Baptist preacher as well as a farmer. Hosea's mother died when he was two years-old. A self-educated man, Hosea Ballou converted to Universalism in 1789 and began preaching in 1791 as a Universalist preacher. Ballou preached in Vermont from 1801 to 1807 and in Portsmouth from 1807 to 1815. In 1815, Ballou became the minister of the Universalist church in Salem Massachusetts. In 1817, he became the pastor of the famous Second Universalist Church in Boston until his death in 1852.

Hosea married Ruth Washburn in 1795 and had thirteen children. Of his nine surviving children, three became Universalist preachers. Ballou has been referred to as the Father of the American Universalist Church. He founded and was the editor of "*The Trumpet*" and "*The Universalist Quarterly Review*", two prominent Universalist publications.

He is credited with writing more than 10,000 sermons. A quick search of Hosea Ballou quotes offers viewers some interesting notables that would capture the attention of his congregation. For example, "Real happiness is cheap enough, yet how dearly we pay for its counterfeit", and "Falsehood is cowardice, the truth is courage". His tenet for his belief is that those who see God as wrathful only lead to followers with hardened hearts. Ballou died in Boston on June 7, 1852.

Rindge

Marker # 0210: Second Rindge Meeting House

Location: Main Street and Todd Hill Road

Sign Erected: 1980

GPS Coordinates-N 42° 45'.008″ W 72° 00'.591″

"This Meeting House was an outgrowth of the time when Proprietors of the town were responsible for the encouragement of religion. It was built in 1796 when church and state were intertwined. Until 1819, regardless of denomination and belief, residents were considered members of this parish and their tax money supported the minister. In 1839 the town became owner of this edifice and the church society its tenant and this arrangement remains today. This building of simple colonial architecture still embraces some of the religious and civil affairs of this community and stands as a monument to pure democracy."

In 1794, citizens of Rindge began construction of the Second Rindge Meeting House. The First Rindge Meeting House was constructed generally on the same tract of property in 1765. The original Masonian proprietors voted to approve the construction on the First Rindge Meeting House in 1750 on twenty acres. The building was supposed to have been completed in four years, but fear of attacks by Indians delayed construction. The settlers began using the First Meeting House in 1766.

With the community growing in population, the citizens voted to build a new and larger Meeting House in the 1790's. The original Meeting House was moved to a location across from the current Town Hall on Payson Hill Road. This building was originally dismantled for its lumber. The Second Rindge Meeting House included a larger meeting area, horse stables, bell and tower. The current Meeting House was listed on the National Register of Historic Places in 1979. A unique trait of this building is the first floor is used for town meetings and the second floor is used for religious services; a lasting example of religious and state functions sharing of space. The Town of Rindge was incorporated on February 11, 1768.

Sharon

Marker # 0068: Toll House and Toll Gate

Location: NH Route 124 East of Prescott Road (⅓ mile east of Jaffrey town line)

Sign Erected: 1990

GPS Coordinates- N 42° 47'.814" W 71° 58'.238"

"A Toll House and Toll Gate stood on this site from 1803 to 1822. For many years droves of cattle passed along this 3rd New Hampshire Turnpike (Incorporated in 1799) four rods wide running from Walpole through Keene and Sharon toward Boston to the Massachusetts line."

The Third New Hampshire Turnpike was incorporated on December 27, 1799 and was fifty miles in length. The turnpike's western terminus was in Keene, New Hampshire and the eastern terminus was in Townsend, Massachusetts. Construction of the Turnpike cost approximately $50,000. The cost was incurred by local proprietors who owned the tracts of land the turnpike crossed. The proprietors set up toll gates, a bar which stopped travelers from continuing until the toll was paid. Travelers (typically a horse and rider) paid one cent per mile and gave the toll to attendants stationed in the Toll House. The road converted to a toll-free road in 1819, but the Toll House and Toll Gate remained on this site until 1822.

The Town of Sharon was originally settled in 1738 but was not named until 1750 when it was named Peterborough Slip due to a surveying error. This name remained until 1768 when the town was renamed Sliptown. On January 24, 1791, the town was incorporated and renamed Sharon from where many of the settlers originated from in Sharon, Connecticut.

Stoddard

Marker # 0027: Stone Arch Bridge

Location: NH Route 9 (mile marker 33.8 at Antrim/Stoddard town line)

Sign Erected: 1965

GPS Coordinates- N 43° 04'.458″ W 72° 02'.714″

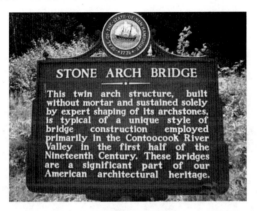

"This twin arch structure, built without mortar and sustained solely by expert shaping of its archstones, is typical of a unique style of bridge construction employed primarily in the Contoocook River Valley in the first half of the Nineteenth Century. These bridges are a significant part of our American architectural heritage."

Of the surviving stone arch bridges in New Hampshire this site may be the most scenic. NH Route 9 runs parallel and has ample parking. Visitors can walk on this bridge and appreciate the beauty and craftsmanship of its construction. Remarkably, Hillsborough County has similar bridges built of native quarried granite and constructed without mortar. Two other historical markers in the Monadnock Region acknowledge this engineering marvel. Gilsum (marker #0168) and Hillsborough (marker #0203) both were built during the same period as this bridge.

The stone bridges constructed in the Monadnock Region were the result of Scottish descent stone masons. These bridges built without mortar was only possible with expertise shaping of the granite blocks to interlock in the archway. The weight of the bridge load is dispersed in the arch framework and the shaped blocks transfer the weight outward from the center to the abutments. The stonework has persevered for more than 150 years. This resiliency is not unlike the settlers who made us the granite state.

Stoddard

Marker # 0052: Stoddard Glass

Location: NH Route 9 (mile marker 31.2)

Sign Erected: 1968

GPS Coordinates- N 43° 03'.101″ W 72° 04'.398"

"Glassmaking in this town covered the years 1842-1873. Nearby stood the South Stoddard Glass Works founded by Joseph Foster in 1842. A second works was erected in 1846 at Mill Village two miles north. In its day a major industry of the State, Stoddard glass products are now highly prized by collectors."

Stoddard was the epicenter of the glass industry in the mid-19th century. At its peak, Stoddard had four glass manufacturers. The Monadnock Region has significant history in the glass industry to include Temple and Keene. Stoddard was a preferred location due to the abundance and quality of finely-grained sand which was used in making glass. Stoddard glass was known for its amber and olive-green hues. Whereas, Keene Glass was a major producer of window glass due to its bluish hue, Stoddard Glass was a major producer of bottles and medicine containers due to the amber and greenish hues.

Like the Keene Glass factory, workers created their own works of art from the leftover glass at the end of the work day. Workers created "whimsicals", or small pieces of glassblower pieces that were not made for sale. These items are highly sought-after collectibles and are recognized by the distinct hues found in Stoddard produced glass.

The decline of the Stoddard Glass industry began in the 1870's. Other manufacturers used gas or coal as their heat source, which was found to be cheaper than the wood-fueling glassworks. Also, other glassworks had mastered the chemistry needed to produce the desired hues of the glass, rather than relying on the organic structure of sand. The sand used in the Stoddard glassworks was also unable to be modified to create the high-demand clear glass.

Surry

Marker # 0093: Surry Mountain Gold Mine and Lily Pond

Location: 8 Village Road off NH Route 12A (on lawn of Reed Free Library)

Sign Erected: 1973

GPS Coordinates- N 43° 01'.152″ W 72° 19'.293″

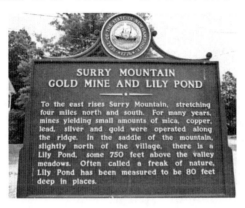

"To the east rises Surry Mountain, stretching four miles north and south. For many years, mines yielding small amounts of mica, copper, lead, silver and gold were operated along the ridge. In the saddle of the mountain, slightly north of the village, there is a Lily Pond, some 750 feet above the valley meadows. Often called a freak of nature, Lily Pond has been measured to be 80 feet deep in places."

According to "History of the Town of Surry, Cheshire County, New Hampshire" written by Frank Burnside Kingsbury in 1925, Surry Mountain has been a source for minerals dating back to the Native Americans of the region. Kingsbury wrote that tradition believes the Native Americans had mined the lead from ledges on Surry Mountain. The book also claims early Spaniards had taken gold ore from this mountain. Another piece of lore claims that in the early 19th century that an extensive forest fire on the mountain had resulted in flows of molten lead over the exposed rocks. In the late 18th century many mining ventures attempted to mine gold, silver, copper, and lead from the mountain. One man even shot pellets of gold from his shotgun into a ledge and brought potential investors up to witness the gold specks. He collected their investments and fled; fleecing them of their money. In 1880, the Granite State Gold and Silver Mining company began mining the metals from the area. While this was the biggest mining operation in the town, it quickly closed in 1887 due to financial problems.

Surry Mountain is now part the Society for the Protection of New Hampshire Forests and known as the French-Harris Memorial Forest. It spans 140 acres to include Lily Pond. Lily Pond is considered a geological anomaly due the eighty-foot deep, cone shape contour of the pond.

The Town of Surry was incorporated on March 9, 1769 and derived its name from Surrey county in southern England where it is believed the original settlers emigrated from. The town was also one of the western New Hampshire towns that attempted to secede and join Vermont in 1781.

Swanzey

Marker # 0022: Denman Thompson 1833-1911

Location: NH Route 32 & Sawyers Crossing Road (Across from Swanzey Town Hall)

Sign Erected: 1964

GPS Coordinates- N 42° 52'.403″   W 72° 16'.891″

"A famous theatrical trouper who lived and died in West Swanzey. he gained a national reputation by his portrayal of the character, "Joshua Whitcomb", the New Hampshire farmer on a trip to Boston. From this he subsequently evolved "The Old Homestead", a play of long runs before enthusiastic audiences."

Henry Denman Thompson was born October 15, 1833 in Erie, Pennsylvania. His parents lived in Swanzey, New Hampshire and moved to Pennsylvania in 1831. Denman Thompson was a direct descendant of the original settlers of Swanzey. Denman Thompson moved back to Swanzey with his family in 1847. Denman Thompson attended school in what is now the Mount Caesar Union Library (which is the steepled building across the street and north of this marker). As a young boy, he began learning his father's trade as a carpenter.

Denman had greater aspirations and moved to Boston at the age of nineteen. He worked for a circus and developed his passion for theater. In 1850, he began his professional acting career. This led to his travels to Toronto, Canada and London, England. Thompson wrote the four-act play "The Homestead" and it debuted in Boston in April 1886. The storyline (with the Uncle Joshua Whitcomb as the main character) portrays life and a collection of characters set in his hometown of Swanzey. This play was widely received by a national audience and ran for several years. The play debuted on Broadway in 1904. Denman Thompson died in Swanzey on April 14, 1911. In 1915, a silent film was produced of Thompson's play and reproduced in 1922.

photo courtesy of Wikipedia

Swanzey (West Swanzey)

Marker # 0232: The Homestead Woolen Mills Dam

Location: Main Street and Spring Street (next to Denman Thompson Covered Bridge)

Sign Erected: 2012

GPS Coordinates- N 42° 52'.300″ W 72° 19'.652"

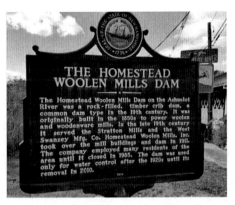

"The Homestead Woolen Mills Dam on the Ashuelot River was a rock-filled, timber crib dam, a common dam type in the 19th century. It was originally built in the 1850's to power woolen and woodenware mills. In the late 19th century it served the Stratton Mills and the West Swanzey Mfg. Co. Homestead Woolen Mills, Inc. took over the mill buildings and dam in 1911. the company employed many residents of the area until it closed in 1985. The dam was used only for water control after the 1920s until its removal in 2010."

Hydro power was the primary means for generating power for manufacturing from the 18th century to early 20th century; with what we know as the Industrial Revolution. New Hampshire manufacturing relied heavily on power generation from our major rivers. With the expansion of electrical power sources, hydropower began to diminish. The dam was located just south (downriver) of the bridge. All that remains is a small ripple of current where the former dam was situated.

With a request from the owner, the New Hampshire Department of Environmental Services removed the dam in 2010. There were no plans to repair the dilapidated wooden dam and removal was a significant ecological step in the return of fish migration.

At this marker site is the West Swanzey Bridge (also known as the Denman Thompson Bridge). The bridge was built in 1832. The bridge at one time had pedestrian walkways on both sides. One was removed sometime after 1915. The bridge still maintains its stone constructed abutments and central pier. The bridge is 136 feet long with a span of 64 feet. It was listed on the National Register of Historic Places in 1980.

Temple (Temple Village)

Marker # 0012: Temple Glass Factory

Location: NH Route 45 and Cemetery Road (General Miller Highway)

Sign Erected: 1963 & 1985   Village Cemetery sign: 1962

GPS Coordinates- N 42° 49'.139″ W 72° 51'.051"

"Was located at a secluded site in the southwest portion of Temple township. Founded in 1780 by Robert Hewes who employed Hessian mercenaries from the British Army trained in the art of glass-blowing. This early attempt to manufacture bottles and crude window-glass was beginning of glass-making in New Hampshire."

"Here were buried most of first settlers in Temple including Rev. Samuel Webster, Patriot-Preacher; Francis Blood-Moses Child whom Gen. Washington sent on spy mission to Nova Scotia-Ebenezer Edwards who fought at Concord Bridge- First Burial in 1772".

The original New England Glassworks was founded by Robert Hewes in 1780. Hewes employed Hessian deserters with experience in glass-blowing. The Hessians were mercenaries from the Hesse-Kassel region of Germany who were hired out to the British army. Hewes built his first glassworks factory, but it succumbed to fire shortly after construction. Hewes had financial difficulty keeping his glassworks in operation and it closed in 1783.

The effort to produce glass products in Temple was the first location for this industry in the Monadnock Region. Some records suggest that Hewes chose Temple as the location for his glassworks for its abundance of hardwood for the kilns. However, the land was not noted for any extensive amount of sand, or waterways for shipping the glassware. While the New England Glassworks was short-lived, it was the beginning of what was to become a prosperous industry in the region. The site of this glassworks (near the Sharon town line) was excavated in the 1970's and many glass artifacts were found onsite. The excavated glassworks site was listed on the National Register of Historic Places in 1975.

Next to this marker is a marker for the Village Cemetery, erected by the Temple Historical Society. As noted on this marker, many patriots made Temple their home and eternal resting place.

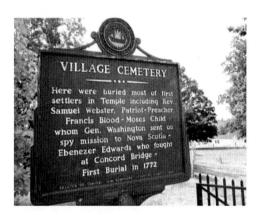

Walpole

Marker # 0061: First Connecticut River Bridge

Location: NH Route 12 at North Walpole Lower Boat Landing (⅓ mile south of RR crossing)

Sign Erected: 1970

GPS Coordinates- N 43° 07'.711″ W 72° 26'.241″

"The first bridge across the river was built approximately ¼ mile north of this location in 1785 by Col. Enoch Hale. This toll bridge, replaced in 1840, was recognized in the 18th century as one of America's outstanding bridges because of its unique engineering style. Its replacement was made a free bridge in 1904."

North of this marker site is the now closed Vilas Bridge. The location of the Vilas Bridge was the site of the First Connecticut River bridge built in 1785. This original bridge was a wooden covered bridge that was replaced in 1840. Prior to the 1840 bridge replacement, the toll for crossing was three cents for a man on horseback. The 1840 toll bridge was known as a Tucker truss-style bridge built by Captain Isaac Damon. This bridge was destroyed on March 16, 1868 when high water and ice destroyed a section of the bridge. It was not until 1870 when the citizens of Walpole voted to fund two-thirds of the new bridge construction and the Vermont town of Westminster voted to fund the remaining one-third.

This bridge remained in use until it was destroyed by fire in 1910. The current bridge, named for Charles Vilas was built in 1930. The bridge was named in honor of a hotelier and philanthropist from nearby Alstead. In 2009, the bridge was closed for vehicle traffic and no agreement between the States of New Hampshire and Vermont have been made to rehabilitate the structure.

Walpole was first granted in 1736 and known as Fort #3. During the early 18th century, early settlements were forts established along the Connecticut River (Charlestown Fort# 4 is the only surviving fort and is now a museum). The town was incorporated in 1756 as Bellowstown and reincorporated as Walpole in 1761 in honor of Great Britain's first Prime Minister Sir Robert Walpole. While visiting Walpole do not be surprised if you come across their most famous resident and noted documentary filmmaker, Ken Burns.

Westmoreland

Marker # 0074: Park Hill Meeting House

Location: NH Route 63 and Dutton Road

Sign Erected: 1971

GPS Coordinates- N 42° 58'.435″ W 72° 27'.423"

"This church, built on the northeast corner of Cole Cemetery in 1762, was moved in sections by ox cart in 1779 to this location, then known as Federal Hill. A steeple with a bell cast by the Paul Revere Foundry was added in 1826. This edifice is recognized as one of the most beautiful churches in New England."

The Westmoreland Historical Society has additional information regarding this building. The marker states the building was moved to this location in 1779. The reason for the initial move in 1779 was due to a shift in the population of Westmoreland to Park Hill.

The Historical Society adds that the building was moved again in 1826 when the bell was installed. This move of approximately 90 feet was made to accentuate the aesthetics of the current site. During the move in 1826, the main meeting room was also enlarged by twenty feet in length. Today, the first floor is used for meetings and exhibitions. The second floor is used for church services. The building was listed on the National Register of

Historic Places in 1980 and is currently owned by the Park Hill Meeting House and Historical Society.

Westmoreland was first granted as Fort #2 in 1735. The town was re-granted by Governor Benning Wentworth in 1752 and named in honor of Sir John Fane, 7th Earl of Westmoreland. The land was primarily settled for its fertile farmlands. Throughout the 19th century many small mills were in operation which made this community a highly sought-after place to live.

Chapter Six

Merrimack Valley Region

The Merrimack Valley Region is the heart of New Hampshire in so many ways. The region is in the south-central part of the state. Named for the river that dominates the region, this area is abundant with notable history relating to the development of the Granite State. With the Merrimack River as its main artery, the river begins in Franklin to the north, through Concord, Manchester and Nashua to the south. The growth of the Granite State throughout the centuries centered on this river. Today, the region offers more than industry along the mighty Merrimack River. The Merrimack Valley Region is the home to our seat of state government with the State Capitol in Concord, as well as the government seat for Merrimack County. The Queen City of Manchester is New Hampshire's largest city and at one time the heartbeat of the Industrial Revolution in the 19th century. Nashua is the Gateway City to the south along the Merrimack River and bordering Massachusetts. Nashua is the second largest city in New Hampshire. Manchester and Nashua share as county seats for Hillsborough County.

In relation to the number of historical markers, this region clearly has the most with approximately twenty-five percent of all the markers. It is not unusual to see a handful or more of our state's historical markers in a relative short drive. Concord has thirteen markers within the city alone. Many are within walking distance from each other.

The Merrimack Valley Region offers visitors a multitude of activities from cultural activities in Concords Arts Center to the Currier Museum of Art in Manchester. The region also has the McAuliffe-Shepard Discovery Center in Concord. Explore the celestial skies at the planetarium. Exhibits include astronomy, air and space science, aviation and space history. This is a fitting tribute to New Hampshire's pioneers of space exploration Christa McAuliffe and Alan Shepard.

Manchester and Nashua are home to New Hampshire's only minor-league sports teams. Most notable are baseball's New Hampshire Fisher Cats and hockey's Manchester Monarchs. The Southern New Hampshire University Center in Manchester is also the venue for many top musicians and other shows. As the New Hampshire Department of Travel and Tourism claims, this region is the destination for entertainment.

The historical significance of this region is clearly recognized with the multitude of state and local markers (Hooksett has several town historic markers). Here we will visit historical markers honoring signers of the Declaration of Independence, famous Revolutionary War heroes, the 14th President of the United States, famous visitors, astronauts and poets. This region has it all!

Merrimack Valley Region

Allenstown- Marker #0193: Meeting House/Burial Grounds

Allenstown- Marker #0205: Bear Brook Civilian Conservation Corps Camp

Allenstown- Marker #0211: Suncook Connection Bridge

Allenstown- Marker #0230: Robert Frost in Allenstown/Buck Street Mills

Amherst- Marker #0003: Birthplace of Horace Greeley

Bedford- Marker #0102: John Goffe

Boscawen- Marker #0049: Hannah Dustin (1657-1737)

Bow- Marker #0036: Andrew Jackson's Visit

Candia- Marker #0141: Sam Walter Foss (1858-1911)

Candia- Marker #0237: East Candia: The Langford District/ Candia: One Town

Chester- Marker #0014: Early American Clocks

Chester- Marker #0139: Chester Village Cemetery

Concord- Marker #0066: State Capitol

Concord- Marker #0067: Bridges House Governor's Residence

Concord- Marker #0080: Franklin Pierce (1804-1869)

Concord- Marker #0105: Mary Baker Eddy (1821-1910)

Concord- Marker #0110: Ratification of the Federal Constitution

Concord- Marker #0125: The Pierce Manse

Concord- Marker #0128: The Concord Coach

Concord- Marker #0147: White Park

Concord- Marker #0148: Sunset Baseball

Concord- Marker #0175: New Hampshire Presidential Primary

Concord- Marker #0184: Turkey Pond- 1938 Hurricane

Concord- Marker #0236: Civil War Mustering Camps

Concord- Marker #0238: The Pennacook

Deerfield- Marker #0025: Major John Simpson

Deerfield- Marker #0145: Deerfield Parade

Deerfield- Marker #0183: First Church Building in Deerfield

Deerfield- Marker #0214: Pawtuckaway Civilian Conservation Corps Camp

Derry- Marker #0048: General John Stark (1728-1822)

Derry- Marker #0058: Scotch-Irish Settlement

Derry- Marker #0126: Robert Frost (1187-1963)

Dunbarton- Marker #0111: Molly Stark House

Epsom- Marker #0199: Major Andrew McClary

Fremont- Marker #0142: Mast Tree Riot of 1734

Fremont- Marker #0156: John Brown Family- Gunsmiths

Fremont- Marker #0157: Spaulding & Frost Cooperage

Fremont- Marker #0167: Meetinghouse and Hearse House

Fremont- Marker #0170: Civil War Riot of 1861

Hooksett- Marker #0132: New Hampshire Canal System

Hopkinton- Marker #0195: Contoocook Railroad Bridge and Depot

Londonderry- Marker #0166: Londonderry Town Pound

Loudon- Marker #0015: Shaker Village

Manchester- Marker #0124: Amoskeag Mills

Manchester- Marker #0208: St. Mary's Bank Credit Union/La Caisse Populair Sainte

Manchester- Marker #0225: Stark Park

Merrimack- Marker #0029: Old Dunstable

Merrimack- Marker #0079: Matthew Thornton (1714-1803)

Milford- Marker #0133: Captain Josiah Crosby (1730-1793), Lieutenant Thompson Maxwell

New Boston- Marker #0146: Home of Molly Stark Cannon

Northwood- Marker #0024: Lafayette's Tour

Northwood- Marker #0181: First New Hampshire Turnpike

Pelham- Marker #0176: Abbott Bridge

Pembroke- Marker #0144: First Meeting House

Pembroke- Marker #0187: Suncook Village

Pembroke- Marker #0250: Watering Trough/Pembroke Street

Pittsfield- Marker #0197: Jonathan "Jocky" Fogg, Patriot

Raymond- Marker #0085: Nottingham Chartered 1722

Salem- Marker #0072: Mystery Hill

Salem- Marker #0221: Armenian Settlement

Salem- Marker #0253: Londonderry Turnpike

Sandown- Marker #0026: The Old Meeting House

Weare- Marker #0143: East Weare Village

Weare- Marker #0192: Piscataquog River Mill Sites

Allenstown

Marker # 0193: Meeting House Burying Ground/Old Allenstown Meeting House

Location: 150 Deerfield Road near Bear Brook State Park north of New Rye Road

Sign Erected: 2005

GPS Coordinates-N 43° 09'.625" W 71° 22'.859"

"The Old Burying Ground is enclosed within the stone walls across the road. Judge Hall Burgin donated land for a meeting house and burying ground about 1807, and both parcels have always been conveyed together. There are five known graves in the cemetery: Ede Hall Burgin; his wife, Elizabeth Burgin; two daughters of Jonathan Sargent; and John Critchett. In the early 1900s, two gravestones remained visible. Buntin Chapter, Daughters of the American Revolution, passed the property to the state in 1991, and the state deeded it back to the town in 2004."

"Built in 1815 for both religious and town meetings, this rare example of a one-story meeting house has slanted floors that offer a clear view of its simple pulpit. The building housed services of the "Christ-ian" sect until about 1860, and evangelical camp meetings until 1886, but ceased to be used for town meetings in 1876. The town deeded it to Buntin Chapter, Daughters of the American Revolution, in 1908. Buntin Chapter's restoration of the building was a pioneering effort at historic preservation."

This two-sided narrative marker marks the center of civic activity of Allenstown in 1815. While other communities in New Hampshire have restored and displayed their historical meeting houses, this building is distinct in that it is an original one-story building with the unique slanted floor. The simple design also makes it unique to buildings that were built with Greek-revival or federalist style in their architecture during the early 19th century. This structure lacks the ornate features of other meeting houses, but the simple "Puritan-style" was very functional. The Allenstown Historical Society shares that during restoration, the original pew holder names from the early 19th century are preserved. At the time of construction, residents could purchase a box pew for twenty dollars. The money raised was used for the cost of construction.

This building remained active for religious and civic meetings until 1876 when the Industrial Revolution caused a shift to the population of Allenstown westward. In 1985, an arsonist caused major damage to the building. Since 1991, efforts were made to restore this significant part of Allenstown history back to its original features. Final restoration efforts were completed in 2013. Peek in the windows and see how simple the design of the building is and check out the slanted floor. The Allenstown Meeting House was listed on the National Register of Historic Places in 2004.

The Meeting House Burying Ground which is located across the street. This burying ground is also known as the Burgin Family Cemetery where many of the original Burgin family descendants were laid to rest. As stated on this marker, there are five known graves within this plot.

Allenstown

Marker # 0205: Bear Brook CCC Camp 1935-1942

Location: 153 Deerfield Road north of New Rye Road (across street from meetinghouse)

Sign Erected: 2007

GPS Coordinates- N 43° 09'.616″ W 71° 22'.829″

"The Bear Brook Civilian Conservation Corps (CCC) Camp was one of 28 work camps established in N.H. between 1933 and 1942. President Franklin D. Roosevelt started the program after the Depression to put young unemployed men to work in conservation. From 1935 to 1938 the 1123rd Co. CCC was here; later this was one of four CCC camps in the state to employ World War I veterans. Bear Brook was the last active CCC camp in N.H. and was given to the state in 1943. It was listed in the National Register of Historic Places in 1992 as one of the country's most intact CCC camp."

The park derives its name from the 10-mile long stream that flows entirely within the park and flows northwest into the Suncook River. Bear Brook Civilian Conservation Corps (CCC) was established in 1935 with the federal government purchasing the land now within the state park. The Civilian Conservation Corps 1123rd company was tasked to construct trails and infrastructure for recreation. Work continued within the park until 1942 when it was closed. In 1942, the property was used by the US Navy for sailor's recreational use during leave while their ships were docked in nearby Portsmouth and Boston.

The original construction of outbuildings was temporary with most built without foundations and directly on the ground. Of the original fifteen outbuildings, eight have survived. Of the twenty-eight camps built under the CCC model, this is the only one in New Hampshire that is intact. This park is also one of a small number nationwide that still exist with much of the infrastructure still standing.

Bear Brook State Park is the second largest state park in New Hampshire and the largest developed state park in the state with over 10,000 acres within its boundary. This state park is also home to the New Hampshire Antique Snowmobile Museum and the Richard Diehl Civilian Conservation Corps (CCC) Museum.

Allenstown

Marker # 0211: Suncook Connection Bridge

Location: U.S. Route 3/Turnpike Street southeast side of bridge

Sign Erected: 2008

GPS Coordinates- N 43° 07'.828″ W 71° 26'.756"

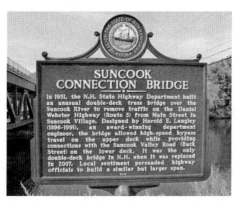

"In 1931, the N.H. State Highway Department built an unusual double-deck truss bridge over the Suncook River to remove traffic on the Daniel Webster Highway (Route 3) from Main Street in Suncook Village. Designed by Harold E. Langley (1896-1991), an award-winning department engineer, the bridge allowed high-speed bypass travel on the upper deck while providing connections with the Suncook Valley Road (Buck Street) on the lower deck. It was the only double-deck bridge in N.H. when it was replaced in 2007. Local sentiment persuaded highway officials to build a similar but larger span."

Finding this marker was initially a challenge using directions from the state website. The first attempt resulted in driving over the upper deck to Pembroke. Once I realized the mistake, a simple U-turn and I was back on track. If a visitor is new the area, they may not realize that the lower-deck is the route to downtown Suncook. With a search online for information regarding this unique bridge, I found the bridge name was the result of a local school contest where students submitted names for the bridge. A student named James Mahon was the winner with the aptly named, "Suncook Connection Bridge".

The village of Suncook was originally settled in the 1730's. The location was ideal for harnessing the hydropower of the Suncook River; particularly where it meets the Merrimack River. In these early days, the village had sawmills and gristmills. Fulling mills were built (these mills cleansed woolen cloth and converted to paper). By the 1830's, glass manufacturing became a major industry. In 1880, the village became a major producer of bricks. The area had an abundance of deep clay beds which allowed for the village to produce more than 5.5 million bricks per year. With many of the mills constructed of wood, most succumbed to fire. But the village adapted, rebuilt with brick and included cotton and other manufacturers. Today, this quaint mill village is a nice place to visit with the village district listed in the National Register of Historic Places in 1986.

Allenstown

Marker # 0230: Robert Frost in Allenstown / Buck Street Mills

Location: NH Route 28 & Deerfield Road

Sign Erected: 2012

GPS Coordinates- N 43° 09'.522"   W 71° 24'.356"

"In the summer of 1896, aspiring poet Robert Frost (1874-1963) and his wife Elinor spent a belated honeymoon in a rented cottage near the Suncook River in Allenstown. Carl Burell, a high school friend and avid naturalist, was foreman at the Moulton box shop at Buck Street dam. Botany walks with Burell awakened Frost to the natural world, coloring his later writings. Frost recalled these walks in "The Quest of the Orchis" (1901). Burell's 1896 injury in a mill accident inspired Frost's poem, "The Self-Seeker"."

"A bridge was built at "Buck Street," by the 1750's. Natural falls were dammed to power saw and grist mills before 1767. The 19th c. added a water-powered fulling mill for cleansing wool cloth by 1813, a bedstead shop by 1845, a spoke shop in the 1850s and twine mills. By the 1890s, the dams powered Charles Fisher's axe handle factory and Reuben C. Moulton's box and trunk shop. Then known as East Pembroke, the area had a post office, store, blacksmith shop, houses and workers' tenements."

Robert Frost is a name which Granite Staters take pride in calling one of their own. While we consider Frost a Granite State icon, he was born in California, attended high school and Harvard University in Massachusetts, had a farm in Derry, New Hampshire and a summer retreat in Franconia and a home in Vermont. Frost died in Boston and is buried in Bennington, Vermont. While Frost was a teacher and lived in New Hampshire for approximately thirty years, this represents less than half of his 88 years.

Frost's poem, "The Quest of the Orchis" was published in *The Independent*, a magazine of poems published in 1901. The poem, "The Self-Seeker" main character is known as "Broken One" and is distraught about the injustice of his factory accident that broke his feet. The poem also identifies the "Broken One" as a naturalist who enjoys the local fauna of orchids where he lives.

Amherst

Marker # 0003: Birthplace of Horace Greeley

Location: NH Route 101 and Horace Greeley Road (mile marker 45.2)

Sign Erected: 1958

GPS Coordinates- N 42° 53'.804″ W 71° 36'.267"

"About five miles north of Amherst is the birthplace of Horace Greeley (1811-1872), founder of the New York Tribune, member of Congress, and candidate for President in 1872."

Horace Greeley was born February 3, 1811 to Zaccheus and Mary Greeley on a small farm nearby. A poor farming family, the Greeley's struggled to make a living in farming. Horace was considered a highly-intelligent child and neighbors offered to pay his tuition to attend Phillips Exeter Academy. But the Greeley's would not accept the offer being too proud to accept charity. To flee their incurring debt, the family moved to Vermont in 1820. By 1826, Horace began learning the trade of a printer's apprentice at a nearby print shop.

In 1831, Horace Greeley moved to New York to seek his fortune. By 1834, he published his first issue of the New Yorker paper. Ten years later, he published his first issue of the daily newspaper the New York Tribune. During his tenure as editor of the Tribune, the paper was the highest circulation paper in the country.

Greeley made his debut as a member of the US Congress in 1848. He was selected by the Sixth District of New York's Whig party to replace their sitting congressman who was ousted for election fraud. Greeley served out the remainder of that term of three months until 1849. Greeley was not nominated to continue serving in Congress where he is believed to have not been popular with any party.

Horace Greeley returned to run the popular newspaper he founded. He continued to remain an active voice in politics while he maintained his position as editor of the Tribune. In 1872, Greeley opted to run against President Ulysses S. Grant for the Republican nomination. Greeley ran as a Liberal Republican Party member and lost to Grant in a landslide. Horace Greeley died shortly thereafter on November 29, 1872 in Pleasantville New York.

Bedford

Marker # 0102: Colonel John Goffe (1701-1786)

Location: US Route 3 (106 South River Road) next to Citizens Bank

Sign Erected: 1975 & 2006

GPS Coordinates- N 42° 57'.346″ W 71° 28'.723″

"This is considered to be the site of Colonel John Goffe's log dwelling. In 1744 Goffe built a gristmill on Bowman's Brook, later run by his son, Major John Goffe (1727-1813), and his grandson, Theodore Atkinson Goffe (1769-1860). The stream eventually powered several other mills. In 1939, Dr. George Woodbury (1902-1973), a Goffe descendant, built a mill that is now part of the hotel complex across the road, as told in his book, "John Goffe's Mill." Prominent in local history, Colonel Goffe lent his name to neighboring Goffstown and Goffe's Falls. Four generations of Goffes lie nearby in Bedford's Old Burying Ground."

Born in Boston in 1701, Colonel "Hunter John" Goffe was a soldier in the colonial army and lived in nearby "Moore's Village" in what was then Derryfield (now known as part of Manchester). He earned his nickname "Hunter John" because of his passion for hunting and trapping at an early age. In 1722, he married Hannah Griggs of Roxbury Massachusetts. They had eight children of which only one son (John Goffe). In 1740, John Goffe was granted land in Bedford as payment for his service in the militia. In 1744, the family moved to this site and built the gristmill.

Colonel Goffe and his militia fought battles of the French and Indian War at Lake George New York, Fort William Henry, Ticonderoga, and Montreal. After the war, Goffe retired back to Bedford and continued his service as a civic leader. He served in the New Hampshire provincial legislature and was Hillsborough County's first probate judge. He was also an original petitioner to the provincial legislature for incorporation of the town of Bedford in 1750. Colonel John Goffe died on October 20, 1786. He is buried in the Old Bedford Cemetery on Black River Road.

Boscawen

Marker # 0049: Hannah Dustin 1657-1737

Location: US Route 4 Park & Ride lot (mile marker 56.8) west side of Merrimack River

Sign Erected: 1967

GPS Coordinates- N 43° 17'.406″ W 71° 35'.424″

"Famous symbol of frontier heroism. A victim of an Indian raid in 1697, on Haverhill, Massachusetts, whence she had been taken to a camp site on the nearby island in the river. After killing and later scalping ten Indians, she and the two other captives, Mary Neff and Samuel Lennardson, escaped down the river to safety."

Hannah Emerson was born on December 23, 1657 in Haverhill, Massachusetts. She married Thomas Dustin in 1677 and they had eight children. During the 17th century, much of what we now know as New Hampshire was considered a wilderness, or frontier. The lands were occupied by tribes of Abenaki Indians. On March 15, 1697 her village of Haverhill, Massachusetts was raided by Abenaki Indians. The objective was to capture white settlers and bring them to Canada where they were sold to the French as slaves or ransomed back to the colonies.

During the raid, Thomas had escaped with seven of the children, but Hannah and their six-day old baby (Martha) and nurse Mary Neff were captured. The Indians had killed the baby and forced

Hannah and Mary along with other captives to walk north for days. Stopping on this island on the Merrimack River (Dustin Island), the Indian raiders joined their families encamped here. Hannah and Mary met fourteen-year-old Samuel Lennardson at this encampment who was held captive for nearly a year. Realizing the need to escape, Hannah, Mary and Samuel plotted to attack their captors once they were asleep. Stealing tomahawks, they killed ten of their captors of which six were children, two women and two men. Hannah insisted they scalp the dead to show proof of their actions, as well as to collect the bounty for the scalps.

The three escaped downstream in a canoe and traveled only at night. After several days of travel, they arrived in Haverhill, Massachusetts and were received as heroes. The Massachusetts General Court paid the bounty for the ten scalps. Hannah Dustin's story became part of early settlers' folklore. Hannah Dustin's story has been retold by famous authors Cotton Mather (1706), John Greenleaf Whittier (1831), Nathaniel Hawthorne (1836) and Henry David Thoreau (1849).

Bow

Marker # 0036: Andrew Jackson's Visit

Location: NH Route 3A and Interstate 89 entrance

Sign Erected: 1966

GPS Coordinates- N 43° 10'.296″ W 71° 31'.622″

"Just north of this point, on the boundary between Bow and Concord a large cavalcade of enthusiastic citizens met President Jackson and escorted him to New Hampshire's Capital. His official reception by the State Government on the following day, June 29, 1833, marked the conclusion of a triumphal New England tour."

According to the book, "*New Hampshire: A guide to the Granite State" (1938)* an excerpt depicts the story of President Jackson's visit to the capital city. The focal point is of the Hillsborough Instrumental Band. It reads, "*A notable incident in its history is connected with President Andrew Jackson's visit to New Hampshire in June 1833 when the band was invited to play. They traveled by wagons to Concord, gay in their uniforms of gray coats with bell buttons, black leather caps with plumes, and white pants. Reaching Concord at night, they struck up a lively tune and awoke General Pierce, who stormed and raved because they had disturbed his guest. President Jackson then laughed and invited them to a feast.*" (p. 463).

During this trip, Jackson had traveled to Massachusetts and followed on to New Hampshire and Maine. In the journal of the Massachusetts Historical Society, "*Andrew Jackson in New England, 1833*" it was believed that Jackson became ill or simply weary of travel during his time in Massachusetts. He went on to his scheduled stop in Concord, accompanied by Vice-President Martin Van Buren but terminated his tour there due to ill health. Jackson stayed in Concord until July 1st and proceeded back to Washington DC.

Andrew Jackson was the 7th President of the United States (1829-1837). Prior to being elected to the presidency, Jackson earned his fame as a general in the War of 1812 and politician from the State of Tennessee. He is considered the Father of the Frontier with an emphasis of westward expansion of the country. His nickname "Old Hickory" describes his unnerving and steady personality. He is also considered the father of the Democratic Party.

Candia

Marker # 0141: Sam Walter Foss (1858-1911)

Location: NH Route 43 South and Main Street

Sign Erected: 1981

GPS Coordinates- N 43° 03'.523" W 71° 17'.378"

"Candia is the birthplace of the well-known poet, journalist and publisher, Sam Walter Foss. Son of Dyer and Polly Foss, he was born June 19, 1858. His homespun verse and country poems were great favorites. "The House By the Side of the Road," the most popular, was believed to have been inspired by his boyhood home, on Brown Road, in this town."

The poem *"The House by the Side of the Road"* was one of the first New Hampshire poems that I was aware of. I grew up in Tilton and there is a house on School Street with a sign attached to a large old tree which reads, "Inspiration for the poem *The House by the Side of the Road* when the poet Sam Walter Foss roomed while attending Tilton Seminary 1878." While this marker suggests that Foss authored his famous poem about his childhood home, others believe the inspiration was drawn from the Tilton home built in 1783 that Foss lived in while he attended the Tilton Seminary in 1877-1878.

Foss published his famous poem in 1897 and since that time there is a strong belief that the Tilton residence was his inspiration. Sam Walter Foss's sister had stated in a later interview that there is no specific house that her brother was referring to, but the general theme could apply to many places. However, Candia residents disagree. The Tilton home was registered in the National Register of Historic Places as the poem's inspiration in 1980. I imagine both communities can be proud of their inspiration of the famous Foss poem.

Sam Walter Foss attended Brown University in Providence, Rhode Island and went on to become the librarian at the Somerville Massachusetts Public Library for thirteen years. Known as the "People's Poet" and "Master of the Yankee Dialect", he is believed to have written a poem a day for publication in the "Saturday Union", a local newspaper where he was the editor and writer. Sam Walter Foss died February 26, 1911 and is buried in Providence, Rhode Island.

Photo courtesy of Dr. Ronald Mills, Tilton NH.

Candia

Marker # 0237: East Candia: The Langford District/ Candia: One Town-Five Villages

Location: Intersection of Langford Road and Depot Street

Sign Erected: 2013

GPS Coordinates- N 43° 02'.888″ W 71° 14'.951"

 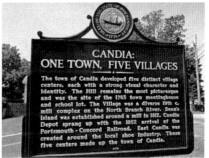

"East Candia was a dense neighborhood of workers' housing developed around the local shoe industry in the 1850's, exemplifying a late-19c. industrial economy made possible by the arrival of the Portsmouth and Concord Railroad in 1852. The area's most significant growth came after 1885, when the first of two mechanized shoe factories opened. The new prosperity resulted in a building boom in the popular Stick Style, characterized by decorative trusses in gable ends, many in porches and door hoods, still visible today."

"The town of Candia developed five distinct village centers, each with a strong visual character and identity. The Hill remains the most picturesque and was the site of the 1763 town meetinghouse and school lot. The Village was a diverse 19th c. mill complex on the North Branch River. Bean's Depot sprang up with the 1852 arrival of the Portsmouth-Concord Railroad. East Candia was created around the local shoe industry. These five centers made up the town of Candia."

Most communities that prospered in New England relied on hydro-power to run the mills and local natural resources. With the addition of railroads and the New Hampshire Turnpike system, communities became focal points for industry. Candia is an example of a 19th century community that thrived from powering the mills along the North Branch River. With the addition of the Portsmouth-Concord Railroad line through Candia goods were easily transported to city centers.

Candia was originally settled in 1743 and was known as Charmingfare, part of Chester, New Hampshire. Colonial Governor Benning Wentworth granted incorporation as Candia on December 17, 1763. According to town historian Ed Fowler, it is believed that Governor Wentworth named the town Candia for the Greek island Candia, now known as Crete.

Chester

Marker # 0014: Early American Clocks

Location: NH Route 121 100 feet north of intersection with NH Route 102.

Sign Erected: 1963

GPS Coordinates- N 42° 57'.461″ W 71° 15'.440"

"Isaac Blasdel, 1738-1791, son and father of clockmakers, settled in Chester in 1762 and commenced manufacturing one-day, striking, wall and tall-case clocks with one weight and metal works. He was an Association Test signer, Revolutionary War soldier, selectman and member of the Committee of Safety."

The wall clock, or tall-case clock is commonly known as a grandfather clock. This original design was made by the Englishman clockmaker William Clement in 1670. Isaac Blasdel had refined the original design to include a longer pendulum. The longer pendulum required less movement and less wear on the gears. The tall-case clock manufactured by Isaac Blasdel was the one-day (30 hour) style requiring winding daily. This clock was less expensive than the eight-day clock which only needed winding once a week. The 30-hour clock winding mechanism had only one keyhole that winds both the timing and striking. An interesting note, some 30-hour clocks included a false keyhole to allude that the clock was of the more expensive 8-day design. Vanity in the 18th century!

Isaac Blasdel served with the Peabody Regiment of the New Hampshire militia during the Revolutionary War attaining the rank of Corporal. The regiment, led by Colonel Stephen Peabody was raised on January 1, 1778 and fought at the Battle of Rhode Island in August 1778. The regiment was disbanded January 1, 1779 when the men's one-year enlistment expired.

The Committee of Safety was an appointed group of six to twelve men who oversaw the function of what would now be viewed as the Commander-in-Chief of the State Militia. This executive power was shifted away from the royal Governor during the Revolutionary War. The Committee of Safety members were deemed respected and knowledgeable of affairs of the militias. The Committee of Safety was disbanded in June 1784 after the drafting of the new state constitution.

Chester

Marker # 0139: Chester Village Cemetery

Location: NH Route 102 northeast of intersection with NH Route 121

Sign Erected: 1980

GPS Coordinates- N 42° 57'.499″ W 71° 15'.368″

"This graveyard, one of the oldest in the state, was purchased from Capt. Jonathan Blunt for 70 pounds in 1751. Signed stones by the finest stone sculptors in New England are found here. Among the craftsmen are: Stephen and Abel Webster, John Marble, John Wright and Timothy Eastman. Revolutionary War heroes rest here as well as two governors of the state, Samuel and John Bell, William Richardson, Chief Justice of the N.H. Supreme Court, Isaac Blasdel, the clockmaker and others."

The Chester Congregational Church was established in 1730 with four other churches in town. At that time, descendants were buried in family plots on private property or adjacent to the local churches. In 1751, Jonathan Blunt sold one acre for the establishment of this cemetery. This parcel is known as the "Revolutionary Section" and makes up the frontage along NH Route 121 and half of the frontage on NH Route 102. The second parcel which comprises of approximately ½ acre is known as the "Jonathan Dearborn" section and was purchased in 1834. In

1852, the town purchased the ½ acre "Coffin French" section. The "French" section was donated to the town by Amos T. French in 1937. These combined parcels make up the 2.5-acre cemetery.

This cemetery was listed in the National Register of Historic Places on November 29, 1979. According to the National Register of Historic Places Nomination Form, the significance of this cemetery to our state history is *"The comprehensive local and regional collection of gravestones in the Chester Cemetery makes this burying ground one of the most significant in the state, providing an ideal index of style, of the traffic in stones from community to community, and of the spread of symbolism from one region or one stonecutter to another"*.

Chester was originally settled in 1719 by inhabitants from Portsmouth, Rye and Hampton; and was known as Cheshire. The town was incorporated on May 8, 1722 as Chester. Chester is the birthplace of three former New Hampshire governors; Samuel Bell (8th governor), John Bell (12th governor), and Charles H. Bell (38th governor).

Concord

Marker # 0066: State Capitol

Location: 107 North Main Street & Park Street

Sign Erected: 1970

GPS Coordinates- N 43° 12'.456″ W 71° 32'.221"

"The State Capitol Building of New Hampshire was built in 1816-19 by Stuart J. Park. It is constructed of New Hampshire granite quarried in Concord. The original part was occupied June 2, 1819 and is the nation's oldest State Capitol in which a legislature meets in its original chambers."

History of the State Capitol is quite interesting. Concord became the state capitol in 1809 having formerly been in Exeter during the Revolution. In 1814, the legislature debated on the location being considered between Concord, Hopkinton, and Salisbury. The town of Salisbury even offered the state seven thousand dollars if chosen. In the end, Concord was selected, and construction began in 1816. The granite blocks were quarried from the nearby Swenson granite quarry with the labor being done by inmates from the prison.

The building was completed for $82,000 and housed both chambers of the General Court, the Executive Council and Governor's chamber, Secretary of State, State Treasurer and

State Library. The first session of the legislature was held in 1819 and is still in use as the chamber for the legislature. Over the last two centuries, additions, and modifications have been made but the original building as we see remains the centerpiece of New Hampshire government.

If you can visit this spectacular building, be sure to spend some time in the main entrance known as the Hall of Flags. The room is adorned with flags, guidons, and streamers of various military campaigns dating back to the Revolutionary War.

New Hampshire politics is serious business. The New Hampshire General Court (House and Senate) make up the third largest legislative, English-speaking bodies worldwide. Only the U.S. Congress and the British Parliament are larger. It is comprised of four-hundred House members and twenty-four senators. The New Hampshire General Court members are volunteer and paid a minimal stipend of $200 per two-year term.

Concord

Marker # 0067: Bridges House Governor's Residence

Location: 21 Mountain Road (NH Route 132 north)

Sign Erected: 1970

GPS Coordinates- N 43° 14'.339″ W 71° 32'.214″

"This house, on land long occupied by Revolutionary Veteran Joshua Thompson, was built by Charles Graham about 1836. Styles Bridges, Governor of New Hampshire (1935-36) and U.S. Senator for 25 years thereafter, lived here from 1946 until his death. Left to the State upon the death of his widow, it became in 1969 the Governor's official residence."

While the history of ownership of this property dates to the 1600's, the current home was built around 1837 and 1843. The uniqueness of this building is that it was not common to see homes constructed of brick and a Greek revival style. The house was purchased by Alfred H. Bath in the 1890's and continued to be in the Bath family until it was purchased by Henry Styles Bridges in 1946. The Bridges family owned this home until 1969. Senator Bridges bequeathed the eleven-acre home and property to the state in late 1940's with transfer of ownership upon his death. The home became the State of New Hampshire official Governor's residence in 1969 after Senator Bridges widow passed.

Henry Styles Bridges served as New Hampshire governor from 1935-1937. He was a U.S. Senator for the State of New Hampshire from 1937 to 1961. While Senator Bridges was an influential member of the U.S. Senate, he was a man who appreciated life back in his home state. The Bridges House foundation even states that Senator Bridges was a gentleman farmer who raised livestock on this property.

While the home became the official Governor's residence in 1969, it needed major renovations and improvements. In 2004, newly elected Governor John Lynch's wife, Dr. Susan Lynch, started a foundation to raise funds to bring the home back to its original splendor. The Bridges House was listed on the National Register of Historic Places December 22, 2005.

Concord

Marker #0080: Franklin Pierce 1804-1869 Fourteenth President of the United States (1853-1857)

Location: Old North Cemetery on North State Street adjacent to US Route 3

Sign Erected: 1971

GPS Coordinates- N 43° 12'.908″ W 71° 32'.620″

"Lies buried in nearby Minot enclosure. Native son of New Hampshire, graduate of Bowdoin College, lawyer, effective political leader, Congressman and U.S. Senator, Mexican War veteran, courageous advocate of States' Rights, he was popularly known as "Young Hickory of the Granite Hills"."

Born November 23, 1804 in Hillsborough New Hampshire, Franklin Pierce was raised in a family that was not wealthy but was more privileged than others. He attended local schools until age fifteen when he attended Bowdoin College in Maine. It was during his time at Bowdoin that Pierce became friends with writer Nathaniel Hawthorne. Franklin Pierce returned to his hometown in Hillsborough and practiced law in the house across the street from where he grew up. He was elected to the New Hampshire state legislature in 1829. He was elected Speaker of the House in 1831. In 1833, Pierce was elected to the U.S. House of Representatives where he served until 1837. A short four years as a congressman, Pierce was elected to the U.S. Senate in 1837 and five years as a senator. In the nine years as a member of Congress, Pierce did not sponsor any major legislation.

Franklin Pierce recognized the importance of military service and petitioned President James Polk for a military commission. Starting his military service as a private, Pierce was commissioned a Brigadier General (most likely as a campaign favor). In 1847, Brigadier General Pierce was leading more than two thousand men in the Mexican-American War.

After the war, Pierce returned to his law profession and actively became a leader in the Democratic Party. Pierce was nominated as candidate for President of the United States under the Democrat Party ticket in 1852. He defeated Whig candidate Winfield Scott (his former commander in the war). Pierce was elected the fourteenth President of the United States and served until 1857. Pierce died in Concord, New Hampshire on October 8, 1869.

Concord

Marker # 0105: Mary Baker Eddy 1821-1910

Location: 227 Pleasant Street (NH Route 9) (Pleasant View Retirement Home)

Sign Erected: 1976

GPS Coordinates- N 43° 11'.775″ W 71° 33'.539″

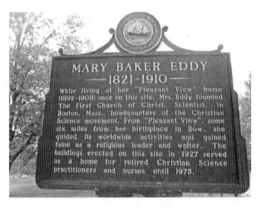

"While living at her "Pleasant View" home (1892-1908) once on this site, Mrs. Eddy founded The First Church of Christ, Scientist, in Boston, Mass., headquarters of the Christian Science movement. From "Pleasant View", some six miles from her birthplace in Bow, she guided its worldwide activities and gained fame as a religious leader and writer. The buildings erected on this site in 1927 served as a home for retired Christian Science practitioners and nurses until 1975."

Mary Baker was born in nearby Bow, New Hampshire, the sixth and youngest child of Mark and Abigail Baker. As a child, she suffered from periods of sickness. While she was out of school gaining back her strength, she spent her time reading books and writing poetry. Her family were devout Congregationalists, yet Mary Baker challenged the doctrine of predestination and dedicated her effort to healing by reading the bible and devotion to prayer.

In 1843, Mary Baker married George Washington Glover. George died six months later and three months before the birth of their son. Mary Baker Glover was still suffering from ill health and had to give up her son to her family nurse. With no known cure for her ailments, Mary Baker studied and practiced homeopathy and other natural remedies in addition to her spiritual health through prayer and devotion. In her studies, she experimented with diluting drugs and concluded that the true path to healing was spiritually grounded. In 1866, Mary Baker had succumbed to a serious fall and injured her back. She requested her Bible while bedridden and read passages about healing. She quickly recovered and considered this moment of self-healing through prayer and became the realization for Christian Science.

Mary Baker married a former student Asa Eddy in 1877. She wrote her first book, *Science and Health* in 1875. In 1879, she founded the Church of Christ Science and began publication of the *Christian Science Monitor* in 1908 which is still in publication. Mary Baker Eddy died December 3, 1910 and is buried in Cambridge, Massachusetts where she started her church.

Concord

Marker # 0110: Ratification of the Federal Constitution

Location: US Route 3 (Bouton Street) and Church Street

Sign Erected: 1976

GPS Coordinates- N 43° 12'.881" W 71° 32'.501"

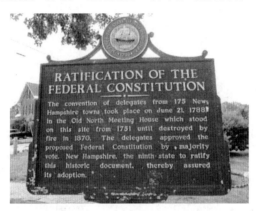

"The convention of delegates from 175 New Hampshire towns took place on June 21, 1788 in the Old North Meeting House which stood on this site from 1751 until destroyed by fire in 1870. The delegates approved the proposed Federal Constitution by majority vote. New Hampshire, the ninth state to ratify this historic document, thereby assured its adoption."

The Constitutional Convention held in Philadelphia that drafted the original Constitution began May 14, 1787. This Constitutional Convention had a rocky start. Rhode Island boycotted and only Pennsylvania and Virginia attended. A quorum of seven states (of the original 13 colonies) was needed. New Hampshire delegates were two months late. Things were not looking good for establishing an agreement. Four months later, a final draft was sent to the thirteen states. An interesting tidbit of information I found on a history website stated that the "We the people of the United States" opening line was a late edit to the document. It originally was drafted as "We the people of New Hampshire, Massachusetts", [add other states here].

The Convention of Delegates of the People of the State of New Hampshire debated whether to accept in its entirety, modify, or reject the Constitution. The federal Constitution is written with twelve provisions/alterations. The New Hampshire delegates made the 12th provision of the Constitution that read, "Congress shall never disarm any citizen, unless such as are or have been in actual rebellion" (Library of Congress). The New Hampshire Convention of Delegates were led by John Sullivan and John Langdon who both presided as President of the Convention of Delegates.

An interesting story I had heard from a volunteer at the Pierce Manse. She informed me that the New Hampshire delegates could not come to agreement on ratification. On June 21st, after a lengthy debate, delegates departed for a break from the afternoon heat. Some delegates left to visit a local tavern and consumed a great deal of rum and did not return. Those who returned voted to ratify the Federal Constitution and we became the ninth state in the new Union. Keep in mind, that ratification required a 2/3 vote majority of the thirteen states. The ninth state to ratify the Federal Constitution would be the deciding delegation. New Hampshire will live with the recognition of being the state that finalized ratification.

Concord

Marker # 0125: The Pierce Manse

Location: US Route 3 (North Main Street) and Horseshoe Pond Lane

Sign Erected: 1978

GPS Coordinates- N 43° 13'.016″ W 71° 32'.698″

"One tenth of a mile east of here stands the only house in Concord owned (1842-1848) by Franklin Pierce, 14th President of the United States. Removed to this site in 1971 from Montgomery Street, it was restored by the Pierce Brigade. Opened to the public in 1974, it is now an important tourist attraction."

This home was built in 1838 and was the only home that the Pierce family owned in Concord. Franklin Pierce purchased this home after he resigned from his seat in the U.S. Senate in 1842 and returned to practicing law. The family lived in this home from 1842 to 1847 when Franklin Pierce left to serve in the Mexican/American War. In 1848, Franklin Pierce returned from the war and sold the home. The Pierce family remained in Concord until he was inaugurated as the fourteenth President of the United States in 1853.

Franklin Pierce married Jane Means Appleton in 1834. Jane's father was a Congregational minister and former president of Franklin's alma mater Bowdoin College. Franklin and Jane had three children. Their first son, Franklin Jr. died three days after birth. Their second son, Franky died at the age of four in this home in 1843 of typhus. Their third son, Benjamin "Benny" died in a train accident on January 3, 1853 in Andover Massachusetts, two months before President-Elect Pierce took office. Benny was the only casualty in this tragedy. The loss of all three children was extremely difficult for Jane Pierce. She fulfilled her role as First Lady during Franklin's term in office even while in ill health. She started the tradition of having a Christmas tree in the White House to honor her children. The Pierce family is buried in the family plot in the Old North Cemetery on North State Street.

The Pierce Manse is a museum that is operated by the Pierce Brigade; a group of devoted volunteers who enjoy sharing in the story of New Hampshire's only son to have been elected to the presidency.

Concord

Marker # 0128: The Concord Coach

Location: US Route 3 near 80 South Main Street (across from Dunkin Donuts)

Sign Erected: 1979

GPS Coordinates- N 43° 11'.880″ W 71° 31'.887"

"The Abbot-Downing Company began in 1813 when Lewis Downing founded a "waggon" factory, located here from 1816 to 1928. In 1828 he was joined by J. Stephens Abbot. The next century saw 14 styles of "stage" coaches, the most famous being the Concord Coach, and 40 styles of commercial and pleasure vehicles carrying the name of Concord all over the United States and around the world."

According to the Concord Historical Society, Lewis Downing a wheelwright from Lexington, Massachusetts came to Concord and made his first carriage for Benjamin Kimball in 1813. In 1826, Downing joined J. Stephen Abbot and they built the first Concord Coach in 1827. The Concord Coach was unique in its design where leather straps were used as a form of a suspension system. The leather straps gave the coach rocking motion rather than a stiff jolting effect from spring suspensions over rough terrain.

By 1847, the Abbot-Downing coach company had manufactured more than seven hundred stage coaches. The partnership between Abbot and Downing disbanded in 1847. Lewis Downing created a new company, Lewis Downing & Sons and began competing for business against his former partner. Stephen Abbot continued making Concord Coaches under the Abbot-Downing name. When Lewis Downing retired in 1865, his sons joined with Abbot in his father's original company. The Abbot-Downing Company went out of business in 1901.

The Concord Coach was the premier stagecoach of its time. Its popularity spread nationwide. During peak production, each stagecoach cost approximately $1,000 to $1,500. The major customer for these stage coaches was Wells Fargo. Today, Wells Fargo has the rights to the Abbot-Downing name, and still uses the iconic Concord Coach as their branding symbol.

Photo courtesy of Concord Historical Society

Concord

Marker # 0147: White Park (This is a cooperative sign with the City of Concord)

Location: Sign Missing (Centre Street and Washington Street-near park entrance)

Sign Erected: 1984

GPS Coordinates- Unknown

Photo retrieved from Pinterest

"One of the oldest municipal parks in New Hampshire, White Park was conveyed to the city by Armenia White in 1884, in memory of her husband Nathaniel. Mr. White, a founder of the American Express Company, was a prominent businessman, legislator, and philanthropist. Both Mr. and Mrs. White were active in the abolition, temperance, and women's suffrage movements. The park was designed by landscape architect Charles Eliot, and retains the character of his original design."

This historical marker was a cooperative effort between the State of New Hampshire and the City of Concord. This was explained that cooperative signs are funded by the entity other than the State of New Hampshire because all State-funded markers must be located along a state highway. Inquiring with a park employee, he was not aware of this marker. Satellite imagery on Google shows the sign missing since at least 2011.

Nathaniel and Armenia White lived on nearby School Street on a four hundred-acre farm. In 1884, in memory of her husband, Mrs. White deeded this property and a $1,700 endowment to the City of Concord. This land was considered undesirable for development and considered viable for development of a city park. Mr. Charles Eliot was a Harvard graduate who specialized in naturalistic park designs. Eliot was employed by the leading landscape architect of the 19th century Frederick L. Olmstead.

According to the National Register of Historic Places nomination form, the twenty-five-acre park was originally known as "The Ring Wood". White Park was listed on the National Register of Historic Places in 1982.

Concord

Marker # 0148: Sunset Baseball

Location: White Park (between baseball diamond and park office building) Liberty Street

Sign Erected: 1976

GPS Coordinates- N 43° 12'.447″ W 71° 32'.861″

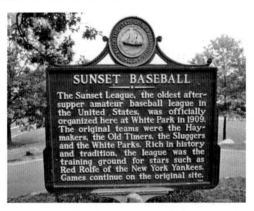

"The Sunset League, the oldest after-supper amateur baseball league in the United States, was officially organized here at White Park in 1909. The original teams were the Haymakers, the Old Timers, the Sluggers and the White Parks. Rich in history and tradition, the league was the training ground for stars such as Red Rolfe of the New York Yankees. Games continue on the original site."

June 21, 1909 article in the Concord Monitor *"The White Parks beat the Old Timers 14-0 in the first game of Concord's Sunset League. The four-team after-supper baseball league will have games daily except Saturday at 6:15 p.m. The teams play till dark or for five innings, whichever comes first. Crowds of 400-500 gather to watch"*. The nation's longest running after-supper baseball league is still in existence. An article in the Concord Monitor dated August 10, 2017 claims the league may be nearing its end. Not due to a lack of interest by players, but rather a lack of support of attendees as well as volunteers to keep the league operating.

Back in 1909, the Sunset League was an opportunity for those who loved the game to continue to play, as well as a means of entertainment for onlookers. Today, the league is primarily an opportunity for college-aged players to remain in playing condition. The league still consists of four teams. The most recent article in the Concord Monitor claims the demise of the league could also be affected by the lack of attendance of observers, and financial support. Let's hope this century-plus year league remains in existence for many more seasons.

Concord

Marker # 0175: New Hampshire Presidential Primary

Location: 20 Park Street in front of NH State Library

Sign Erected: 2000

GPS Coordinates- N 43° 12'.442″ W 71° 32'.311″

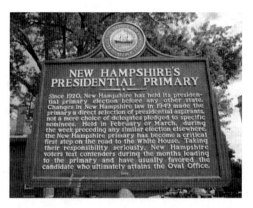

"Since 1920, New Hampshire has held its presidential primary election before any other state. Changes in New Hampshire law in 1949 made the primary a direct selection of presidential aspirants, not a mere choice of delegates pledged to specific nominees. Held in February or March, during the week preceding any similar election elsewhere, the New Hampshire primary has become a critical first step on the road to the White House. Taking their responsibility seriously, New Hampshire voters test contenders during the months leading to the primary and have usually favored the candidate who ultimately attains the Oval Office."

New Hampshire's tradition of First in the Nation voting in the presidential elections is something Granite Staters take seriously. Dixville Notch (marker #0171) proclaims the first votes taken at midnight on Primary Day. The New Hampshire Presidential Primary is an opportunity for locals and the nation to observe true retail politics. The New Hampshire Presidential Primary is the opportunity for candidates to "shake hands and kiss babies". This is the opportunity for citizens to meet all the candidates in diners, churches and living rooms and ask questions directly to the candidates.

In 1913, Democratic State Representative Stephen Bullock of Richmond authored legislation that created the first presidential primary to be held in May 1916. In 1915, Republican State Representative John G.M. Glessner of Bethlehem sponsored a bill to change the date to the second Tuesday in March. The state's first presidential primary election was held on March 14, 1916. With the Iowa Caucus typically the week before the New Hampshire Primary, both states are bound by state law to adjust their caucus/primary to occur prior to any other state. Larger states argue that Iowa and New Hampshire do not represent the diversity of our country. The truth is that our small state affords the common citizen the opportunity to meet candidates and ask questions that are important to them. Granite Staters take this civic responsibility very seriously.

Concord

Marker # 0184: Turkey Pond- 1938 Hurricane

Location: NH Route 13 South (1 mile from I-89)

Sign Erected: 2003

GPS Coordinates- N 43° 10'.128″   W 71° 34'.974″

"The Great Hurricane of 1938 devastated New England's forests. As a result, Turkey Pond was used to store almost 12 million board feet of salvaged white pine logs, more than anywhere in New England. From 1941 to 1943, the H.S. Durant mill, operating on this site, sawed most of the volume floating in Turkey Pond. On the pond's north side, the U.S. Forest Service constructed a sawmill that was operated by a group of local women. Led by sawfiler Laura Willey, the women proved themselves to be an exemplary crew. "Snow, rain, or sub-zero weather never slowed them up," wrote one Forest Service manager."

The Category 3 Hurricane was one of the most devastating storms to hit New England. New England had not had a major hurricane in nearly a century. In addition, the technology for prediction of storm tracks was not yet developed. This hurricane hit the Northeast practically without warning. The hurricane made landfall on Long Island, New York on September 21, 1938. In one day, the hurricane resulted in seven hundred deaths (600 in Long Island, NY), nine thousand homes destroyed, and three thousand ships sunk or wrecked.

In New Hampshire, thirteen citizens died due to the high winds. On Mount Washington, the observatory measured winds gusts more than 160 mph. Even 2,500 feet of the Cog Railway tracks were destroyed, including the infamous Jacob's Ladder trestle.

While New Hampshire was less devastated from the brunt of the hurricane compared to Connecticut, Rhode Island, and Vermont, the Granite State suffered major loss of trees. It is believed that at least 1.5 billion of board feet of timber was destroyed or damaged. In 1940, the U.S. Forest Service deemed 110,000 acres of White Mountains National Forest land was so severely damaged that it would become a fire hazard. The massive effort to reclaim the timber and repair damage led to the reopening of several Civilian Conservation Corps camps in the state to include Bear Brook CCC in Allenstown.

Concord

Marker # 0236: Civil War Mustering Camps

Location: Loudon Road & Airport Road (next to NH National Guard flagpole)

Sign Erected: 2013

GPS Coordinates- N 43° 12'.701″ W 71° 30'.961"

"We have but 'one country, one Constitution and one destiny;' the Union must be preserved." Gov. Nathaniel S. Berry.

From May 1861 to December 1864, twelve New Hampshire Civil War regiments and a cavalry unit mustered on "The Plains" and other nearby locations in Concord. Here they gathered to equip, train, and await orders, living in tents or temporary barracks. 32,486 soldiers from NH served in the war, which cost the state at least 4,840 lives, more than 1% of the population. 21 soldiers from NH units were awarded the Medal of Honor, established in 1861."

"1st Regiment N.H. Volunteer Infantry, 3rd Regiment N.H. Volunteer Infantry, 5th Regiment N.H. Volunteer Infantry, 9th Regiment N.H. Volunteer Infantry, 11th Regiment N.H. Volunteer Infantry, 12th Regiment N.H. Volunteer Infantry, 13th Regiment N.H. Volunteer Infantry, 14th Regiment N.H. Volunteer Infantry, 15th Regiment N.H. Volunteer Infantry, 16th Regiment N.H. Volunteer Infantry, 17th Regiment N.H. Volunteer Infantry, 18th Regiment N.H. Volunteer Infantry, 1st Regiment N.H. Volunteer Cavalry"

The New Hampshire National Guard has a storied history dating back to the earliest settlements along the Piscataqua River in New Castle dating to 1623. In 1679, the provincial governor officially established the New Hampshire Militia. New Hampshire militiamen have fought and protected our land against Indian attacks to British troops at Fort William & Mary (now Fort Constitution) and every engagement since.

During the Civil War, New Hampshire volunteers came forward to preserve the Union. In addition to the twelve infantry regiments and cavalry regiment listed above, New Hampshire sent artillery and three companies of sharpshooters to fight for the Union. New Hampshire regiments are honored at the fields of Gettysburg with monuments for their gallantry and service. The New Hampshire light artillery was a forefront regiment against Pickett's Charge on July 3, 1863.

Concord

Marker # 0238: The Pennacook

Location: Fort Eddy Road at New Hampshire Technical Institute athletic field

Sign Erected: 2013

GPS Coordinates- N 43° 13'.396″ W 71° 31'.607"

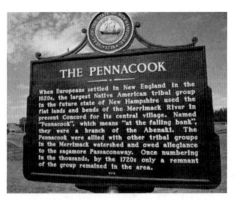

"When Europeans settled in New England in the 1620s, the largest Native American tribal group in the future state of New Hampshire used the flat lands and bends of the Merrimack River in present Concord for its central village. Named "Pennacook", which means "at falling bank", they were a branch of the Abenaki. The Pennacook were allied with other tribal groups in the Merrimack watershed and owed allegiance to the sagamore Passaconaway. Once numbering in the thousands, by the 1720s only a remnant of the group remained in the area."

The Abenaki Nation were a confederacy of tribes that inhabited northern New England from Lake Champlain in Vermont to the coast of Maine. The Pennacook tribal group were the major inhabitants along the Merrimack River. The Pennacooks had extended their lands as far south as southern New Hampshire on land along the Merrimack River until the 1670's. Their loss of lands along the southern banks of the Merrimack River were due to the encroachment of English settlements. By 1730, much of the lands along the Merrimack River were abandoned by the Pennacooks. Much of the abandonments of lands was also the result of disease brought by white settlers such as smallpox. The native population had no immunity to the European diseases and caused mass epidemics to the native population.

With a depleted population and loss of native land, the tribes of the Abenaki to include the Pennacooks moved north towards the Quebec region of Canada. At its peak, it is believed that the Pennacook tribal group consisted of more than 12,000 inhabitants and established more than thirty settlements along the Merrimack River.

The legendary Pennacook sachem "Passaconaway" was believed to be the first chieftain to lease lands to the English settlers. This beloved Pennacook chieftain has a mountain in the Sandwich Range named in his honor. Just west of the Merrimack River is the town of Penacook named in honor of the tribal peoples who once inhabited this land along the banks of the Merrimack River. This marker was sponsored by the New Hampshire Technical Institute student council who worked in conjunction with faculty to construct the narrative.

Deerfield

Marker # 0025: Major John Simpson

Location: NH Route 107/ NH Route 43 (North Rd) and Meetinghouse Hill Rd.

Sign Erected: 1964

GPS Coordinates- N 43° 08'.636″ W 71° 14'.081″

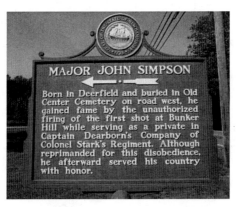

"Born in Deerfield and buried in Old Center Cemetery on road west, he gained fame by the unauthorized firing of the first shot at Bunker Hill while serving as a private in Captain Dearborn's Company of Colonel Stark's Regiment. Although reprimanded for this disobedience, he afterward served his country with honor."

New Hampshire's participation in the battles of the Revolutionary War are well documented. However, Major John Simpson may be credited with notoriety for an action he may not have committed. Records of the Battle of Bunker Hill depict statements of who fired the first shot. Private John Simpson is among them. According to the Deerfield Historical Society, John Simpson was only following the orders given by his commanders. That command was to not shoot until you can see the "whites of their eyes". So, local defendants claim Simpson had better sight than others and took down the British officer he was aiming at.

Private John Simpson was serving under the command of Captain Henry Dearborn and arrived at Bunker Hill on June 17,1775. Dearborn's company joined the regiments of Colonel John Stark of the New Hampshire 1st Regiment and Colonel James Reed of the New Hampshire 3rd Regiment. Stark believed the British would be attempting to flank the colonist from a position from the shore and constructed a makeshift barrier. The order was to hold fire until the British set foot on the beach. Folklore suggests that Private Simpson stood up and shot a British officer prior to the order to fire was given. After the battle, Simpson was arrested but not punished for the alleged action.

Simpson served honorably throughout the remainder of the Revolutionary War and was promoted to the rank of Major. He retired back to his hometown, married Mary Whidden and had six children. He farmed his land until his death on October 28, 1825. He was buried in the family plot but later moved to the Old Center Cemetery where he now rests.

Deerfield

Marker # 0145: Deerfield Parade

Location: Nottingham Road at intersection with NH Route 107/ NH Route 43

Sign Erected: 1983

GPS Coordinates- N 43° 08'.505″ W 71° 14'.062″

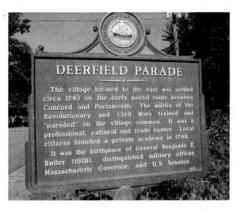

"The village located to the east was settled circa 1740 on the early postal route between Concord and Portsmouth. The militia of the Revolutionary and Civil Wars trained and "paraded" on the village common. It was a professional, cultural and trade center. Local citizens founded a private academy in 1798. It was the birthplace of General Benjamin F. Butler (1818), distinguished military officer, Massachusetts Governor, and U.S. Senator."

The Deerfield Historical Commission shares that Deerfield Parade which was a central village of the community in the 18th century was popular due to its route along the well- traveled postal route from Portsmouth to Concord. Post roads were the main travel ways prior to the construction of the turnpike system in the later 1790's. The villages along the post roads were common to have inns for weary travelers to rest their horses, have a meal and overnight accommodations.

At the height of population for Deerfield Parade, the area included inns, taverns, stores, and an academy for the children of the professional citizens of the area. While much of the towns had significant farming populations, Deerfield Parade was noted for the draw of professionals such as lawyers, doctors, and other intellectual professions. According to the Deerfield Heritage Commission Bicentennial book (1966) it describes the citizenry of Deerfield Parade as, *"The families that settled here on the Parade were to an unusual degree, possessed of wealth and intellectual culture and these people supported an Academy"*.

The village of Deerfield Parade was located on elevated land along the Portsmouth to Concord route. The open and flat fields made an ideal location for the local militia to train and practice their drill and ceremony routines. Deerfield was incorporated in 1766 as a separated parish of neighboring Nottingham. The Deerfield Academy was established in Deerfield Parade in 1798.

Deerfield

Marker # 0183: First Church Building in Deerfield

Location: NH Route 43(Stage Rd)/South of NH Route 107 across from Ladd Cemetery

Sign Erected: 2003

GPS Coordinates- N 43° 06'.335″ W 71° 14'.646"

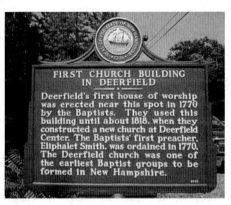

"Deerfield's first house of worship was erected near this spot in 1770 by the Baptists. They used this building until about 1818, when they constructed a new church at Deerfield Center. The Baptists' first preacher, Eliphalet Smith, was ordained in 1770. The Deerfield church was one of the earliest Baptist groups to be formed in New Hampshire."

The records depicted on the Deerfield Historic Commission's website describes that the Congregationalists of the community worshipped at the meetinghouse beginning in 1772 with pastor Reverend Timothy Uphand as their first minister. Deerfield's first church building was constructed on this site. The first church constructed was for the Baptists and not the earlier Congregationalists due to conflicts in the latter. With a population leveling off and competition with the Baptists, the Congregational Church began losing parishioners.

The Baptist Church built on this site was for practicing Baptists. Eventually, the church split into two distinct sects, the First Baptist Society and the Freewill Baptists. Both sects worshipped in the same building. The record claims that while the two sects shared the building their relationship was not always amiable.

In 1834, the First Baptist Society built a new church in Deerfield Center and worshiped there until the late 1880's. By the early 20th century, a declining population in the community resulted in the First Baptists and Freewill Baptists merging churches once again. Their place of worship was in Deerfield Center. In 1921, the church engaged Reverend Christina MacKenzie as their pastor. It is believed she was the first ordained female Baptist minister in New Hampshire.

Over time, church population declined to a point where the Baptist and Congregational churches merged to form the Community Church of Deerfield in 1929. This federation of two churches survived until the 1970's. Today, Deerfield has the Deerfield Community Church, and the Deerfield Bible Church located in the second building of the original First Baptist Society.

Deerfield

Marker # 0214: Pawtuckaway CCC Camp

Location: NH Route 43 at Deerfield Fairgrounds entrance

Sign Erected: 2009

GPS Coordinates- N 43° 06'.056" W 71° 14'.824"

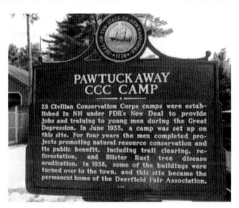

"28 Civilian Conservation Corps camps were established in NH under FDR's New Deal to provide jobs and training to young men during the Great Depression. In June 1933, a camp was set up on this site. For four years the men completed projects promoting natural resource conservation and its public benefit, including trail clearing, reforestation, and Blister Rust tree disease eradication. In 1938, some of the buildings were turned over to the town, and this site became the permanent home of the Deerfield Fair Association."

The first Deerfield Fair took place in 1876 but it was held at a different location near the old Town Hall in Deerfield Center. During these early years, the fair was known by different names such as the Sanborn Company Creamery Fair, and the Grange Fair. The first Deerfield Fair to take place on this site was 1924.

The Depression was the catalyst for the creation of the Civilian Conservation Camps initiative. Workers provided services that benefited their communities. With the Pawtuckaway Civilian

Conservation Camp (company #123), the men constructed nature trails, fire towers, surveyed lands and performed mapping. This provided men the wages needed to support their families and learn a skill.

By 1937, an improved economy resulted in the closing of the camp. As stated on this marker, workers were used to eradicate the Blister Rust disease that devastated the white pines common in this area. Much of the white pines found in Pawtuckaway State Park are the result of the eradication efforts made by these CCC workers. Today, visitors can see the original CCC recreation hall building where the "Deerfield Fair: Past and Present" exhibit is now located.

In 1938, the federal government relinquished ownership of the camp to the State of New Hampshire. The state transferred ownership to the town who in turn made this the permanent home of the Deerfield Fair under the stewardship of the Deerfield Fair Association. The Deerfield Fair is considered the largest and oldest agricultural fair in New Hampshire.

Derry

Marker # 0048: General John Stark 1728-1822

Location: NH Route 28 and South Range Road (148 Londonderry Turnpike)

Sign Erected: 1967

GPS Coordinates- N 42° 51'.855″ W 71° 17'.344″

"Rogers' Ranger and Revolutionary hero, served at Bunker Hill and in Washington's New Jersey campaign of 1776-77, and commanded the American militia which decisively defeated two detachments of Burgoyne's army near Bennington, Vermont, August 16, 1777. A stone marks his birthplace on Stark Road, six-tenths of a mile easterly on Lawrence Road."

Born on Stark Road in 1728, this town was then known as Londonderry. General John Stark is to New Hampshire as George Washington was to our newly formed country. General Stark is referred to on three New Hampshire historical state markers. This marker was erected in 1967 for his birthplace. In Charlestown, a marker memorializes Stark's march to the Battle of Bennington and was erected in 1977. In Manchester, a marker details the life and heroics of General John Stark on the site of Stark Park. This marker was installed in 2011. The Stark name is an integral part of our state history.

John Stark grew up in Manchester (what was then known as Derryfield) on the family farm now known as Stark Park. He served under Major Robert Rogers in the French and Indian War. On April 28, 1752, John Stark was part of a hunting party who was captured by Indians to be ransomed to the French. Stark and fellow hunter Amos Eastman escaped while their colleague David Stinson was killed and scalped. John Stark fought with Rogers Rangers until the end of the war and he returned to his farm in Manchester.

The Revolutionary War brought Captain Stark back into military service. He was promoted to Colonel and led the 1st New Hampshire Regiment at the Battle of Bunker Hill in June 1775. Stark became a commander in Washington's Continental Army and led campaigns in the Battles of Trenton and Princeton under General Washington. The Battle of Trenton is also famously known as Washington's crossing of the Delaware on Christmas Eve 1776. Stark resigned his Continental Commission and returned to New Hampshire.

The New Hampshire Provincial Legislature sought out Stark to lead the militia in Bennington Vermont. He was promoted to Brigadier General and his regiment heroically defeated the British at this famous battle.

Derry

Marker # 0058: Scotch-Irish Settlement

Location: East Derry Road & Cemetery Road (across street from East Derry post office)

Sign Erected: 1969

GPS Coordinates- N 42° 53'.646″ W 71° 17'.687″

"In April 1719, sixteen Presbyterian Scotch-Irish families settled here in two rows of cabins along West Running Brook easterly of Beaver Brook. Initially known as Nutfield, the settlement became Londonderry in 1723. The first year, a field was planted, known as the Common Field, where the potato was first grown in North America."

The early settlers to this area were from the Ulster region of Northern Ireland. Many Scots from the Highlands of Scotland migrated to Ulster for promises of cheap rent on the fertile farmlands captured by the British. With the Irish uprising against the newly-arrived Scots, life became difficult for these Presbyterian Scots. In 1718, the Scots left Aghadowey County in Ulster in search for a place to call home. They arrived in Boston on August 4, 1718 and were met with hostility by the British colonists.

These sixteen immigrant families were granted a one hundred-acre tract of land in what was then known as Nutfield. The name was believed to be from the abundance of nut trees in the area as well as marshy grass fields. This congregation was led by their Presbyterian pastor Reverend James McGregor. These new settlers arrived on this site on April 11, 1719.

In 1722, the Nutfield settlers petitioned to rename the town Londonderry in honor of their home sake in Northern Ireland. The town of Londonderry was chartered that year. By the time of the Revolutionary War, these Scotch-Irish families had suffered decades of discrimination and hostility from the British Crown. It was an easy decision for these immigrants to take up the cause of the patriots in the pursuit independence. Many of the families from this settlement fought against the British in the Revolutionary War.

The settlers are known for planting the first potato in North America here on the Common Field. These families also were famous for their linens having raised the flax on their land. The Town of Derry claims that this famous Londonderry Linen was worn by George Washington and Thomas Jefferson.

Derry

Marker # 0126: Robert Frost 1874-1963

Location: NH Route 28 (122 Rockingham Road)

Sign Erected: 1978

GPS Coordinates- N 42° 52'.280″ W 71° 17'.708"

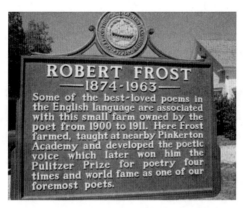

"Some of the best-loved poems in the English language are associated with this small farm owned by the poet from 1900 to 1911. Here Frost farmed, taught at nearby Pinkerton Academy and developed the poetic voice which later won him the Pulitzer Prize for poetry four times and world fame as one of our foremost poets."

Robert Frost was born March 26, 1874 in San Francisco, California. The Frost family moved to Massachusetts in 1885 after the death of his father. Robert Frost attended college at Dartmouth in 1892 but dropped out after two months. He later went on to attend college at Harvard University from 1897-1899 but left due to ill health. Frost earned his first wage for his literary skills with a poem he had published in the New York Independent in 1894. The poem was entitled, "My Butterfly. An Elegy" and he was paid $15.

Robert Frost moved to this farm in 1900. It was purchased by his grandfather as a wedding gift for Robert and his wife Elinor. The

Frost's resided here while Robert farmed the land and worked at Pinkerton Academy as an English teacher from 1906 to 1911. At this time, Robert continued works of poetry for publication. Robert and his family moved to Great Britain in 1912 and it was here that he published his first book, "*A Boy's Will*" in 1913 and "*North of Boston*" in 1914.

Frost returned to the United States in 1915 and moved his family to their new home on Ridge Road in Franconia. Frost maintained this as his home until 1938. Today, it is the Frost Place Home and Museum. Each year, Dartmouth College selects a Poet in Residence to summer at this home where Robert Frost wrote numerous prose of the beauty of rural New Hampshire.

Robert Frost was awarded the Pulitzer Prize for poetry in 1924, 1931, 1937, and 1943. Frost was also named Poet Laureate for Vermont in 1961. On January 20, 1961 Robert Frost read his poem, "*The Gift Outright*" at President John F. Kennedy's inauguration.

Dunbarton

Marker # 0111: Molly Stark House

Location: NH Route 13 and intersection with NH Route 77 (346 Jewett Road)

Sign Erected: 1976

GPS Coordinates- N 43° 08'.966″ W 71° 37'.786"

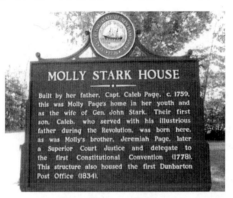

"Built by her father, Capt. Caleb Page, c. 1759, this was Molly Page's home in her youth and as the wife of Gen. John Stark. Their first son, Caleb, who served with his illustrious father during the Revolution, was born here, as was Molly's brother, Jeremiah Page, later a Superior Court Justice and delegate to the first Constitutional Convention (1778). This structure also housed the first Dunbarton Post Office (1834)."

Elizabeth "Molly" Page was born February 16, 1737. The Page family built and moved to this home in 1759. Molly Page married John Stark on August 20, 1758. John and Molly Stark had eleven children. This home is located at what is known as Page's Corner and was the site of Dunbarton's first post office, where Caleb Page served as its first postmaster.

General John Stark is infamous in the history of the Granite State as a successful soldier from the French and Indian War through the Revolutionary War. Molly Stark also served her state and country as well. During the Revolutionary War, Molly Stark tended to soldiers who suffered from injuries at the Battle of Bennington. The Stark farm was used as a place for Stark's men to recuperate from their injuries. Molly Stark also treated soldiers who suffered from a smallpox outbreak. The Stark's eldest son, Caleb fought alongside his father at the Battle of Bunker Hill and the Battles of Trenton and Princeton.

Dunbarton was part of the Mason's Grant in 1748 to Archibald Stark. The township was known as Starkstown and renamed Dunbarton in 1765 after Dunbartonshire Scotland, the town where Archibald Stark emigrated from. Famous Dunbarton residents include General John & Molly Stark, Robert Rogers of Rogers Rangers, and John Ordway a member of the Lewis & Clark Expedition. Major Robert Rogers was the son of one of the original settlers to this area, James Rogers. James Rogers was killed while he was in the woods. The history of Dunbarton states that James was wearing a bear pelt and a hunter mistook him for a bear and shot him.

Epsom

Marker # 0199: Major Andrew McClary

Location: US Route 4 (Epsom Public Library-1606 Dover Rd.) mile marker 74.6

Sign Erected: 2006

GPS Coordinates-N 43° 13'.391″ W 71° 20'.046″

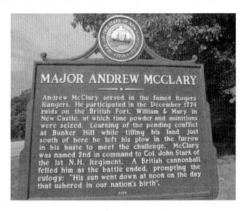

"Andrew McClary served in the famed Rogers Rangers. He participated in the December 1774 raids on the British Fort, William & Mary in New Castle, at which time powder and munitions were seized. Learning of the pending conflict at Bunker Hill while tilling his land just south of here he left his plow in the furrow in his haste to meet the challenge. McClary was named 2nd in command to Col. John Stark of the 1st N.H. Regiment. A British cannonball felled him as the battle ended, prompting the eulogy: "His sun went down at noon on the day that ushered in our nation's birth"."

The Epsom Historical Association's excellent website details biographies of their well-known citizens. The biography for Andrew McClary is derived from the book "McClary Family" written in 1896 and explains how the McClary family had settled in the area as early as 1726. Andrew fought with New Hampshire's own Rogers Rangers in the French and Indian War. After the French and Indian War, McClary returned to his home in Epsom where he farmed, was a successful businessman and was active in local town and church affairs. Andrew McClary also served as a New Hampshire legislator from 1764-1769.

In 1774, McClary was part of the raid at Fort William & Mary which was a British fort in New Castle, New Hampshire. The raiders took much needed ammunition, guns, and cannons to be turned over to the patriots. It is believed that on April 20, 1775 while McClary was tilling his fields, a messenger came and informed him of the Battle at Lexington. Within twenty-four hours, McClary had mustered volunteers and was in Medford, Massachusetts.

Major McClary was second in command of the 1st New Hampshire Regiment under Colonel John Stark. On June 16th, the Regiment was ordered to Boston to secure Bunker Hill with the 3rd NH Regiment under the command of Colonel James Reed. On the final British assault, Major Andrew McClary was killed. The irony is the first shot of the Battle of Bunker Hill was fired by Private John Simpson of Derry; and the last casualty of the battle was Major Andrew McClary of Epsom.

Fremont

Marker # 0142: Mast Tree Riot of 1734

Location: NH Route 107 & NH Route 111A-southern split (to 936 Main Street)

Sign Erected: 1982

GPS Coordinates- N 42° 58'.020″ W 71° 05'.497″

"Local lumbermen illegally cut Mast Trees reserved for the King's Royal Navy. When David Dunbar, Surveyor General, visited nearby Copyhold Mill to inspect fallen lumber, local citizens assembled, discharged firearms and convinced Dunbar to leave. Returning with 10 men, Dunbar's group was attacked and dispersed at a local tavern by citizens disguised as "Indians"."

This area was once part of Exeter and was densely populated with large, high-quality eastern white pine trees. These trees were highly valuable as timber for constructing ship masts for the British Royal Navy. The mast trees were measured to be twenty-four inches in diameter at twenty-four inches from the ground. Settlers who moved to this area relied on subsisting off the land. This included building cabins and heating with firewood. Generally, the large tracts of land which had valuable resources were under the ownership of the elite or established British loyalists. Settlers and colonists attempted to survive on less favorable lands.

In April 1734, Surveyor General David Dunbar of the Kings Woods visited the region to inspect local sawmills for their lumber. If mast trees were cut, they were confiscated and the mill owners severely fined. This incensed the local settlers and they surrounded the Copyhold mill and fired shots from their guns which resulted in Dunbar leaving the mill. Dunbar demanded the local populace turn over those who interrupted his official duties. No one would offer him any assistance. Dunbar departed but was determined to return.

Dunbar believed his authority established under British law entitled him to the lumber and he collected ten men and returned. On April 23rd, Dunbar and his men were staying at the inn of Captain Samuel Gilman. That evening, Dunbar and his men were assaulted by local settlers who were disguised as Indians. Dunbar and his men escaped and retreated to Exeter. This act known as the Mast Tree Riot is considered one of the earliest acts of aggression between the colonists and British authority.

Fremont

Marker # 0156: John Brown Family- Gunsmiths

Location: NH Route 107 (390 Main Street)

Sign Erected: 1988

GPS Coordinates- N 42° 59'.190″ W 71° 07'.981"

"Around 1845 John Brown of Poplin, now Fremont, built this gun shop, and with sons Andrew & Freeman spent 62 years producing fine target and hunting rifles, shotguns, and pistols. During the Civil War these prominent gunsmiths made firearms for the U.S. Government, and in 1861 their gun shop served as a recruiting office for enlisting Union sharpshooters."

The town of Fremont has the most (while still limited) information about the history of the Brown family gunsmiths. John Brown was born in the town of Poplin (now Fremont) in 1806. He had married three times and had five children. In 1830, John Brown built his home which is now 402 Main Street. Around 1845, John Brown built his gunsmith shop on this site. Brown manufactured rifles, pistols, and shotguns at this shop. John Brown manufactured a unique firearm known as a "side by side", which was a rifled barrel on one side and a shotgun barrel on the other.

John and his son Andrew were well respected gunsmiths. At the time of the Civil War, they were contracted by the U.S. government to manufacture firearms for the Union Army. This site was also used as a recruiting station for enlisting men for the New Hampshire Volunteer Sharpshooter companies in September 1861. New Hampshire had three sharpshooter companies that were assigned to either the 1st or 2nd United States Volunteer Sharpshooter Regiments. Both regiments had made significant contributions at the Battle of Gettysburg in July 1863.

John Brown continued the business on this site with his sons until his death in 1895. His son Andrew built a new gunsmith shop at 291 Main Street in 1899. The business continued until Andrew's death in 1907.

Fremont

Marker # 0157: Spaulding & Frost Cooperage

Location: NH Route 107 (near 314 Main Street) in front of water tower

Sign Erected: 1989

GPS Coordinates- N 42° 59'.360″ W 71° 08'.339"

"The Cooperage was founded here in 1874 by Jonas Spaulding, Jr. After his death in 1900, his sons, two of whom became New Hampshire governors, served as company officers; Stephen Frost, who bought into the firm in 1893, served as manager. Rebuilt after devastating fires in 1921 and 1973, the Spaulding & Frost Cooperage is now the oldest white pine cooperage in the United States."

The original cooperage was built on this site in 1874. Jonas Spaulding Jr. had come to Fremont in search of quality white pine lumber. Realizing the availability of quality white pine, he established the cooperage on this site. Spaulding was also aware that the railroad was planned to go through Fremont, making this a prime location for the new business. This factory has produced millions of barrels, buckets and firkins in its 125 years of operation. Firkins are buckets used for beer and other liquids which measure approximately a quarter of a keg, or about 8 gallons.

In 1893, it became known as Spaulding & Frost Barrel Cooperage after Stephen Frost bought into the company and became its general manager. The cooperage was originally named Barnes and Spaulding's Kit factory in 1884. In 1888, the name was changed to Spaulding & Wallace. These two divisions merged in 1893 under the ownership and name Spaulding & Frost creating one manufacturing company. The world's largest barrels were made here in 1976 and again in 1998 measuring 15 and 17 feet high respectfully. The cooperage closed in 1999 after financial hardships resulting from the major fires in 1921 and 1973.

The Spaulding sons who went on to serve as New Hampshire governors are Huntley and Rolland Spaulding. Huntley served as Governor from 1927-1929. His brother, Rolland served as Governor from 1915-1917. The Spaulding brothers are recognized with a historical marker in the town of Rochester (marker #0042) located in front of the Governors Inn.

Fremont

Marker # 0167: Meetinghouse and Hearse House

Location: NH Route 107 (464 Main Street) North of Scribner Road

Sign Erected: 1991

GPS Coordinates- N 42° 58'.980″ W 71° 07'.706″

"Built in 1800, this steepleless structure, originally unheated, was used for both town and church meetings. This and a similar building in Rockingham, Vt., are the only two survivors of some 70 meeting houses with twin end "porches" (stairwells) built in New England in the 1700s. The building retains box pews (once privately owned) and a high pulpit. "Singing seats" in the gallery reflect the introduction of choral music in the late 1700s. The nearby hearse house (1849) marks a transition in local funerals from a hand-carried bier to a horse-drawn vehicle."

Also known as the Poplin Meetinghouse, this early republic Federal-style building is the only one of its kind still standing in New Hampshire. It is believed that nearly seventy meetinghouses once existed in New Hampshire built to this design. The uniqueness of its structure is the stairwells on each side and the high pulpit used for church services. According to Fremont town historian Matthew Thomas, in the early years of the 19th century, town selectmen paid local tavern keepers to sell liquor from these porches during the military muster days held in May and September.

Another unique feature of this building is that on the second-floor gallery are pews for slaves who attended church. Thomas also clarifies slaves were not what we consider today, but also included indentured servants who worked for generally seven years before being "freed" of their indebtedness. The gallery (or balcony) also has a row of seats that face the pulpit and is known as the singing gallery. One of the major improvements made to the original building was the addition of the chimney to accommodate two wood stoves for heating in 1840.

The adjacent Hearse house which was built in 1849 still contains an original horse-drawn hearse which was last used in a funeral procession in 1961. The town burying ground is across the street. The Meetinghouse and Hearse House were listed in the National Register of Historic Places in 1993. Visitors can take a tour of the buildings annually on Memorial Day in May and Old Home Day in August.

Fremont

Marker # 0170: Civil War Riot of 1861

Location: NH Route 107 and Sandown Road (272 Main Street)

Sign Erected: 1996

GPS Coordinates- N 42° 59'.439" W 71° 08'.515"

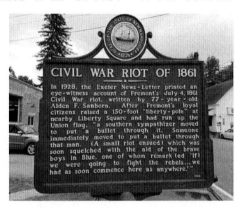

"In 1928, the Exeter News-Letter printed an eye-witness account of Fremont's July 4, 1861 Civil War riot, written by 77-year-old Alden F. Sanborn. After Fremont's loyal citizens raised a 150-foot "liberty-pole" at nearby Liberty Square and had run up the Union flag, "a southern sympathizer moved to put a bullet through it. Someone immediately moved to put a bullet through that man. (A small riot ensued) which was soon squelched with the aid of the brave boys in Blue, one of whom remark (ed 'If) we were going to fight the rebels...we had soon commence here as anywhere.'"

Fourth of July is typically a day of celebration for Americans. But this was not the case in Fremont, New Hampshire in 1861. The start of the American Civil War was just a few months removed in April 12, 1861. The citizens of Fremont were (and still are) considered one of the most patriotic towns in New Hampshire. A fact that in 2009, New Hampshire magazine selected Fremont as one of two most patriotic towns in New Hampshire.

The patriotic citizens of Fremont raised a towering 150-foot liberty pole and flew the Union Colors in honor of the country. Many citizens were in attendance and local Union soldiers were present to celebrate prior to their departure to the battlefronts. When a rebel sympathizer shot a bullet through the Union flag, attendees commenced to assault the culprit. It was the Union soldiers who broke up the mayhem. While this riot was one of four to break out in the United States (the first was in Baltimore Maryland), it was the first Civil War riot in New England.

The town of Fremont was originally part of colonial Exeter. This area was granted by colonial Governor Benning Wentworth as Poplin on June 22, 1764. It is unknown where this name is derived from. On July 8, 1854, the town of Poplin petitioned the State to be renamed Fremont in honor of American West pathfinder John C. Fremont; who also became the first Republican Presidential candidate of the newly created Republican party in 1856.

Hooksett

Marker # 0132: New Hampshire Canal System

Location: 78 Merrimack Street at Lambert Town Park

Sign Erected: 1979

GPS Coordinates- N 43° 06'.051″ W 71° 27'.806″

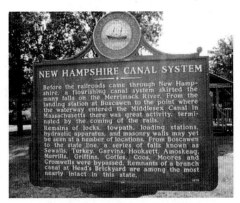

"Before the railroads came through New Hampshire, a flourishing canal system skirted the many falls on the Merrimack River. From the landing station at Boscawen to the point where the waterway entered the Middlesex Canal in Massachusetts there was great activity, terminated by the coming of the rails.

Remains of locks, towpath, loading stations, hydraulic apparatus, and masonry walls may yet be seen at a number of locations. From Boscawen to the state line, a series of falls known as Sewalls, Turkey, Garvins, Hooksett, Amoskeag, Merrills, Griffins, Goffes, Coos, Moores and Cromwells were bypassed. Remnants of a branch canal at Head's Brickyard are among the most nearly intact in this state."

The earliest means of transportation in the region were river and roads. However, roads were expensive to build, and primitive compared to today's standards. Waterways were the most efficient way to transport goods from manufacturing sites. This was also common sense since most manufacturing was located on waterways for its hydro power. While the Merrimack River afforded industrialists excellent means for transportation and hydro power, the falls along the river hindered transportation. The falls along the river required the installation of a canal system to detour the unnavigable falls. The canal system provided a way for barges to travel in both directions to and from the manufacturing centers and to the shipping ports of Boston.

Here at Hooksett Falls, the elevation drop along the river is approximately sixteen feet in a ¼ mile span. One of the largest falls on the Merrimack River is Amoskeag Falls in Manchester. The Amoskeag Falls spans a half mile of river with a descent of drop of fifty-four feet. The canal system to bypass the Amoskeag Falls was built in 1793. The Amoskeag Falls was the major provider of power for the infamous Amoskeag Manufacturing mills that was the major industrial linen center of New Hampshire in the early 19th century to the mid-20th century.

Hopkinton (Village of Contoocook)

Marker # 0195: Contoocook Railroad Bridge and Depot

Location: Intersection of NH Route 127 and NH Route 103 (sign at covered bridge)

Sign Erected: 2005

GPS Coordinates- N 43° 13'.398″ W 71°42'.849″

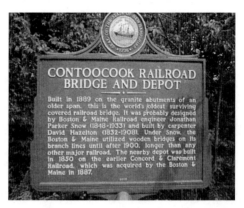

"Built in 1889 on the granite abutments of an older span, this is the world's oldest surviving covered railroad bridge. It was probably designed by Boston & Maine Railroad engineer Jonathan Parker Snow (1848-1933) and built by carpenter David Hazelton (1832-1908). Under Snow, the Boston & Maine utilized wooden bridges on its branch lines until after 1900, longer than any other major railroad. The nearby depot was built in 1850 on the earlier Concord & Claremont Railroad, which was acquired by the Boston & Maine in 1887."

This covered railroad bridge built in 1889 and depot station are along the original Contoocook Valley Railroad line. The original bridge on this site was built in 1849-1850 and was redesigned in 1889 to accommodate heavier trains. This line was later renamed the Concord & Claremont and then the Boston & Maine Railroad.

Spanning the Contoocook River, this covered railroad bridge was operational until 1960. As stated on the sign, this structure is the last known surviving railroad covered bridge in the United States. The bridge has a span of 157 feet and had a switching system partially on the bridge when it was in use. The switching system directed the engines between the Hillsboro and Claremont lines.

After the railroad closed this line in 1960, it was later converted to a warehouse and flea market until 1989. It was then returned to the public with state funding for restoration. The Contoocook Railroad bridge was listed in the National Register of Historic Places in 1980.

The Contoocook Railroad Depot built in 1849 was listed in the National Register of Historic Places in 2006. Today, the Railroad Depot is the Contoocook Railroad Museum and visitor center located at 896 Main Street. I suggest a visit inside the museum for viewing the exceptional photos and memorabilia as well as the 1907 vintage passenger rail car. This mid-19th century depot is exceptionally restored to its original splendor.

Londonderry

Marker # 0166: Londonderry Town Pound

Location: NH Route 128 (330 Mammoth Road)

Sign Erected: 1991

GPS Coordinates- N 42° 52'.706″ W 71°22'.853″

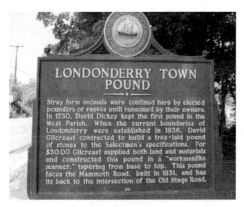

"Stray farm animals were confined here by elected pounders or reeves until ransomed by their owners. In 1730, David Dickey kept the first pound in the West Parish. When the current boundaries of Londonderry were established in 1836, David Gilcreast contracted to build a free-laid pound of stones to the Selectmen's specifications. For $30.00 Gilcreast supplied both land and materials and constructed this pound in a "workmanlike manner." tapering from base to top. This pound faces the Mammoth Road, built in 1831, and has its back to the intersection of the Old Stage Road."

This structure was one of two built on this site. The town of Londonderry records suggest that one was built in 1730 and the second was built in 1735. The engraving on the granite arch over the gate reads, "Ye Old Londonderry Pound 1730". The additional engraving shows that this arch was engraved by the Community Club in 1930. The original pound was in what was known as West Parish and is now part of the town of Derry.

David Dickey was the original keeper (pounder) for the pound on that site.

This livestock pound was built by David Gilcreast in 1836. It was necessary for a new pound to be constructed once the new boundaries were marked between Derry and Londonderry. A second pound located at another location had a keeper named John Stewart. These structures were commonplace in New England communities in the 18th century. Other surviving pounds are in Atkinson, Danville, Derry, Chester, Gilmanton, Salem, Sanbornton, Sandown and Windham. The use of pounds was necessary when life in the 1700's was mostly agricultural, and livestock was abundant on these farms. When the livestock broke loose, pound keepers would hold the livestock inside the structure until the owner could come and claim their livestock.

This pound measures nearly six feet in height thirty feet by thirty feet. The stone placement appears to be in excellent shape. While stonework was completed decades ago to repair parts of the pound, except for the gate and hinges, this pound is much like it was in 1831.

Loudon

Marker # 0015: Shaker Village

Location: NH Route 106 and Shaker Road (sign location) Village is 2.6 miles on Shaker Rd.

Sign Erected: 1963

GPS Coordinates- N 43° 19'.530" W 71°28'.672"

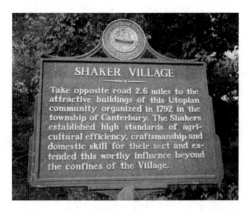

"Take opposite road 2.6 miles to the attractive buildings of this Utopian community organized in 1792 in the township of Canterbury. The Shakers established high standards of agricultural efficiency, craftsmanship and domestic skill for their sect and extended this worthy influence beyond the confines of the Village."

The Canterbury Shaker Village is a contender for one of the most beautiful places to visit in New Hampshire. The Canterbury Village was established in 1792 by founder Mother Ann Lee. This was the seventh of nineteen Shaker communities established in the United States. The Shaker religion was formed in England in the 1750's from believers of the Methodist and Quaker faiths. The sect known as the United Society of Believers in Christ's Second Appearing, or Shaking Quakers was named for their movements, or dancing resembling "shaking" during worship.

This utopian society believed in equality of genders, celibacy, pacifism, and communal living. On this site, the Village contains twenty-five restored original buildings to include the Meetinghouse built in 1792, four reconstructed buildings, and 694 acres of forests and fields. The Shakers were famous for their ingenuity and quality craftsmanship. Shaker furniture is functional and without adornment. For example, ladder back chairs were designed to be hung up on wall posts to clear the floor and during cleaning. Shakers also invented the clothespin.

The Shakers had their "Golden Age" of members from 1820 to 1860. Due to their belief in celibacy, orphans were brought into communities but could leave of their choosing once they reached adulthood. The last elder to have lived at Canterbury Shaker Village was Sister Ethel Hudson who died in 1992. The property has been a living museum since 1992. The property was listed in the National Register of Historic Places in 1975. There are 75-minute guided tours which will detail what the life of a Shaker was like in the 19th century. Please visit their website at www.shakers.org for more information.

Manchester

Marker # 0124: Amoskeag Mills

Location: 771 Canal Street & Pennacook Street at the National Guard parking lot

Sign Erected: 1978

GPS Coordinates- N 43° 00'.066″ W 71° 28'.026″

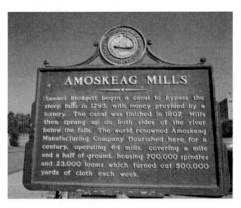

"Samuel Blodgett began a canal to bypass the steep falls in 1793, with money provided by a lottery. The canal was finished in 1807. Mills then sprang up on both sides of the river below the falls. The world renowned Amoskeag Manufacturing Company flourished here for a century, operating 64 mills, covering a mile and a half of ground, housing 700,000 spindles and 23,000 looms which turned out 500,000 yards of cloth each week."

The Amoskeag Manufacturing Company was world renowned in the textile industry. The Industrial Revolution began in England in the mid-1700's and shifted to the United States. New England was a prime location for expansion of the Industrial Revolution due to the rivers and proximity to seaports. Manchester's location along the Merrimack River provided an excellent waterway to Boston shipping ports. The Amoskeag Falls provided an ideal source of hydropower for the mills. The invention of the cotton gin by Eli Whitney in 1794 resulted in improved efficiency in the harvesting and refining of cotton.

Englishman Samuel Slater brought his technical knowledge of cotton spinning machines to the United States and ignited the textile industry to compete with England.

The Amoskeag Cotton & Wool Manufacturing Company started in 1809. With assistance from the state legislature's appropriation of one million dollars, the factories were built, and machinery installed. Manchester was built and designed with the mills as the focal point. The housing was built by the company. The bricks for the mills were made at a local brickyard and the machinery was tooled at a local foundry.

The boom in the textile industry required additional workers. Many immigrants moved to Manchester to work in the mills. The work was hard, with long hours and even children worked in the mills. The results of the Amoskeag Manufacturing Company made the mills one of the leading textile manufacturers in the world. Over a century in business, the last yard of cotton was woven in March 1975.

Manchester

Marker # 0208: St. Mary's Bank Credit Union/La Caisse Populair Sainte-Marie

Location: 420 Notre Dame Avenue and Amory Street (America's Credit Union Museum)

Sign Erected: 2007

GPS Coordinates- N 42° 59'.597″ W 71° 28'.543"

"The first credit union in the U.S. was founded here in 1908, the inspiration of Monsignor Pierre Hevey, the pastor of Sainte-Marie Parish. Monsignor Hevey sought to improve the economic stability and independence of the French-speaking mill workers by giving them a safe and welcoming place to save and borrow money. Until 1913 the credit union was located here in the home of attorney Joseph Bolvin, its first president and manager. Initially open just evenings and holidays, the credit union grew to become one of the state's most stable financial institutions."

"La première caisse populaire aux États-Unis fut fondée ici en 1908, inspiration of de abbé Pierre Hévey, curé de la paroisse Ste-Marie, qui cherchait à améliorer la stabilité et l'independencé économiques des ouvriers francophones en leur offrant un endroit accueillant et sécuritaire pour déposer et pour emprunter de l'argent. Jusqu'en 1913, elle avait ses bureaux ici, chez Me Joseph Bolvin, son premier président et directeur. Ouverte au début

uniquement en soirée et les Jours fériés, la caisse populaire est devenue une plus stables institutions financiers de l'état."

The La Caisse Populaire Sainte Marie (The Bank of the People) was spurred on by the influx of immigrants to the city to work in the Amoskeag Mills. The west side of Manchester is commonly known as the French section, particularly the Notre Dame and Rimmon Heights neighborhoods. With a large population of French-speaking immigrants from Quebec Canada, the workers were drawn to the city for work in the mills. While these immigrant families had steady work, they were not afforded the opportunities to save and borrow money from local banks. Monsignor Hevey of Saint Mary's Parish, an anchor for this neighborhood created the credit union.

The credit union was open to members of the parish and was known as St. Mary's Cooperative Credit Association, which operates under the concept of the members as shareholders. The cost of $5 for a single share was required to become a member of the credit association. This opportunity provided the French immigrants a means to become financially stable, purchase a home and raise their families. This building was listed on the National Register of Historic Places in 2002.

Manchester

Marker # 0225: Stark Park

Location: River Road and Park Avenue

Sign Erected: 2011

GPS Coordinates-N 43° 00'.900″ W 71° 28'.107″

"This 30 acre tract along the Merrimack River was the family farm of Revolutionary War hero General John Stark and his wife Molly. When soldiers were stricken with smallpox at Ticonderoga, the General sent them here to his farm to recover. General Stark returned here at the end of the war. He died in 1822 and is buried in the family plot in the park. The city of Manchester purchased this site from Stark descendants in 1891, and it was dedicated as a public park in 1893."

John Stark was born on August 28, 1728 in Nutfield (which is now Londonderry). At the age of eight, his family moved to this location known where his father Archibald built a home along the banks of the Merrimack River and Amoskeag Falls. Archibald and Eleanor Stark were immigrants from Scotland and were members of the Scotch-Irish Settlement in Derry (Marker #0058). The Stark family property was divided into parcels for each son after Archibald's death. John Stark retained the property of the house which he was raised in.

Captain John Stark took leave in June 1758 from his duties as a commander for Roger's Rangers during the French and Indian War at the death of his father. He spent time as a guest of the Page homestead in Dunbarton (Molly Stark House in Dunbarton). John married Elizabeth "Molly" Page on August 20, 1758. In 1760, Stark returned from the war and purchased the properties of his siblings. He and Molly lived in the home on this site until their deaths. The property remained in the Stark family until 1891 when it was purchased by the city to be made into a park.

The statue of General Stark has an inscription, "Tonight our flag floats over yonder hill or Molly Stark sleeps a widow" was made at the Battle of Bennington on August 16, 1777; a turning point in the Revolutionary War. Another inscription is the state motto of "Live Free or Die" was adopted in 1945. The full quote, "Live Free or Die, Death is not the worst of evils" was from a letter written by General Stark to veterans of the Battle of Bennington in 1809. John and Molly Stark had ten children born on this estate. Molly died in 1814. John died on May 8th, 1822. The Stark family is buried on this property.

Merrimack

Marker # 0029: Old Dunstable

Location: U.S. Route 3 and Woodbury Street at Watson Park

Sign Erected: 1965

GPS Coordinates- N 42° 51'.732″ W 71° 29'.601"

"Was the original town, chartered by Massachusetts Bay Colony in 1673, which embraced parts of New Hampshire and Massachusetts. The New Hampshire portion of this area, following determination of the province boundary in 1741, was subsequently divided into Hollis, Hudson, Litchfield, Merrimack and Nashua."

According to the book written by Ezra Stearns, *Early generations of the founders of Old Dunstable: Thirty families* (1911), this area was once part of the Massachusetts colony until a revision of the boundary made this part of New Hampshire. Originally, this area which now includes Nashua, Hollis, Hudson, Litchfield and Merrimack was part of the original grant of Dunstable, Massachusetts. The original land mass for Dunstable exceeded two hundred square miles.

By 1655, land grants were created to provide an incentive for grant owners to recruit families to settle within these expanded land grants. The land grant of Dunstable was petitioned by the settlers to be made a plantation "for the common good" in 1673.

The northern stretches of the town of Dunbarton prior to 1741 were considered wilderness and susceptible to Indian raids. The 1741 revision of the land boundary encompassed an area that is bisected by the Merrimack River. The significance of having this major means of transportation is instrumental in the development of this township. The Merrimack River and valley were also settled by local Indian tribes. The *History of the Old Township of Dunstable* written by Charles J. Fox in 1846 depicts settlers and Indians trading and coexisting in Old Dunstable.

However, white settlers brought disease that the Indians had no immunity to and many died. While the white settlers and Indians traded together, that may have been more out of necessity than friendship. Many skirmishes broke out between the two groups. In one account, the Indians suspected a local trader named Cromwell of having cheated them in trading furs. Cromwell heard that the Indians realized his unfair trading and left town. The Indians returned and burned down his house and trading post. As towns began to separate from Dunstable New Hampshire, the city of Nashua retained the name of Dunstable until December 31, 1836.

Merrimack

Marker # 0079: Matthew Thornton (1714-1803)

Location: U.S. Route 3 and Greely Street (north side of road adjacent to monument)

Sign Erected: 1971

GPS Coordinates- N 42° 50'.422″ W 71° 29'.451"

"One of three New Hampshiremen to sign the Declaration of Independence, Matthew Thornton, physician, soldier, patriot, agitated against the Stamp Act of 1765, presided over the Provincial Congress in 1775, served in the State Senate and as an associate justice of the Superior Court. The nearby monument honors his memory. He is buried in the adjacent cemetery. His homestead stands directly across the highway."

Matthew Thornton can be considered a Son of New Hampshire, even though he was born in Limerick Ireland. The Thornton family immigrated to America in 1717 moving to Wiscasset, Maine and then to Worcester, Massachusetts. He became a physician and practiced medicine in Londonderry, New Hampshire. In 1745, he became the surgeon to the New Hampshire militia.

While continuing his practice of medicine, Matthew Thornton became involved in politics. Initially, he was a selectman in

Londonderry. He went on to become a member of and president of the Provincial Assembly (today's state legislature). Thornton was also a member of the Committee of Safety which was responsible for drafting a plan after the dissolution of the royal government. This draft was accepted as the state's first Constitution. The New Hampshire State Constitution was the first to be adopted of any of the colonies.

Matthew Thornton was above all a patriot for the rights of citizens of New Hampshire. As president of the New Hampshire legislature, he traveled to Philadelphia, Pennsylvania for the meeting of the Second Continental Congress. He arrived late but was present in time to sign the Declaration of Independence. Since his arrival was late, he was unable to sign next to the other New Hampshire delegates. So, his signature is the last one on the document.

Thornton retired from his medical practice in 1780 and stayed involved in state political affairs. He farmed his land in Derry and operated the ferry across the Merrimack River. The area is still known as Thornton's Ferry. Matthew Thornton died on June 24, 1803 and is buried in the adjacent cemetery. The bottom inscription on his grave reads, "The Honest Man".

Milford

Marker # 0133: Captain Josiah Crosby (1730-1793)

Lieutenant Thompson Maxwell (1742-1832)

Location: 115 Emerson Road (1/10 mile east of NH Route 13)

Sign Erected: 1979

GPS Coordinates- N 42° 48'.952″ W 71° 38'.705″

"These two Revolutionary soldiers were settlers near here in the town of Monson (afterward Amherst, now Milford). Captain Crosby served with distinction at Bunker Hill and marched in defense of Ticonderoga in 1777 and of Rhode Island in 1778. He also served in Amherst as moderator, selectman, and representative to the General Court. Lieutenant Maxwell had the unusual record for a New Hampshire resident of participating in the Boston Tea Party, Battle of Lexington-Concord, and Battle of Bunker Hill. He returned to Massachusetts and later migrated west and served in the War of 1812."

Captain Crosby was a millwright by trade having apprenticed for Joseph Fitch in Bedford, Massachusetts. Josiah Crosby married Fitch's daughter in 1750 and they moved to Monson, New Hampshire which is now Milford. Crosby began his military service in 1748 on the frontier wilderness along the Connecticut River. In 1775, Captain Josiah Crosby led his company of local militia to Cambridge, Massachusetts and became part of the 3rd New Hampshire Regiment where he continued to fight in the Battle of Bunker Hill under Colonel James Reed. Captain Crosby also served under the command of New Hampshire's General Sullivan at the Battle of Rhode Island in 1778. After the war, Crosby returned to his home in Monson where he was involved in town government. Captain Josiah Crosby died October 15, 1793. He is buried in the Elm Street cemetery in Milford.

Lieutenant Thompson Maxwell was born in Bedford, Massachusetts in 1742. There is not much written about the life of Thompson Maxwell except for his participation in so many of our nation's battles for liberty and independence. Thompson Maxwell fought in the French and Indian War as a Ranger from 1757-1763. A publication, *The History of Milford* reads that Maxwell moved to Monson in 1764 and served with Crosby in the local militia. There is an account of Thompson Maxwell departing Milford to join in the Boston Tea Party in December 1773.

Maxwell is also believed to have fought in the skirmish at Lexington and Concord. In this event, Maxwell was traveling to Boston to sell produce. On his way home, he rested at his brother in-law's home. Maxwell joined his brother in-law and other patriots at Concord Bridge. Lieutenant Maxwell also served with Captain Crosby at the Battle of Bunker Hill in June 1775.

In 1800, Captain Maxwell moved to Ohio. In 1811, Major Maxwell fought under the command of General William Henry Harrison at the Battle of Tippecanoe. General Harrison went on to become the ninth president of the United States. Thompson Maxwell has the distinction of fighting in three of our nation's most significant wars; French and Indian, Revolution, and War of 1812.

New Boston

Marker # 0146: Home of the Molly Stark Cannon

Location: Meetinghouse Hill Road and NH Route 13 at the Town Common

Sign Erected: 1984

GPS Coordinates- N 42° 58'.567" W 71° 41'.481"

"This brass four-pounder, cast in 1743, was captured August 15, 1777 at the Battle of Bennington by Gen. John Stark's troops. Gen. Stark presented "Old Molly" to the New Boston Artillery Company of the 9th Regiment of New Hampshire Militia, for its part in the battle. The artillery company was reorganized in 1938 and maintains a permanent home for "Molly Stark" in New Boston."

The Molly Stark cannon was cast in Paris France in 1743. It was one of two identical cannons cast. According to the New Boston town website, the cannon is "ornately decorated with a shield and crown flanked by American Indians armed with bows and arrows". The French cannons were captured by the British at the Battle of the Plains of Abraham in Quebec, Canada in 1759. The British army used the cannons until both were captured by General John Stark and his troops at the Battle of Bennington, Vermont on August 16, 1777. The cannons remained in use by the American forces until the War of 1812 when the Molly Stark cannon was recaptured by the British at Fort Detroit in Michigan. American forces took back possession of the cannon at the Battle of Fort George in Ontario, Canada in 1813. General Stark gave the cannon "Old Molly" to the New Hampshire militia's 9th Regiment sometime between 1813 and 1822 (the death of General John Stark). The New Boston Artillery Company was reorganized in 1938 and became the official custodian of this famous artillery piece.

The cannon located on display here at the New Boston Historical Society is affectionately named the Molly Stark cannon in honor of General Stark's wife, Molly Stark. The cannon is fired three times each Fourth of July. An inscription has been carved into the cannon that reads, *"Molly Stark - Taken at the Battle of Bennington, August 16th, 1777. Presented to the New Boston Artillery Company 9th Regt N.H. Militia by Gen. John Stark"*. The cannon known as "Old Molly" had served under the French flag once and twice under the British and American flags.

Northwood

Marker # 0024: Lafayette's Tour

Location: US Route 4 in front of Northwood Town Hall (mile marker 81.4)

Sign Erected: 1964

GPS Coordinates- N 43° 12'.938″ W 71° 12'.161″

"Upon invitation of President Monroe, issued at the request of the Congress, Marquis de LaFayette, Revolutionary War hero, revisited the United States for a goodwill tour which included an extensive visit to New Hampshire towns. He passed this spot June 23, 1825, traveling between Concord and Dover."

Marquis de LaFayette was born September 6, 1757 in Chavaniac, France. Orphaned at a young age, he joined the French army at the age of fourteen. At the age of sixteen, he married his wife who was related to the King of France. LaFayette had learned of the challenges faced by the American militias and Continental Army. He decided to travel to America and assist the Americans in their war against Britain.

LaFayette was instrumental in the training of the American militia and fought alongside them during the Revolutionary War. LaFayette was also integral in assisting the Americans in getting support from the French government against the British. France provided soldiers, warships, and logistical support to the American forces.

A close friend and ally to General George Washington, LaFayette provided integral tactical advice and intelligence to support the Americans. LaFayette fought alongside General Washington in several engagements from the Battle of Brandywine to Valley Forge.

After the Revolutionary War concluded, LaFayette returned to France in December of 1781. He maintained his friendship with George Washington and the new government in the United States. LaFayette expanded further trade with the United States with U.S. Ambassador Thomas Jefferson.

LaFayette's success and popularity led him to being known as the "Hero of Two Worlds" for his influence in strengthening the relationship between the United States and France. LaFayette returned to the United States on a goodwill tour in 1825. General Marquis de LaFayette died in Paris, France in 1834.

Northwood

Marker # 0181: First New Hampshire Turnpike

Location: Intersection of US Route 4 and NH Route 107 (mile marker 78.8)

Sign Erected: 2002

GPS Coordinates- N 43° 13'.408″ W 71° 15'.250″

"Extending 36 miles from Piscataqua Bridge in Durham to the Merrimack River in East Concord, this highway was originally a toll road. The first of more than 80 New Hampshire turnpikes built by private corporations in the nineteenth century, this was the only one connecting Portsmouth, the state's seaport, with the interior settlements. Chartered in 1796, the corporation began to build the road about 1801. Much of the present Route 4 follows the four rod (66 foot) right-of-way of this first turnpike."

The First New Hampshire Turnpike was incorporated in 1796. The state legislature had authorized a committee to survey the route from Durham to Concord in 1791. The legislature had specified that the road would be public (a non-toll road). However, as stated on this marker, the funding for construction was through private corporations. Their investment was returned through the collection of tolls from the users. Construction began in 1801 and was opened for travel in April 1803.

The new route increased the business trade between the seaport of Portsmouth to the interior population along the Merrimack River. Industry along the Merrimack River now had a viable route for moving their goods to major cities along the coast.

With Northwood located nearly central on the 36-mile route, it became a popular spot for weary travelers to rest. Many inns, stores and taverns were situated in this town. The First New Hampshire Turnpike was the primary route of transportation to the Merrimack Valley region until two major events. The expansion of rail became a competitor for highway travel. Rail offered less time and cost to ship goods in either direction. The second was the construction of the canal system at Amoskeag Falls in 1809. Merchants and producer of goods were able to ship their goods along the Merrimack River to larger cities such as Lowell and Boston.

Pelham

Marker # 0176: Abbott Bridge

Location: 15 Old Bridge Street and NH Route 38 (at bank parking lot)

Sign Erected: 2001

GPS Coordinates- N 42° 43'.610˝ W 71° 19'.138"

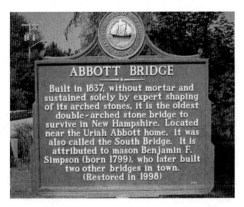

"Built in 1837, without mortar and sustained solely by expert shaping of its arched stones, it is the oldest double-arched stone bridge to survive in New Hampshire. Located near the Uriah Abbott home, it was also called the South Bridge. It is attributed to mason Benjamin F. Simpson (born 1799), who later built two other bridges in town. (Restored in 1998)"

The Pelham Historical Society has a detailed account of the history and restoration of this unique New Hampshire treasure. The bridge construction was attributed to an excess of federal funds in 1836. President Andrew Jackson had sent surplus federal funds back to the states (25 states total in 1836). Of the federal surplus funds to New Hampshire, Pelham received $3,800. At the March 14, 1837 Town Meeting, the citizens voted to appropriate funds for the construction of this bridge over Beaver Brook. While the bridge was called South Bridge, it was also known as Abbott Bridge due to its proximity to one of Pelham's first settlers, the Abbott family. I have discovered in my travels for this book project, that the Granite State has some beautiful, artisan bridges. From stone arched bridges to covered bridges, we are fortunate to have these in our state.

Another point of interest in Pelham is Pulpit Rock on NH Route 38 (across from Pulpit Rock Rd). I first became aware of this piece of history from *New Hampshire Chronicle* commentator Fritz Wetherbee. Scotch-Irish immigrants from Ireland landed in Boston Harbor in late fall of 1710. They were supposed to land in Casco Bay, Maine but were unable to do so due to bad weather.

 In 1719, the governor of Massachusetts granted the immigrants a tract of land in Nutfield what is now known as Derry (marker #0058). As they traveled north to their new settlement, they made a stop here to honor the Sabbath on April 11, 1719. Reverend James McGregor preached his sermon from this rock. General John Stark's parents Archibald and Eleanor Stark were present at this Sabbath Day sermon. By the way, there is another notable rock formation in Sandwich, New Hampshire known as Pulpit Rock. This site is in Sandwich Notch and was the pulpit for sermons as well.

Pembroke

Marker # 0144: First Meeting House

Location: Pembroke Street (across from 369 Pembroke Street) adjacent to cemetery

Sign Erected: 1982 & 2008

GPS Coordinates- N 43° 09'.375″ W 71° 28'.009″

"This is the site of the first meeting house in Suncook, incorporated as Pembroke in 1759. Granted to soldiers in Lovewell's Indian War (1722-25) or their survivors, the land was largely settled by Congregationalists from Massachusetts Bay. Their first meeting house was "made of Good Hewn Loggs" in 1733, it measured 24 by 30 feet and housed town meetings and religious services. The building was improved in 1735 with seats, window glass, and a pulpit. In 1746, it was replaced by a two-story framed building, which was moved around 1806 and converted to the barn standing to the northwest."

The original sign posted at this 1982 location was titled, "First Church and Meetinghouse" and read: *"Site of the First Meetinghouse built on The Suncook Grant. Built in 1733, it was moved, rebuilt and enlarged several times. Its timbers were finally used in the red barn northwest of the site. The Christian community it nurtured still exists and flourishes as The First Congregational Church of Pembroke, United Church of Christ."*

According to the book, *History of Pembroke, N.H.: 1730-1895 Volume 1* (1895) by Nathaniel Carter and Trueworthy Ladd Fowler dedicated a chapter relating to the history of the North, or Ambrose Meetinghouse (debate is written on the actual name). Some called it the North Meetinghouse since it was located north of the cemetery. While the marker denotes that over the years, the Meetinghouse received upgrades and was replaced in 1746. Both markers read that the structure was replaced and made into a barn. Standing at this marker and follow the white fence north to the next driveway. The red barn is located behind the home and visible from this marker.

In reading of the justification of relocating the new meetinghouse was simply that the demographics of Pembroke shifted from this location to the area of Buck Street with the increased emphasis of industry in this town. Citizens wanted a meetinghouse that was centrally located.

Pembroke

Marker # 0187: Suncook Village

Location: Main Street and Union Street

Sign Erected: 2003

GPS Coordinates- N 43° 07'.895″ W 71° 27'.171″

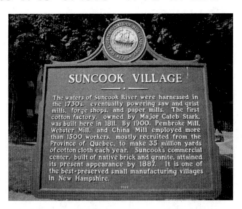

"The waters of Suncook River were harnessed in the 1730's, eventually powering saw and grist mills, forge shops, and paper mills. The first cotton factory, owned by Major Caleb Stark, was built here in 1811. By 1900, Pembroke Mill, Webster Mill, and China Mill employed more than 1500 workers, mostly recruited from the Province of Quebec, to make 35 million yards of cotton cloth each year. Suncook's commercial center, built of native brick and granite, attained its present appearance by 1887. It is one of the best-preserved small manufacturing villages in New Hampshire."

Suncook is situated in both Pembroke and Allenstown separated by the Suncook River. Suncook Village is in and is part of Pembroke. This area was part of the Suncook Grant given to soldiers and heirs of Captain Lovewell's soldiers in 1728 and named Lovewell's Town. The town was later incorporated in 1759 as Pembroke.

Suncook Village lies along the banks of the Suncook and Merrimack Rivers. This ideal location was utilized in the days of the earliest settlers for operating saw and grist mills powered by the Suncook River. The falls along the Suncook River drops seventy feet in a span of ½ mile. Major Caleb Stark (son of Major General John Stark) built the first cotton factory along the falls. As manufacturing increased in New Hampshire during the early 19th and 20th century, ideal locations required sufficient hydropower and means to transport goods to the major cities.

Suncook Village was accessed by railroad with the Concord & Portsmouth line in 1852. This brought a boom to industry and more factories were built along the Suncook River. A second rail line, the Suncook Valley Railroad came to the village in 1869. Most buildings were constructed of wood. Due to susceptibility of fires, buildings were later constructed of brick from a nearby brickyard. The Pembroke, China and Webster mills are still standing. In addition to the major industry of cotton cloth production, the village also had a major glass manufacturing business. The Suncook Village district was listed in the National Register of Historic Places in 2005.

Pembroke

Marker # 0250: Watering Trough/Pembroke Street

Location: Pembroke Street and 203 Pembroke Hill Road

Sign Erected: 2016

GPS Coordinates- N 43° 09'.519″ W 71° 28'.114"

 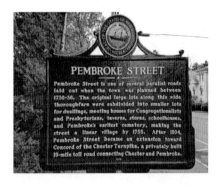

"Clean water was essential to the health of horses, particularly on heavily traveled roads and in extreme weather. A state statute of 1858 authorized towns to reimburse private citizens who provided and maintained watering troughs for the use of travelers' horses. In 1884, Pembroke took the added step of providing "good drinking water for man and beast" at public expense, purchasing this trough from the C.A. Bailey Granite Company in Allenstown for $124 and adding a bronze drinking fountain for human refreshment."

"Pembroke Street is one of several parallel roads laid out when the town was planned between 1730-36. The original large lots along the wide thoroughfare were subdivided into smaller lots for dwellings, meeting houses for Congregationalists and Presbyterians, taverns, stores, schoolhouses, and Pembroke's earliest cemetery, making the street a linear village by 1755. After 1804, Pembroke Street became an extension toward Concord of the Chester Turnpike, a privately built 19-mile toll road connecting Chester and Pembroke."

Visiting this new marker was an interesting change. There are significant number of historical markers for prominent New Hampshire citizens, significant events, bridges and homes of particular craftsmanship. But this is the only marker in the Granite State of a watering trough for man and beast!

A visit to this site, you will see the trough is still in place (albeit now an incredible flowerpot) with the inscription of "1884". It is believed this eight-foot long granite trough was originally supplied with water from the Meetinghouse Brook just a short distance south of this site. Considering what it may have been like traveling by horse in the late 19th century and 20th century, the commitment of a community to provide drinking water for riders and their horses is a part of history worth preserving. In 2014, consideration was made to move the trough to allow for an expansion of the intersection. Fortunately, decision makers understood the significance of historical preservation.

Pembroke Street (U.S. Route 3) is the major road through the town of Pembroke and its population center. The unique feature of this marker narrative is the community planning of linear roads in the 1730's. If anyone has driven in Boston understands that many 18th century roads are haphazard and nonlinear. An aerial map view of US Route 3 will show that south of Pembroke from Hooksett south, the road lays along the Merrimack River with similar bends and curves. The same is true north of Pembroke as US Route 3 curves west into Concord. The Pembroke Street segment is straight and parallel with the Merrimack River to the west. I would suggest this planning made it more accessible for additional businesses and civic buildings to be arranged closer together and easier to travel.

Pittsfield

Marker # 0197: Jonathan "Jocky" Fogg, Patriot

Location: 15 Main Street

Sign Erected: 2005

GPS Coordinates- N 43° 18'.324″ W 71° 19'.755"

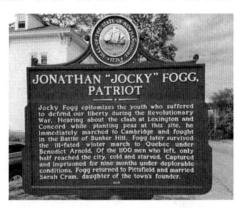

"Jocky Fogg epitomizes the youth who suffered to defend our liberty during the Revolutionary War. Hearing about the clash at Lexington and Concord while planting peas at this site, he immediately marched to Cambridge and fought in the Battle of Bunker Hill. Fogg later survived the ill-fated winter march to Quebec under Benedict Arnold. Of the 1100 men who left, only half reached the city, cold and starved. Captured and imprisoned for nine months under deplorable conditions, Fogg returned to Pittsfield and married Sarah Cram, daughter of the town's founder."

Born May 22, 1757 this local boy went on to leave his mark on the fight for liberty in the Revolutionary War battles of Lexington & Concord, Bunker Hill and Quebec City. In September 1775, Colonel Benedict Arnold (yes, the one who later became a traitor) led a force of 1,100 men from Massachusetts into Quebec City. At the time, Quebec City was under the control of British forces. Colonel Arnold's expedition was to travel through Maine and north via the Kennebec River. General Richard Montgomery was to lead his troops from Lake Champlain.

Colonel Arnold's expedition was fraught with hardship. Damage to boats, loss of supplies and drownings dwindled his force to a mere 600 men who were starving and exhausted. The route taken was nearly 350 miles of wilderness. The expedition was nearly twice the distance of what was initially planned.

The Battle of Quebec City occurred on December 31, 1775. The attack was a blunder and Arnold's men were captured. General Montgomery was killed in battle and Colonel Arnold was wounded. The prisoners were held for nine months with many months of captivity in the frigid winter.

Jonathan Fogg survived some of the most significant battles of the Revolutionary War. In my research, New Hampshire patriot Henry Dearborn led militia in these same three battles fought by Fogg. I would not be surprised if Fogg served under Dearborn's command. Returning to his home in Pittsfield, Jonathan Fogg married Sarah Cram. Jonathan Fogg died December 15, 1839 and is buried alongside his wife Sarah in the Old Meetinghouse Cemetery on Broadway Street.

Raymond

Marker # 0085: Nottingham- Chartered 1722

Location: NH Route 27 & NH Route 107, .2 miles east of Harriman Road

Sign Erected: 1972

GPS Coordinates- N 43° 02'.631″ W 71° 10'.692″

"Two miles north on Route 156 (one mile ahead) is Nottingham, home of Revolutionary War patriots, Generals Thomas Bartlett, Henry Butler, Joseph Cilley, and Henry Dearborn who was later a Congressman, Secretary of War, and Minister to Portugal. Monuments in Nottingham Square, five miles north, commemorate these men and the 1747 massacre of Elizabeth Simpson, Robert Beard and Nathaniel Folsom by Indians of the Winnipesaukee Tribe."

The Nottingham Grant of 1722 made up the area that now includes Nottingham, Deerfield and Northwood. Keep in mind, during the early 1700's the land of New Hampshire was mainly wilderness with limited settlements and occupied by Indian tribes. These grants to include Old Dunstable (1673), Scotch-Irish Settlement of Londonderry (1719) and the Two-Mile Streak in Barrington (1719) comprised a settlement boundary north from the population centers near Boston. The original petition for the grant occurred on April 21, 1721. By May 1723, one hundred thirty-two persons signed to be proprietors of lands in the grant. Each proprietor was required to build a house and plow and fence a three-acre plot.

In these outlying land grants, it was not uncommon to have men of military experience settle here. The Scotch-Irish settlement in Londonderry had Archibald Stark and son John Stark. In Nottingham, heroes of the Revolutionary War including Joseph Cilley, a member of Rogers Rangers and fought alongside John Stark. General Henry Dearborn fought at Bunker Hill and the Battle of Quebec. He went on to become a member of the staff for General George Washington at the Battle of Yorktown.

The massacre of September 1747 took the lives of Elizabeth Simpson, Robert Beard and Nathaniel Folsom by raiders of the Winnipesaukee Tribe. The Nottingham Square monument commemorates the town's Generals Bartlett, Cilley, Dearborn and Butler and adorned with a Minuteman. This is located at NH Route 156 and Ledge Farm Road. The monument is also located across from the General Butler homestead.

Salem

Marker # 0072: Mystery Hill

Location: NH Route 28 (332 North Broadway Road) south of Lake Street

Sign Erected: 1970

GPS Coordinates- N 42° 48'.162″ W 71° 14'.556″

"Four miles east on Route 111 is a privately owned complex of strange stone structures bearing similarities to early stone work found in western Europe. They suggest an ancient culture may have existed here more than 2,000 years ago. Sometimes called "America's Stonehenge", these intriguing chambers hold a fascinating story and could be remnants of a pre-Viking or even Phoenician civilization."

The website for the attraction (http://www.stonehengeusa.com) suggests that the rock formations were the work of Native Americans or early European explorers. This thirty-acre archeological site is a dichotomy of beliefs. Some suggest that it was constructed by Native American Indians as a worship site. Others believe it was constructed by early explorers from the Mediterranean civilization of Phoenicia. Lastly, some believe it is a well-designed hoax.

Early studies of the structures and layout began in 1937 by William Goodwin. Goodwin purchased this property and named it Mystery Hill. There is speculation that Goodwin had made attempts to move some of the boulders to place in their original settings. Goodwin believed the site was used by ancient Irish monks known as Culdees. Some archaeologists believe the structures are simply the workings of early farmers. Other notable archaeologists debunk the site due to its lack of bronze-age artifacts. What has been discovered is potential stone chips that suggest local Indians had forged stone tools.

In 1982, the property changed its name to America's Stonehenge to focus on the archeological significance and away from a tourist oddity exhibit. I recall visiting this attraction back in the 1970's. As a young person, my curiosity was peaked. My suggestion is for readers to visit the attraction located at 105 Haverhill Road and make your own decision of its origin.

Salem

Marker # 0221: Armenian Settlement Salem, NH

Location: Intersection of Brady Street & Salem Street

Sign Erected: 2010

GPS Coordinates- N 42° 45'.324″ W 71° 13'.651″

"Around 1900, this area was settled by Armenian immigrants fleeing massacres and religious persecution in their homeland. They established a community here where they maintained their heritage and religious traditions. Farming was the primary occupation until the 1940's. They built the nearby Ararat Armenian Congregational Church in 1913, and it remains a symbol of their freedom to worship and the center of community life."

The United States began to receive immigrants from Armenia which is in the Caucasus mountains between Europe and Asia. Armenia is one of the oldest Christian countries in world. In the 1890's, neighboring Ottoman Empire (now Turkey) began a relentless persecution of Armenians. Many fled to the United States and a group settled here in Salem in the early 1900's. The Armenian Genocide of 1915 resulted in the killing of hundreds of thousands of Armenian Christians by the Ottoman government.

The Armenians who settled here purchased land and created farmsteads where they marketed their produce locally. The

Armenian Settlement in Salem encompasses approximately 105 acres with this church being the center of their civic and religious life. The original settlement extended to the Massachusetts border. The Ararat Armenian Congregational Church is across the road on Salem Street. Prior to this church being built, local settlers traveled to Lawrence, Massachusetts to attend church. On October 25, 1912, local Armenians decided to build this church. The first service was held on July 25, 1913.

Business enterprise expanded to other ventures to include heavy construction. The Armenians who settled here found refuge from the persecution in their homeland. They were free to practice their Christian faith and create a livelihood in their new homeland. While the settlers made this region home, they never forgot the suffering their peoples endured under the Ottoman rule.

Salem

Marker # 0253: Londonderry Turnpike

Location: 75 Old Rockingham Road

Sign Erected: 2016

GPS Coordinates- N 42° 48'.061″ W 71° 14'.523"

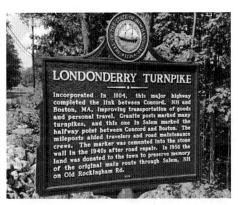

"Incorporated in 1804, this major highway completed the link between Concord, NH and Boston, MA, improving transportation of goods and personal travel. Granite posts marked many turnpikes, and this one in Salem marked the halfway point between Concord and Boston. The mileposts aided travelers and road maintenance crews. The marker was cemented into the stone wall in the 1940s after road repair. In 1956 the land was donated to the town to preserve memory of the original main route through Salem, NH on Old Rockingham Rd."

As stated on this marker, the Londonderry Turnpike was the major highway between Concord, New Hampshire and Boston. Earlier turnpikes in New Hampshire typically originated in the Portsmouth area and travelled north or northwest. The Londonderry Turnpike provided direct access to Boston. As with other turnpikes, the roads were designed and constructed by turnpike corporations. Local communities purchased shares and maintained their section of the roads. In return, the communities could charge tolls for travelers using their segment of the highway.

Construction began in 1804 and was a straight line from Concord to the Massachusetts state line. The Londonderry Turnpike section in Salem was the midway point between Concord and Boston. The distance from Concord to this marker was approximately thirty-five miles. This turnpike passed through Salem, Londonderry, Chester, Hooksett, Bow and the terminus in Concord. The Londonderry Turnpike remained a toll road until 1831 when the State of New Hampshire retained ownership and it became a public freeway.

Salem Historical Society member Wilbur Blackey stated to the *Union Leader* newspaper that he would walk by the granite post every day and did not know the significance it had in the local history. He continued that it is hard to envision the heyday when this turnpike's main traffic was stagecoaches and cattle drives. Blackey even commented that the road was also used for turkey drives. The Turnpike was lined by stonewalls on both sides to corral the livestock. Now that would be a sight to see!

Sandown

Marker # 0026: The Old Meeting House

Location: NH Route 121A & Fremont Street (in front of Sandown Historical Society)

Sign Erected: 1964

GPS Coordinates- N 42° 55'.716″ W 71° 11'.209″ (marker)

N 42° 55'.962″ W 71° 11'.158″ (Meetinghouse)

"The erection of this distinctive type of New England Meeting House, located at .3 mile on road to northeast, was begun in 1773 and finished in 1774. A former center of civic and church affairs in Sandown, this excellent example of period architecture is carefully maintained for its historical significance."

The Sandown Old Meetinghouse also known as the Congregational Meetinghouse was built in 1774 to replace a smaller building. This unique building is mostly in the original condition it was in 1774. According to the National Register of Historic Places records, the building is in the geographical center of town which was common in the 18th century. The town pound is located across the street as well. Some of the minor modifications that took place include a row of family pews be turned over to singers in 1798. In 1860, this row was removed to make room for the organ and choir. In 1835, wood stoves were installed. Heated meetinghouses were uncommon until the middle to late 1800's. This meetinghouse was used for Congregational church services until 1834 but town meetings continued until 1929. Today, the building is maintained by the Old Meeting House Historical Association. The Sandown Old Meeting House was listed in the National Register of Historic Places in 1978.

Another noteworthy building of historical significance is the Sandown Railroad Depot located near this historical marker. The depot was built in 1874 by the Nashua and Rochester Railroad. The rail line eventually became part of the Boston & Maine railroad. The rail service through this depot was central to many larger cities in the region and was heavily used. Train service continued here until 1934. The abandoned depot was converted into the town highway garage. The depot was restored to its' original condition in 1977 and has been the home to the Sandown Historical Society and Railroad Depot museum. The depot was listed on the National Register of Historic Places in 1986.

Weare

Marker # 0143: East Weare Village

Location: NH Route 77 East (Concord Stage Rd) and South Sugar Hill Road

Sign Erected: 1982

GPS Coordinates- N 43° 08'.251″ W 71° 41'.092″

"In 1960 their beautiful community was sacrificed for the Everett Flood Control Project. Their village was the home for over 60 families and was a self supporting thriving community. Farming and lumbering was the way of life for the villagers.

East Weare formerly had a train depot, churches, school, post office, toy shop, garage, grocery store, lumber mills, grist mill, also Grange Hall, cemeteries, blacksmith shop and creamery."

A short distance to the east of the marker, NH Route 77 crosses over the channel for the Everett Flood Control plain. To the north of here (across the road) along Windsong Heights Road is the Everett Dam which construction began in 1959 and completed in 1962. The control dam is part of the Hopkinton-Everett Lakes Flood Management Project. The flood control project protects properties along the Contoocook and Piscataquog rivers, both which are tributaries for the Merrimack River. With the potential of heavy rains and spring runoff, the legislatures of New Hampshire and Massachusetts worked to control flooding on the Merrimack River.

Similar to the Hill Village relocation in 1941 along the Pemigewasset River, U.S. Army Corps of Engineers designed flood control systems that included canals and dams to control exceedingly high waterflow. In the early 20th century, much of Weare was situated along the Piscataquog River. With increased manufacturing industries in Manchester and Concord, there was less demand for industry in Weare. Most of the mills in Weare were destroyed in the Hurricane of 1938.

Today, the area which was once the East Weare Village is managed by the U.S. Army Corps of Engineers and the New Hampshire Parks Trails Bureau. Trail maintenance is maintained by a local riders' club. Many recreational activities are available along the trail system as well as hiking, fishing and winter trail access sports.

Weare (North Weare)

Marker # 0192: Piscataquog River Mill Sites

Location: NH Route 114 (310 N. Stark Highway) next to bridge over Piscataquog River

Sign Erected: 2005

GPS Coordinates- N 43° 06'.565˝ W 71° 45'.012"

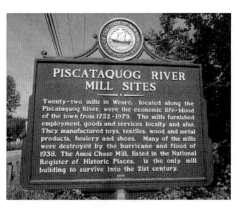

"Twenty-two mills in Weare, located along the Piscataquog River, were the economic life-blood of the town from 1752-1979. The mills furnished employment, goods and services locally and afar. They manufactured toys, textiles, wood and metal products, hosiery and shoes. Many of the mills were destroyed by the hurricane and flood of 1938. The Amos Chase Mill, listed in the National Register of Historic Places, is the only mill building to survive into the 21st century."

The first settlers known to inhabit the lands along the Piscataquog River are believed to be from a Masonian Grant in 1749. By 1764, the area was incorporated as Weare by colonial Governor Benning Wentworth. The town was named for its first town clerk and first New Hampshire president Meshech Weare.

Settlers found an abundance of white pine and red oak trees. Many of the larger white pines were claimed by the King of England for masts of ships. The falls along the Piscataquog River provided hydropower for early grist and sawmills. According to the National Register of Historic Places, it is believed the first commercial shoe factory was in operation on this site in 1823. Prior to this time, shoes were made by cordwainers for individual customers. This factory was believed to have manufactured more than 23,000 boots in its first year.

Industry flourished with the addition of rail service through the town. This provided timely and cost-effective transportation of goods to Manchester and other cities via the Merrimack River. In 1849, the Amos Chase Mill was built. The Amos Chase house (299 N. Stark Highway) was built in 1836 and is adjacent to the mill. The mill is the only surviving water-powered mill in Weare. The Amos Chase House was built as the primary residence of Amos Chase and remained in the family for more than a century. The Amos Chase Mill and home were listed in the National Register of Historic Places in 1992.

Chapter Seven

Seacoast Region

The Seacoast Region holds title of being the first settled region of New Hampshire. With the first English settlements of Hampton, Portsmouth, Exeter and Dover. This region may be the smallest in area, but it does not lack in vast richness and historical significance. From the first settlements at Odiorne's and Dover Point in 1623 to the colonial capitals in Portsmouth and Exeter, much of what makes New Hampshire the state as we know it has a deep-rooted foundation in the seacoast region.

New Hampshire's seacoast is the shortest in the United States. The shoreline of the Atlantic Ocean spans a mere eighteen miles from Newcastle to Seabrook. But do not let the size fool you. Much of our country and state's history began here. The first white settlers to what is now New Hampshire is believed to have settled at Odiorne's Point in 1623, known as Pannaway Plantation. In Newcastle, Fort Constitution was originally built by the British as early as 1632. This fortification was raided by colonists on December 14, 1774 which resulted in the pilfering of gunpowder and ammunition later used against the British at the Battle of Bunker Hill.

In addition to the extensive amounts of history, the seacoast is also a popular vacation destination. Visitors flock to the beaches of Hampton and Rye for summer sun and fun. Hampton also has an abundance of shops that cater to the tourist population, as well as the infamous Hampton Beach Casino Ballroom. The Casino Ballroom hosts top named musical artists and is a historical landmark having opened in 1900. A worthwhile trip to explore is along the coastal NH Route 1A. There are majestic oceanfront homes that reflect the architecture prevalent in the 19th and early 20th century.

While visiting the seacoast region, it would not be authentic if you did not stop and enjoy the delicious seafood. One example includes two famous establishments in Seabrook; Brown's Lobster Pound and Markey's Lobster Pound. These two institutions are directly across the street from each other. Now that is convenient! A visit to the seacoast must include a stop and walking visit to historic Portsmouth. The cobblestone streets and eclectic shops and buildings make this a great place to take a break and enjoy the beauty of this colonial-era seaport city.

While visiting the picturesque New Hampshire seacoast, take the time to enjoy the attractions this region affords its visitors. Add the abundance of history this region has, and you will see why the New Hampshire seacoast region is a favored destination in the Granite State.

Seacoast Region

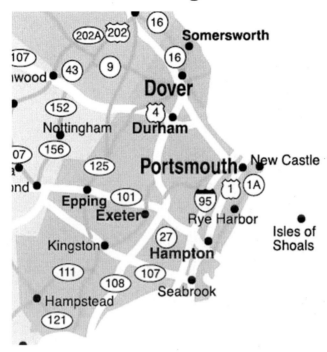

Barrington- Marker #0096: The Two-Mile Streak

Barrington- Marker #0212: Deputy Sheriff Charles E. Smith

Brentwood- Marker #0180: Rockingham Memorial

Brentwood- Marker #0249: Crawley Falls Road Bridge

Danville- Marker #0169: Hawke Meeting House

Dover- Marker #0051: Dr. Jeremy Belknap (1744-1798)

Dover- Marker #0092: Hilton's Point- 1623

Dover- Marker #0165: The Alexander Scammell Bridge over the Bellamy River

Durham- Marker #0008: Site of Piscataqua Bridge

Durham- Marker #0050: Oyster River Massacre

Durham- Marker #0089: Major General John Sullivan (1740-1795)

Durham- Marker #0154: Packer's Falls

Exeter- Marker #0032: Revolutionary Capital

Exeter- Marker #0097: Exeter Town House

Exeter- Marker #0131: Brigadier General Enoch Poor

Exeter- Marker #0161: Ladd-Gilman House

Exeter- Marker #0240: Lincoln Speaks in New Hampshire

Greenland- Marker #0113: Weeks House

Hampstead- Marker #0247: Hampstead Meeting House

Hampton- Marker #0028: First Public School

Hampton- Marker #0119: Old Landing Road

Hampton Falls- Marker #0037: George Washington's Visit

Kingston- Marker #0046: Josiah Bartlett (1729-1795)

New Castle- Marker #0004: William & Mary Raids

Newington- Marker #0151: Newington

Newmarket- Market #0209: Wentworth Cheswill

North Hampton- Marker #0062: Breakfast Hill

Portsmouth- Marker #0075: Portsmouth Plains

Portsmouth- Marker #0114: North Cemetery

Portsmouth- Marker #0127: John Langdon (1741-1819)

Portsmouth- Marker #0194: Wentworth-Coolidge Mansion

Portsmouth- Marker #0234: US Route 1 Bypass of Portsmouth, NH (1940)

Rollinsford- Marker #0088: Charles Cogswell Doe (1830-1896)

Rye- Marker #0018: Isle of Shoals

Rye- Marker #0063: Atlantic Cable Station and Sunken Forest

Rye- Marker #0078: Odiorne's Point

Seabrook- Marker #0103: Shapley Line

Seabrook- Marker #0120: Bound Rock

Barrington

Marker # 0096: The Two-Mile Streak

Location: NH Route 125 (mile marker 29.2) north of Winkley Pond Road & South of NH Route 9

Sign Erected: 1974

GPS Coordinates- N 43° 11'.571″ W 70° 59'.885″

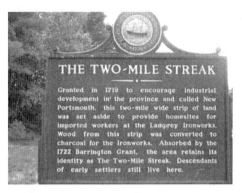

"Granted in 1719 to encourage industrial development in the province and called New Portsmouth, this two-mile wide strip of land was set aside to provide homesites for imported workers at the Lamprey Ironworks. Wood from this strip was converted to charcoal for the Ironworks. Absorbed by the 1722 Barrington Grant, the area retains its identity as The Two-Mile Streak. Descendants of early settlers still live here."

The early 1700's began the growth of settlements expanding outward from Boston, Portsmouth, and Portland Maine. With these three vibrant shipping ports, the demand for industry was booming in Great Bay of Portsmouth, the center of industry and trade in colonial New Hampshire. Shipbuilding was a major industry in the Portsmouth area, masts for ships and iron works were in high demand. The 1719 grant provided natural resources and room to expand for the growing economy. By 1722, the original Barrington Grant added what is known as the Two-Mile Streak to its grant. The original Two-Mile Slip of land near Dover was renamed New Portsmouth and the Two-Mile Streak grant was renamed Barrington.

Captain Archibald MacPheadris, a Scotsman and shrewd entrepreneur established the Lamprey Ironworks along the Lamprey River in Newmarket. His ironworks needed huge amounts of wood to fuel the factory, iron ore from local bogs and a place to settle his workforce. The Two-Mile Streak provided all of this. First settlements to this land were made between 1732 and 1740. Many of the immigrants brought here to settle were Scottish and English.

The grant of The Two-Mile Streak was two miles wide and six miles long. Today, much of what was the original grant is now eastern Barrington. In 1722, the Two-Mile Streak became part of the Barrington Grant that created that township, part of what is now Strafford. Within this charter, the new towns of Chester, Nottingham and Rochester were created. The illustration below depicts the linear grant of the Two-Mile Streak.

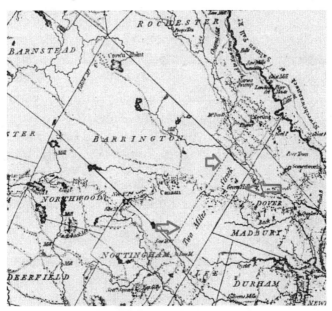

Photo courtesy of Mikenh.wordpress.com

Barrington

Marker # 0212: Deputy Sheriff Charles E. Smith 1843-1891

Location: 668 NH Route 202 and north of Pine Road (in front of cemetery)

Sign Erected: 2009

GPS Coordinates- N 43° 15'.279″ W 71° 02'.150"

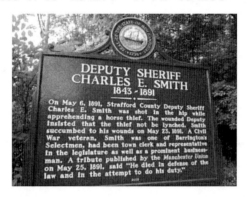

"On May 6, 1891, Strafford County Deputy Sheriff Charles E. Smith was shot in the hip while apprehending a horse thief. The wounded Deputy insisted that the thief not be lynched. Smith succumbed to his wounds on May 23, 1891. A Civil War veteran, Smith was one of Barrington's Selectmen, had been town clerk and representative in the legislature as well as a prominent businessman. A tribute published by the Manchester Union on May 25, 1891, said "He died in defense of the law and in the attempt to do his duty."

Charles E. Smith was born and raised in Barrington. He was appointed Deputy Sheriff in Strafford County by High Sheriff John H. Pingree for his stellar character and reputation in the community. Smith was a veteran of the Civil War, having served in the 18th New Hampshire Volunteer Infantry Regiment. No records indicate any battles he may have been part of during his service in the 18th Volunteer Regiment. The unit did participate in the Battle of Appomattox, as well as the Third Battle of Petersburg; both engagements were in Virginia.

On April 30, 1891, Deputy Sheriff Smith was responding to a complaint of a boarder staying at a house in town. The boarder was reported to have stolen two horses and a buggy from a nearby stable. The thief left with the horses and buggy and camped in nearby Strafford. A posse of men tracked down the thief and when they confronted him the thief shot at the men and attempted to escape.

In the melee, the thief was shot and wounded. Surrounded, the thief declared if anyone attempted to get closer that he would shoot. Deputy Smith attempted to persuade the thief to surrender his weapon. But as Deputy Smith approached the wounded man, the thief shot Smith in the hip and abdomen. Even while severely wounded, Deputy Smith was able to subdue the shooter. The posse began attacking the thief and wanted to lynch him for his crimes. Smith demanded that he be brought to trial and let justice be served.

Deputy Smith was brought to a doctor to be treated for his wound. Even though he was showing improvement, he developed an infection and died six days later. As for the thief, he was jailed in Dover, eventually escaped from jail and was never seen again. Deputy Charles E. Smith was the first law enforcement officer in New Hampshire to die in the line of duty.

Brentwood

Marker # 0180: Rockingham Memorial

Location: NH Route 111A & Haigh Road (197 Middle Rd. at Pilgrim United Church of Christ)

Sign Erected: 2002

GPS Coordinates- N 42° 59'.436″ W 71° 02'.393″

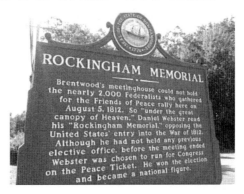

"Brentwood's meetinghouse could not hold the nearly 2,000 Federalists who gathered for the Friends of Peace rally here on August 5, 1812. So "under the great canopy of Heaven," Daniel Webster read his "Rockingham Memorial," opposing the United States entry into the War of 1812. Although he had not held any previous elective office, before the meeting ended Webster was chosen to run for Congress on the Peace Ticket. He won the election and became a national figure."

Statesman, constitutional lawyer, orator, and native-born Daniel Webster was a figure that was revered by many and respected by all. Daniel Webster born in Salisbury (now part of Franklin) in 1782 was widely known as a defender of the U.S. Constitution. It was not until his famous *"Rockingham Memorial"* speech that catapulted the constitutional lawyer and orator to enter politics.

Up until this speech, Daniel Webster had written orations for Fourth of July events in 1802 (Fryeburg, ME), 1805 (Salisbury), 1806 (Concord) and 1812 (Portsmouth). These speeches helped

Webster gain popularity as an orator. Also leading up to his famous *Rockingham Memorial*, Webster wrote, *Considerations on the Embargo Laws.* This paper declared the harm caused by the trade embargo imposed by President Thomas Jefferson against Great Britain and France. Tensions were growing, and Daniel Webster became a voice for New England merchants.

The *Rockingham Memorial* was an anti-war paper. America was engaged in a fight with Great Britain once again. President James Madison felt compelled to declare war with Great Britain due to the British compulsion of American sailors under British authority. While this is a mere segment of British coercion of American citizens, the United States declared war with Great Britain on June 18, 1812.

Daniel Webster went on to serve in the U.S. House of Representatives for New Hampshire and later for Massachusetts. He also served as a U.S. Senator for Massachusetts. Daniel Webster holds the distinction of also serving as the U.S. Secretary of State for three presidents.

Brentwood

Marker # 0249: Crawley Falls Road Bridge

Location: NH Route 111A (Middle Road) and Crawley Falls Road

Sign Erected: 2015

GPS Coordinates- N 42° 58'.690″ W 71° 04'.361″

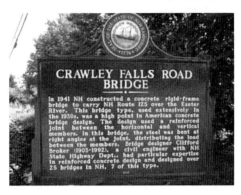

"In 1941 NH constructed a concrete rigid-frame bridge to carry NH Route 125 over the Exeter River. This bridge type, used extensively in the 1930s, was a high point in American concrete bridge design. The design used a reinforced joint between the horizontal and vertical members. In this bridge, the steel was bent at right angles at the joint, distributing the load between the members. Bridge designer Clifford Broker (1903-1992), a civil engineer with NH State Highway Dept., had particular expertise in reinforced concrete design and designed over 25 bridges in NH, 7 of this type."

While this historical maker references the significance of the bridge design, the story is relevant to share who Clifford Broker was. Born in 1903, this structural engineer received his secondary school education at the Tilton School in Tilton, New Hampshire. He received his engineering degree from Worcester Polytechnic Institute in 1929. Specializing in reinforced concrete designs, Broker's design was built on this site in 1941. The New Hampshire State Highway Department built it with funding from the State-aid account totaling $1,800. This bridge replaced an earlier wooden pony-truss bridge located at this site. The current concrete bridge uses the original abutments of the earlier wooden bridge.

In the 1920's and 1930's, bridge engineers recognized the importance of concrete bridge design. Reinforced concrete bridges were able to carry more weight and increased small to medium-sized vehicle traffic. This was necessary for the increased traffic into the industrialized center of Brentwood. This bridge has a span of thirty-six feet.

Clifford Broker was instrumental in the increased construction and standardization of bridges in the New Hampshire Highway's bridge inventory during his tenure with the State Highway department. Broker left the State Highway Department in 1945 and established his own structural and consulting firm.

The town of Brentwood was incorporated in 1742. Much of the industry of this community was situated along the Exeter River and Little River.

Danville

Marker # 0169: Hawke Meeting House

Location: NH Route 111A (466 Main Street) north of Long Pond Road

Sign Erected: 1995

GPS Coordinates- N 42° 56'.224″ W 71° 07'.125″

"Erected prior to June 12, 1755, this is New Hampshire's oldest meeting house in original condition. Built by 27 local proprietors who conveyed it in 1760 to the newly-incorporated Parish of Hawke (now Danville), the building was used for religious services through 1832 and for town meetings through 1887. The Rev. John Page, only regular minister of the parish, died of smallpox in the 1782 epidemic which ravaged the area of "Tuckertown" and is buried in "Ye Old Cemetery" just north of here."

According to the National Register of Historic Places, the Hawke Meeting House was built in 1759. Original construction may have begun as early as 1755 as denoted on the marker. At the time of its construction, this area was part of Kingston and known as the Parish of Hawke; named in honor of British Royal Navy admiral Edward Hawke. In 1760, the residents petitioned the royal governor for incorporation. The request was granted, and the town of Hawke was incorporated on February 22, 1760.

The Hawke Meeting House was the center of all public and religious gatherings in the small community. This meeting house retains most of its original design. The windows were enlarged in 1800 and limited decoration was added.

In the book, *Colonial Meeting Houses in New Hampshire* (1938), it states that this building has the oldest high pulpit in New Hampshire. The book also describes a claim of "vandalism" that occurred in the early 19th century. No longer used as a house of worship, some folks tore out the pews to make way for floorspace for dancing. *"You see, some of them wanted to dance. So, they ripped out the pews of the lower floor one night.... They never did dance a step there. The people were so enraged that no one dared to attempt it."* By the way, the pews were later removed and placed in storage only to be reinstalled in 1936.

When the Free-Will Baptists membership grew, they built a new building to meet in 1832. In 1837, the town hall was built, and the Hawke Meeting House was no longer used. In 1836, the town of Hawke changed its name to Danville. This building was listed on the National Register of Historic Places in 1982.

Dover

Marker # 0051: Dr. Jeremy Belknap (1744-1798)

Location: NH Route 16 Spaulding Turnpike-northbound (just south of tollbooth)

Sign Erected: 1968

GPS Coordinates- N 43° 08'.159″ W 70° 50'.436″

"Noted preacher, educator, naturalist and historian. Born Boston, Mass. Harvard College 1762. School teacher at Portsmouth and Greenland. Pastor of First Congregational Church at nearby Dover, 1766-1786. Published first History of New Hampshire. Founded Massachusetts Historical Society, 1794. A New Hampshire county perpetuates his name."

Jeremy Belknap was born June 4, 1744 in Boston. His parents were members of the Old South Church. In 1758, at the age of 15 years old Jeremy Belknap attended Harvard College and graduated in 1762. Jeremy Belknap pursued his profession as a teacher moving to Portsmouth and teaching until 1766. Belknap entered the ministry and became the Pastor of First Congregational Church in Dover in 1766.

Belknap continued his ministry and was named by the New Hampshire Committee of Safety as the Chaplain for American troops in Cambridge Massachusetts. Unfortunately, he had to decline the appointment due to ill health. While he was unable to serve in this capacity, he was a staunch patriot.

As a naturalist, Belknap participated in a scientific expedition to the White Mountains in July 1784 with six men. On this trip, he recorded details of their travels which were later published as one of three volumes of the *History of New Hampshire*. These volumes detailed the many notes he collected during his years of travel around the state. These volumes are considered the first comprehensive collection of the history of New Hampshire. Much of what Belknap collected over the years was with the approval from colonial Governor John Wentworth.

Jeremy Belknap was conferred the degree of Doctor of Divinity from Harvard College in 1792. Dr. Belknap died June 20, 1798 and is buried in the Granary Burying Ground in Boston with signers of the Declaration of Independence, victims of the Boston Massacre, and Paul Revere. He was later re-interred in Cambridge, Massachusetts. Belknap County in the Lakes Region was named in honor of Dr. Jeremy Belknap as well as Mount Belknap in Gilford.

Dover

Marker # 0092: Hilton's Point - 1623

Location: US Route 4 inside entrance to Hilton State Park- Exit 5 (north side of road)

Sign Erected: 1973

GPS Coordinates- N 43° 07'.303" W 70° 49'.710"

"The first settlement at Dover was made here at the southernmost point of Dover Neck and was called Hilton's Point after Edward and William Hilton. They were fishmongers from London who, in 1623, established their fishing industry at this scenic site."

In 1623, under the authority of the English land grant, Captain John Mason sent David Thompson to establish settlements along the Piscataqua River. Thompson was accompanied by two Englishmen, Edward and William Hilton who were fishmongers (a fish merchant). David Thompson established his settlement at the mouth of the river known as Pannaway Plantation in Rye (Odiorne's Point). The Hilton's established their permanent fishing settlement eight miles upstream on this neck of land and named it Cocheco Plantation (Hilton's Point). This site was favorable due to being situated between the Piscataqua River to the east and the Great Bay estuary and Bellamy River to the west. This settlement was later named Northam and changed to Dover in 1637.

The Pannaway Plantation at Odiorne's Point included salt-drying fish racks and a building to store the fish which was named Mason Hall. The Cocheco Plantation settlement at Hilton's Point contained fish stages to collect and transport their catch down river to Pannaway Plantation. Both historic sites lay claim as having been the first settlement in New Hampshire.

According to Jeremy Belknap's *History of New Hampshire: Volume 1* (1784), both settlements maintained a congenial relationship with the native population. All was peaceful until a man from Massachusetts named Morton from Mount Wollaston went against the King's proclamation to sell firearms and ammunition to the Indians. Morton hired the Indians to hunt for him. When the settlers saw Indians in the woods with firearms, it caused terror and panic. Morton was eventually captured and imprisoned for his actions against the King.

Dover, the "Garrison City" is the oldest settlement in New Hampshire and seventh oldest in the United States. Today, Hilton Point is a state park.

Dover

Marker # 0165: The Alexander Scammell Bridge over the Bellamy River

Location: US Route 4 (eastbound) westside of bridge at Durham/Dover town line

Sign Erected: 1991

GPS Coordinates- N 43° 07'.795″ W 70° 51'.166"

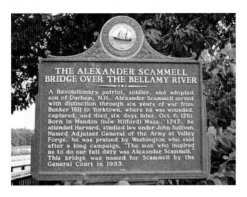

"A Revolutionary patriot, soldier, and adopted son of Durham, N.H., Alexander Scammell served with distinction through six years of war from Bunker Hill to Yorktown, where he was wounded, captured, and died six days later, Oct. 6, 1781. Born in Mendon (now Milford) Mass., 1747, he attended Harvard, studied law under John Sullivan. Named Adjutant General of the Army at Valley Forge, he was praised by Washington who said after a long campaign, "The man who inspired us to do our full duty was Alexander Scammell." This bridge was named for Scammell by the General Court in 1933."

Alexander Scammell was born March 27, 1747 in what is now Milford, Massachusetts. His father died when Alexander was six years old. Raised by his mother and with the mentorship of his minister, Alexander went on to study at Harvard College, graduating in 1769. For a short time, Scammell taught at schools in Plymouth, Massachusetts. In 1772, he moved to Durham New Hampshire to work under the mentorship of John Sullivan.

When the Revolutionary War commenced, Scammell was appointed a Major in Brigadier General John Sullivan's brigade. He served in the Continental Army under General Sullivan in the Battle of Long Island. In November 1776, Scammell was recognized for his success as a leader and was appointed Colonel and took command of the Third New Hampshire Regiment. Colonel Scammell commanded his regiment at the two Battles of Saratoga. Colonel Scammel went on to become the aide-de-camp for General George Washington and later as the Adjutant General for the Continental Army from January 5, 1778 to January 1, 1781.

In 1781, Scammell resigned his Continental commission and returned to New Hampshire to command the First New Hampshire Regiment. At the Battle of Yorktown, Colonel Scammell led four hundred of his men on a reconnaissance mission behind British lines. In a skirmish, Scammell was shot in the back and taken prisoner. Seeing that Scammell was mortally wounded, the British released him to the Americans where he died a few days later. Colonel Alexander Scammell is buried in an unknown location in Yorktown, Virginia.

Durham

Marker # 0008: Site of Piscataqua Bridge

Location: US Route 4 (eastbound) and intersection of Cedar Point Road & Back River Road

Sign Erected: 1962

GPS Coordinates- N 43° 07'.788″ W 70° 51'.664"

"At end of next road southeast, this engineering feat was used from 1794 to 1855. It joined Fox Point, Newington and Meader's Neck, Durham via Goat Island. Also site, in same period, of proposed state capital, Franklin City, and beginning of First New Hampshire Turnpike ~ vital route for instate traffic."

To fully appreciate the engineering needed to complete this bridge, simply drive to where Cedar Point Road meets the shoreline. Keep in mind that this bridge was built in 1794. The Piscataqua Bridge was built by Timothy Palmer of Massachusetts. He had extensive experience building long-span wood truss bridges. In December 1792, the legislature authorized construction of the toll bridge and a charter was granted in 1793. The proprietors of the bridge purchased the property at both ends of the bridge.

The bridge was in three separate spans. The first from Fox Point to Ram Island spanned 600 feet. The second span from Ram Island to Goat Island was 330 feet. From Goat Island to Tuttle Point (where Cedar Point Road meets shoreline) was a span of

1818 feet. Once completed, this bridge was the longest span bridge in the United States, holding this record until 1812. The bridge records indicate that the depth of water at high tide along the bridge varied from 42 to 54 feet deep.

The purpose for construction was to provide a link from mainland Durham to Newington leading to the tidewaters of Portsmouth over the Great Bay of the Piscataqua River. The route included the First New Hampshire Turnpike (incorporated in 1796) which connected the seaport city of Portsmouth to Concord via what is now known as US Route 4.

In 1830, the bridge was rebuilt but gave way to ice jams in 1855. With the introduction of the railroad, the bridge was no longer deemed a necessity. Today, visitors can simply look across the Great Bay towards Goat Island and Fox Point and imagine the bridge which spanned this river more than two hundred years ago.

Photo captured from Google Earth

Durham

Marker # 0050: Oyster River Massacre

Location: NH Route 108 (Newmarket Rd) north of bridge over Oyster River

Sign Erected: 1967 & 1993

GPS Coordinates- N 43° 07'.875″ W 70° 55'.126″

"On July 18, 1694, a force of about 250 Indians under the command of the French soldier, de Villieu, attacked settlements in this area on both sides of the Oyster River, killing or capturing approximately 100 settlers, destroying five garrison houses and numerous dwellings. It was the most devastating French and Indian raid in New Hampshire during King William's War."

This attack was not the first between Indians and settlers. It was the first attack by Indians which was organized by the French. Peace between the Abenaki tribes and settlers had been in place since the Cocheco Massacre in 1689. Jeremy Belknap wrote in *History of New Hampshire* volume 1, *"The Sieur de Villieu, who had distinguished himself in the defense of Quebec...being now in command of Penobscot...with a body of two hundred and fifty Indians marched to Oyster River"*.

The French, weary of an Abenaki and English alliance persuaded the Indians to attack the English at Oyster River. The settlers having a peaceful alliance with the Indians and seeing them in the woods thought they were simply hunting. The attack on the garrison at Oyster River came quickly and without defense.

The Abenaki Indians along with their French commander Villieu had staged their raiding party on the evening of July 17th near the falls and in locations around Oyster Plantation. The engagement of the raid was to take place at the first shot fired at the settlers. During the massacre, one hundred settlers were killed and twenty-seven were captured and taken to Canada. Five of the twelve garrison houses were destroyed as well as the livestock and crops.

Those who survived were left with little to no shelter or supplies. Many families attempted to surrender under terms to the raiders only to be killed. Jeremy Belknap's depiction includes, *"Drew surrendered his garrison on the promise of security but was murdered when he fell into their hands. One of his children, a boy of nine years old, was made to run through a lane of Indians as a mark for them to throw their hatchets at."* The Oyster River Massacre is considered the worst of its kind during the King William's War.

Durham

Marker # 0089: Major General John Sullivan 1740-1795

Location: NH Route 108 (Newmarket Rd) south of bridge over Oyster River

Sign Erected: 1972

GPS Coordinates- N 43° 07'.818″ W 70° 55'.087″

"Revolutionary patriot, soldier, politician, first Grand Master of Masons in New Hampshire, and a resident of Durham. He left the Continental Congress to serve under Washington from Cambridge to Valley Forge. Commanded at Rhode Island in 1778, and led campaign against the Six Nations in New York in 1779. Re-entered Congress, then served three terms as Governor of New Hampshire. Led fight for ratification of U.S. Constitution and became a federal district judge."

Like John Stark, General John Sullivan had a significant impact on the history of the State of New Hampshire. John Sullivan was born February 17, 1740 in nearby Somersworth. Sullivan's profession began by studying law with Samuel Livermore (marker #39) in Portsmouth. Sullivan married Lydia Worcester and they moved to Durham where he opened his own law office. In 1773, Alexander Scammell (marker #0165) joined Sullivan's law practice. Sullivan was not a popular figure in Durham. As the only lawyer in town, he was part of foreclosures and other legal proceedings that made him unpopular.

John Sullivan was a friend of colonial Governor John Wentworth who in 1772 appointed Sullivan a Major in the New Hampshire militia. As tensions rose between the royal government and the colonists, Major Sullivan separated himself from the loyalists and aligned himself with the patriots. This new alliance led to Sullivan being elected as a delegate to the First Continental Congress which met in Philadelphia, Pennsylvania in 1774. In 1775, John Sullivan was elected to be a delegate of New Hampshire at the Second Continental Congress in Philadelphia. He was appointed Brigadier General in the Continental Army at this convention.

General John Sullivan also distinguished himself in the Revolutionary War. He and John Langdon were responsible for the raid on Fort William & Mary in Newcastle. He commanded soldiers in many campaigns to include the Siege of Boston in 1775, Battle of Long Island (1776), Battle of Trenton (1776) with General George Washington and the Battle of Princeton in 1777. After the war, John Sullivan returned to public service where he served as New Hampshire Attorney General. He served as governor for three terms, and in 1788 was chairman of the state convention that ratified the federal constitution making New Hampshire the ninth state in the union to do so. Major General John Sullivan died in Durham on January 23, 1795.

In addition to the historical marker and monument commemorating Major General John Sullivan there is a plaque onsite that marks the location of the meetinghouse where gunpowder confiscated from the raid of Fort William & Mary was stored. These munitions were used by the patriots in their battle against the British at the Battle of Bunker Hill on June 17, 1775.

Durham

Marker # 0154: Packer's Falls

Location: NH Route 108 (Newmarket Road) and Bennett Road

Sign Erected: 1985 & 1989

GPS Coordinates- N 43° 06'.860″ W 70° 55'.512"

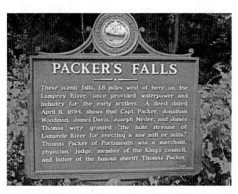

"These scenic falls, 1.6 miles west of here on the Lamprey River, once provided waterpower and industry for the early settlers. A deed dated April 11, 1694, shows that Capt. Packer, Jonathan Woodman, James Davis, Joseph Meder, and James Thomas were granted "the hole streame of Lamprele River for erecting a saw mill or mill." Thomas Packer of Portsmouth was a merchant, physician, judge, member of King's council, and father of the famous sheriff Thomas Packer."

Thomas Packer, along with other partners were granted this segment along the Lamprey River to establish a settlement and construct sawmills and other manufacturing sites along the river. The early 18th century brought an expansion outside of the major seaports and inland to points where resources could be harvested, and manufacturing centers established to produce goods for England. Thomas Packer retained most of the grant totaling fifty acres along the Lamprey River and established mills at the site of Packer's Falls. His partners Woodman, Davis, Meder, and Thomas shared ownership of the remaining fifty acres. The falls located along the bridge 1.6 miles down Bennett

Road are known as Packer's Falls. In the earlier settlement, the namesake also included subsequent falls upstream. Originally, these falls were known as Second Falls. Packer's Falls was named for Thomas Packer's father, Colonel Thomas Packer who was a local doctor, judge, and member of the royal governor's council. According to the book, Landmarks *of Ancient Dover* (1892), the name Packer's Falls can be traced back as far as early as 1718. The first written report in Durham of the name Packer's Falls can be found June 13, 1750 where the road was named Packer's Falls. This segment of Durham comprising the southeastern part of the town was known as Packer's Falls and consisted of its own village and school.

The marker denotes the fame of Sheriff Thomas Packer who was granted this land. He earned his fame as a ruthless sheriff who was responsible for the public hanging of three local women. These executions were the first of their kind in Portsmouth. Notably, a Ruth Blay who was charged with the death of her infant child. While it was believed the child was stillborn, Sheriff Packer continued with the hanging, even with a stay from the governor enroute. Sheriff Packer moved up the time of the hanging, so he would not miss his dinner.

Exeter

Marker # 0032: Revolutionary Capital

Location: 8 Front Street at Exeter Town Offices building (across street from Town Hall)

Sign Erected: 1965

GPS Coordinates- N 42° 58'.867" W 70° 56'.787"

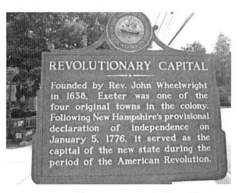

"Founded by Rev. John Wheelwright in 1638, Exeter was one of the four original towns in the colony. Following New Hampshire's provisional declaration of independence on January 5, 1776, it served as the capital of the new state during the period of the American Revolution."

Exeter was settled as early as the 1630's by exiles of the Massachusetts General Court. The landmass now known as Exeter which was included in the Mason's Grant was preferred for its confluence of freshwater from the Exeter River to the tidewater of Squamscott. The falls provided power to operate saw and grist mills. Yet, this land was not under any central form of government. John Mason, proprietor of the land grant had died in 1635 and his son was a minor and could not lay claim to the grant. The land was then settled by Reverend John Wheelwright and his followers who were banished from Massachusetts. Wheelwright helped to establish an independent puritan community which prospered. Exeter came under the jurisdiction of the Massachusetts Bay Colony in 1643.

Exeter grew in population and importance in the region. Manufacturing provided goods to nearby Portsmouth. Exeter became a center of influence in New Hampshire. By 1692, Exeter residents were prominent in providing interference to British authority. Citizens of Exeter supported colonial actions against the Crown. The Provincial Congress met here after being banned in Portsmouth by Royal Governor John Wentworth. Exeter was the central muster location for New Hampshire militias for the Battles at Lexington & Concord, as well as Bunker Hill.

From 1774 to 1788, Exeter was considered the colonial seat of government for New Hampshire. The first state constitution was written here and the first declaration of independence from Britain was created here. The state government met in the old townhouse until 1782. This building site is located one block south of this marker.

The Committee of Safety which functioned as the executive branch of state government met in Exeter. Throughout the American Revolution, Exeter was the capital of New Hampshire. After the Constitutional Convention met in Exeter in 1788, it was then adjourned to Concord and became the next capital city for the State of New Hampshire.

Exeter

Marker # 0097: Exeter Town House

Location: Intersection of Court Street (NH Route 108) and Front Street (NH Route 111)

Sign Erected: 1974

GPS Coordinates- N 42° 58'.823″ W 70° 56'.819″

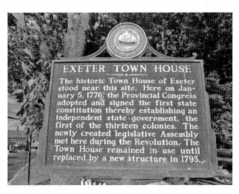

"The historic Town House of Exeter stood near this site. Here on January 5, 1776, the Provincial Congress adopted and signed the first state constitution thereby establishing an independent state government, the first of the thirteen colonies. The newly created legislative Assembly met here during the Revolution. The Town House remained in use until replaced by a new structure in 1793."

The original Exeter Town House was built in 1732 and was primarily used for town meetings. The Exeter Historical Society notes that the original building also had stocks and a whipping post on the property. During the American Revolution, this Town House was the central building of New Hampshire government and served as its State House. The Provincial Congress was banned from Portsmouth by Royal Governor John Wentworth. Patriots stole government records and brought them here. On January 5, 1776 the New Hampshire Provincial Congress drafted and signed the first state constitution among the original thirteen colonies. Eleven colonies had draft new constitutions with only Rhode Island and Connecticut opting to function under their colonial charters. This state constitution begins, *"WE, the members of the Congress of New Hampshire, chosen and appointed by the free suffrages of the people of said colony, and authorized and empowered by them to meet together, and use such means and pursue such measures as we should judge best for the public good; and in particular to establish some form of government, provided that measure should be recommended by the Continental Congress: And a recommendation to that purpose having been transmitted to us from the said Congress: Have taken into our serious consideration the unhappy circumstances, into which this colony is involved by means of many grievous and oppressive acts of the British Parliament"*

On July 16, 1776 the Declaration of Independence was read to the citizens of Exeter from the steps of the Town House by a young man named John Taylor Gilman. While the original Town House served the citizens of Exeter and the State of New Hampshire, it was rebuilt in 1793.

Exeter

Marker # 0131: Brigadier General Enoch Poor

Location: NH Route 85 (Newfields Road) just north of intersection with Swasey Parkway

Sign Erected: 1979

GPS Coordinates- N 42° 59'.388″ W 70° 56'.953"

"Born in Andover, Mass. June 21, 1736, Enoch Poor settled in Exeter, becoming a successful merchant and ship-builder. In 1775 he was appointed colonel in the 3rd New Hampshire Regiment. Poor was at Stillwater, Saratoga and Monmouth, and served under Washington, Sullivan and Lafayette. Congress commissioned him Brigadier General in 1777. Mortally wounded in a duel fought September 8, 1781, he was buried in the First Reformed churchyard in Hackensack, New Jersey."

Enoch Poor began his military service in 1755 when he enlisted as a private and served in the militia commanded by General Jeffery Amherst and fought against the French at Louisburg, Nova Scotia. This action caused the expulsion of the Acadians from Canada where they fled to Louisiana, hence the Acadians we now know who speak Cajun in the southern United States.

Enoch Poor eloped with Martha Osgood and moved to Exeter. He began his profession as a shipbuilder and was quite successful. He was involved in government and in 1775 was elected to the

Provincial Assembly (what we now know as the state legislature). When word spread of the Battle of Lexington, the Provincial Assembly stood up three militia regiments. Enoch Poor was appointed Colonel of the Second New Hampshire Regiment. Colonel John Stark was appointed commander of the First New Hampshire Regiment. Colonel James Reed was appointed commander of the Third New Hampshire Regiment. Colonel Stark and Colonel Reed were sent to the Battle of Bunker Hill. Colonel Poor was ordered to secure Exeter and Portsmouth from British forces.

In 1776, Colonel Poor and his militia was renamed the 8th Continental Regiment and served under General George Washington. Poor was appointed Brigadier General in 1777 and led his brigade at both Battles of Saratoga. That same year, Brigadier General Poor wintered over at Valley Forge with General Washington. He led his men at the Battle of Monmouth and Newtown. Conflicting stories exist of Poor's cause of death. The army surgeon reports that he died of typhus. Other stories claim he was mortally wounded in a duel.

Exeter

Marker # 0161: Ladd-Gilman House

Location: NH Route 27 (189 Water Street) across from intersection with Swasey Parkway

Sign Erected: 1991

GPS Coordinates- N 42° 58'.922″ W 70° 56'.943"

"Built about 1721 as one of New Hampshire's earliest brick houses, and enlarged and clapboarded in the 1750's, this dwelling served as the state treasury during the Revolution. Here was born John Taylor Gilman (1753-1828), who was elected governor for an unequalled total of fourteen years, and his brother Nicholas Gilman, Jr. (1755-1814), a signer of the U.S. Constitution. The house has been maintained since 1902 by the Society of the Cincinnati."

Exeter has a unique claim to having ten structures listed on the National Register of Historic Places. The Ladd-Gilman House, also known as Cincinnati Memorial Hall was listed on December 2, 1974. The Ladd-Gilman House was built around 1721 by Captain Nathaniel Ladd. Nathaniel Ladd lived in the brick home until 1747 when he sold it to Daniel Gilman who he was related to by marriage. While the home appears to have a wood exterior, the facade covers the original bricks. Daniel and Ann Gilman's son Nicholas Gilman Jr. was born in this house August 3, 1755. Nicholas Gilman Jr. was a soldier in the Continental Army, a New

Hampshire delegate to the Constitutional Convention and was a signer of the U.S. Constitution. Also born in this house is his brother John Taylor Gilman on December 19, 1753. John Taylor Gilman, at the age of twenty-two had the distinct privilege of reading the Declaration of Independence from the front steps of the Exeter Town House on July 16, 1776.

The Ladd-Gilman House was used as the New Hampshire State Treasury building during the Revolutionary War. Today, the Ladd-Gilman House is the home for the American Independence Museum. The building was purchased by the Society of Cincinnati in New Hampshire in 1902. The American Independence Museum has a unique and rare collection of items to include furniture and artifacts from the 1700's, as well as a copy of the *Regulations for the Order and Discipline of the Troops of the United States* by Baron von Steuben. While the home held an important role in our state government during the Revolutionary War, the historical significance is showcased for the prominence of the Gilman family members who lived here and their contribution to the history of the State of New Hampshire.

Exeter

Marker # 0240: Abraham Lincoln Speaks in New Hampshire

Location: 10 Front Street in front of the Exeter Town Hall

Sign Erected: 2014

GPS Coordinates- N 42° 58'.858″ W 70° 56'.810"

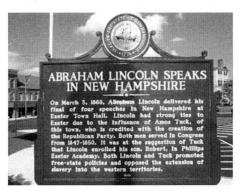

"On March 3, 1860, Abraham Lincoln delivered his final of four speeches in New Hampshire at Exeter Town Hall. Lincoln had strong ties to Exeter due to the influence of Amos Tuck, of this town, who is credited with the creation of the Republican Party. Both men served in Congress from 1847-1850. It was at the suggestion of Tuck that Lincoln enrolled his son, Robert, in Phillips Exeter Academy. Both Lincoln and Tuck promoted free-state policies and opposed the extension of slavery into the western territories."

On February 29, 1860 Abraham Lincoln was giving an anti-slavery speech at the Cooper Union in New York City. Lincoln extended his tour to travel to New Hampshire and give four speeches. In addition to the speech he gave in Exeter, Lincoln spoke in Concord at the Phenix Hall, at Manchester's Smyth Hall, and Dover City Hall. Lincoln included Exeter as a stop, so he could visit his son Robert who was attending Phillips Exeter Academy. Exeter was also the hometown of Lincoln's friend and congressional colleague Amos Tuck.

Abraham Lincoln was a prominent figure who was gaining popularity in the Republican Party, but he still had not gained the name recognition in the New England states. The United States was at a fragile point of balancing the free states and slavery states. Lincoln strongly opposed expanding the slave states into the new western territories as did many in the northern states. The speeches given by Lincoln in New Hampshire assured many men that Lincoln was a viable presidential candidate. The New Hampshire delegates to the Republican Convention overwhelmingly favored Lincoln and cast their ballots for his nomination in the first round. Abraham Lincoln went on to gain the nomination and was elected our sixteenth president of the United States on Tuesday, November 6, 1860.

During Lincoln's stay in Exeter, it was believed that had stayed with friend, Amos Tuck. However, records show that Tuck was not home. The Exeter Historical Society believe that Lincoln may have stayed at the Squamscott House on Front Street or the Granite House on Center Street.

Greenland

Marker # 0113: Weeks House

Location: 1 Weeks Avenue- NH Route 33(Greenland Rd) near intersection of Portsmouth Road

Sign Erected: 1976

GPS Coordinates- N 43° 02'.195" W 70° 50'.481"

"Leonard Weeks settled here in 1658 on 33 acres of land which he left to his son, Samuel, who built the house about 1710. The bricks were made on the premises. Hand hewn oak beams support the 18 inch thick walls, which were cracked by the earthquake of 1755. Occupied by the family over 250 years, it is considered the oldest native brick house in New Hampshire."

The tract of land settled by Leonard Weeks had expanded to sixty acres by 1707 and extended behind this home to the town landing on the Winnicut River. During this time, this homestead and farm were the center of the community with the access to the Winnicut River. The Winnicut River was the access point to the Piscataqua River and the seaport of Portsmouth. Leonard Weeks willed this property to his son, Samuel in 1706. Around 1710, Samuel built this home of bricks fired onsite. During this era, most bricks used in construction came from the ballast of ships. It is believed that due to the likelihood of Indian attacks, Samuel Weeks constructed the 2 ½ story home of bricks as a means of security. The original farmstead is believed to have had two barns, an outbuilding, in addition to the brick house.

The home remained in the Weeks family for nine generations. During this time, the farmstead grew to one hundred acres at its peak in the early 19th century. The homestead was sold in 1968. With the boom of commercial development along NH Route 33, the Week's family was concerned their ancestral property would be lost forever. In 1975, the Weeks family created a non-profit corporation (Leonard Weeks & Descendants in America, Inc.) and purchased the original thirty-three-acre plot and homestead. In 1975, the property also was designated a New Hampshire Historic Site. The Weeks House, also known as the Old Brick House was listed on the National Register of Historic Places on June 20, 1975.

Today, the Leonard Weeks & Descendants in America organization rents the home to tenants to provide security. While the house is not open to the public, visitors can explore the nature trails and "housewife's garden" onsite. The trail includes interpretive signage of the property.

Hampstead

Marker # 0247: Hampstead Meeting House

Location: 20 Emerson Avenue (across from Hampstead Central School)

Sign Erected: 2015

GPS Coordinates-N 42° 52'.525" W 71° 10'.751"

"The Community began preparing framing timbers for a meetinghouse in 1745, erecting it before the town was incorporated in 1749. The completed building featured a balcony on 3 sides and a pulpit across from the entrance on the long side. In 1792, the town added the west tower and east porch. A bell was donated in 1809. In 1856 the 2nd floor was added inside. The last town meeting was held here in 1963, but the meetinghouse remains an active local landmark, one of four colonial period meetinghouses of this type in southeastern NH."

"Donated in 1809 by Mr. Thomas Huse, this bell is likely from Paul Revere Jr.'s foundry. The inscription reads, "The living to the church I call, and to the grave I summons all." The town elected a bell ringer annually, and the bell was rung for church services, funerals, emergencies, and for many years, to mark the time thrice each day. By local tradition, it is still rung at 12:01 am on the 4th of July each year."

Prior to the construction in 1745, settlers in this community traveled twelve miles for civic meetings and church services. The town was chartered by Governor Benning Wentworth when the state boundary was marked in 1749 and named Hampstead. While construction began in 1745, it was not completed until 1792 after townspeople felt a sense of disgrace for the building's lack of completion. Clapboards were replaced and whitewashed. The townspeople began to take pride in their meetinghouse. The steeple and tower were added in 1793.

In 1809, Deacon Thomas Huse told the minister that the belfry needed a bell. He claimed if the church members would see Mr. George Holbrook in Brookfield, Massachusetts that he would purchase the bell. The minister acted upon the gracious offer and the bell was made. In addition to the "The living to the church I call, and to the grave I summon all", one side of the bell is inscribed, "Presented by Thomas Huse, Esq. 1809" and the other side, "Revere, Boston". The bell cost $600. The Hampstead Meetinghouse was listed on the National Register of Historic Places on January 29, 1980. Today, the building is maintained by the Hampstead Historic District Commission.

Hampton

Marker # 0028: First Public School

Location: 53 Winnacunnet Road (NH Route 101E) and Towle Avenue (at Centre School)

Sign Erected: 1965

GPS Coordinates- N 42° 56'.246" W 70° 50'.085"

"In New Hampshire, supported by taxation, was opened in Hampton on May 31, 1649. It was presided over by John Legat for the education of both sexes. The sole qualification for admission of the pupils was that they be "capable of learning."

The area now known as Hampton was first settled around 1638 when Reverend Stephen Bachiler and followers were granted lands by the Massachusetts General Court to be known as the Plantation of Winnacunnet. Winnacunnet was an Algonquian word believed to mean "Beautiful place of pines".

As settlers migrated north to this plantation, school law of 1647 required settlements with at least fifty households to maintain a free school. In 1649, the leaders of this community sought out a teacher qualified to instruct the children to write, read, and teach lessons of Christianity. The leaders selected John Legat to be the first public school teacher in this plantation. He was a member of the community, having been elected to join the community in 1640. For his work, he would be compensated twenty pounds in corn, cattle and butter monthly. Hampton town history depicts that John Legat was not paid timely for his work and he filed a suit against the town for lack of payment. Eventually, Legat and the town leaders settled and Legat dropped his case as plaintiff.

The marker states that the education was available for children of both sexes who were capable of learning. There was also no age restriction or social status requirement for the children to attend. This is contrary to the general belief that girls and children of lower social status were denied an education up to the early 19th century; that belief was not valid at least in Hampton, New Hampshire.

Hampton was incorporated in 1639 and amassed an area that stretched from Salisbury Massachusetts to Portsmouth, New Hampshire. The total land area totaled 100 square miles. In the Fall of 1639, the Massachusetts General Court made claim to rename the Plantation of Winnacunnet to Hampton at the request of Reverend Bachiler.

Hampton

Marker # 0119: Old Landing Road

Location: US Route 1 at Park Avenue and Landing Road (across from Tuck Museum)

Sign Erected: 1977

GPS Coordinates- N 42° 55'.993″ W 70° 50'.134″

"This was the roadway from the ancient landing on Hampton River taken on October 14, 1638 by Rev. Stephen Bachiler and his small band of followers, when they made the first settlement of Hampton, originally named Winnacunnet Plantation. For the next 160 years this area was the center of the Town's activity. During that period and into the Town's third century, Landing Road provided access for fishing, salt-marsh haying, mercantile importing and exporting, and transportation needs of a prospering community."

Located at a triangular-shaped park, locally known as Founders Park, the stones that encompass the boundaries were placed in honor of the original families to settle at Winnacunnet Plantation. In the center, is the stone monument commemorating Reverend Stephen Bachiler, the founder of Winnacunnet Plantation. In addition to the plaques commemorating the settler families, other stones reflect the ten towns that originally were part of the Winnacunnet Plantation.

The Old Landing Road is named for its origin at the Landing along a bend on the Hampton River. According to Joseph Dow's book "*History of Hampton N.H.*" (1988) the Landing was believed to be where the inlet from Hampton Beach to the salt marshes at the end of Landing Road meet. (the site of Defiant Lobster Company at 125 Landing Road). It is believed the shallops (a small sailing boat used for coastal fishing) would bring their bounty to the Landing where it could be transported inland and to merchants. The first mill was built on this site in 1640 when the town and Richard Knight came to an agreement to build. Joseph Dow writes, "The Landing, being on the southerly side of the road, opposite the Benjamin Perkins house; and is, very likely, the place where the first settlers brought their shallop to shore."

Today, visitors can view the monuments at Founders Park and possibly find a name of an ancestor who settled here in the early 17th century. Another point of interest is the Tuck Museum of Hampton History located across from this marker on Park Avenue. The museum is also the home of the Hampton Historical Society.

Hampton Falls

Marker # 0037: George Washington's Visit

Location: US Route 1 and NH Route 84 at Village Triangle

Sign Erected: 1966

GPS Coordinates- N 42° 54'.880″ W 70° 51'.909"

"On his way to Portsmouth after entering New Hampshire on Saturday, October 31, 1789, President Washington accompanied by a splendid procession of the military and state dignitaries, halted for a short time here in Hampton Falls. He greeted and shook hands with a number of soldiers of the Revolution."

After the American War of Independence, General George Washington resigned his commission as Commander-in-Chief of the Continental Army. George Washington intended to return to his home at Mount Vernon and live simply as a citizen. However, his retirement was short-lived. In 1787, he attended the Constitutional Convention in Philadelphia as a delegate of Virginia. Washington was elected president of the Convention to strengthen the central government with the thirteen colonies. In 1789, George Washington was elected our first president with a unanimous vote of the Electoral College. President Washington had a lofty mission to unite all the colonies in supporting a stronger federal government. The weariest were the New England states.

President Washington arrived in New Hampshire the morning of October 31, 1789 and was greeted by hundreds of militiamen, to include New Hampshire President John Sullivan (the title was president for what we now know as governor), and John Langdon (patriot organizer of the Fort William & Mary raid in New Castle).

Along the travel route of President Washington, he was greeted by streets lined with well-wishers from the Massachusetts border to Portsmouth. President George Washington stayed four days in Portsmouth. During his stay, he participated in many local functions as well as went fishing on the Piscataqua River. President Washington was accompanied on his tour by his personal secretary, Portsmouth native Tobias Lear.

President George Washington completed his four-week tour of New England and was successful in solidifying the bond among the newly-formed states. Some may say that President George Washington was not only the father of our country, but also a masterful politician.

Kingston

Marker # 0046: Josiah Bartlett (1729-1795)

Location: Near 163 Main Street on west side of Kingston Green (Across from Town Hall)

Sign Erected: 1967

GPS Coordinates- N 42° 56'.136″ W 71° 03'.248″

"Distinguished participant in the founding of the Republic as signer of the Declaration of Independence and Articles of Confederation, and prominent in this State as Chief Justice of two courts and first holder of the title of Governor. An innovator in medicine, he practiced in this town for forty-five years."

Josiah Bartlett was born November 21, 1729 in nearby Amesbury, Massachusetts. Bartlett studied medicine under the mentorship of a local physician. By 1750, young Bartlett moved to Kingston to start his own practice. While the marker depicts Josiah Bartlett's influence as a statesman, he was also a soldier. Josiah Bartlett served under Brigadier General John Stark at the Battle of Bennington.

Josiah Bartlett gained notoriety as a New Hampshire statesman. He began his political influence as a member of the provincial general court (state legislature) in 1765. Bartlett was known as a member of the general assembly not influenced by the royal governor. Bartlett was an advocate of the colonists against

British oppression. He went on to serve as a member of the Committee of Safety at the start of the Revolution. In 1775, he was elected to the Continental Congress for New Hampshire. He was considered a man of principle and well-respected.

Bartlett was a delegate for New Hampshire at the Second Constitutional Conventions in Philadelphia. Bartlett was second only to John Hancock in signing the Declaration of Independence on July 2, 1776. After the war, Josiah was elected a delegate to draft the first U.S. Constitution. In 1777, he was the first signer of the Articles of Confederation that defined the role of the federal government after the separation from Britain.

Josiah Bartlett served the state as a judge, having risen to the position of Chief Justice of the New Hampshire Supreme Court even though he was not formally educated in law. In 1790, Bartlett was elected the state's first governor in 1790 to 1794. Earlier chief executives for the state were identified as president. Bartlett resigned in 1794 due to ill health. He died May 19, 1795 and is buried in Kingston.

New Castle

Marker # 0004: William & Mary Raids

Location: Wentworth Road at entrance to Fort Constitution & US Coast Guard Station

Sign Erected: 1958

GPS Coordinates- N 43° 04'.243″ W 70° 42'.852″

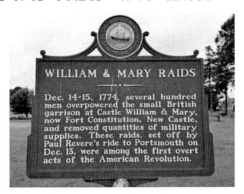

"Dec. 14-15, 1774, several hundred men overpowered the small British garrison at Castle William & Mary, now Fort Constitution, New Castle, and removed quantities of military supplies. These raids, set off by Paul Revere's ride to Portsmouth on Dec. 13, were among the first overt acts of the American Revolution."

Fort William & Mary is located on what is known as Great Island and was first constructed in 1631. The site overlooks where the Piscataqua River meets the Atlantic Ocean. This strategic point was critical in the defense of Portsmouth Harbor. The original fort consisted of earthen embankments, and four "great guns". In 1666, a timber-framed blockhouse was built. By 1692, the fortress expansion included additional guns and was named Fort William & Mary. The fortress was used to defend against French vessels during King William's War.

Most people know of Paul Revere's "Midnight Ride" that occurred on April 18, 1775. But Paul Revere had also made an important ride on December 13, 1774 to warn of the impending arrival of British soldiers to seize munitions. The "Sons of Liberty" consisting of about four hundred men stormed the fort in two separate raids. The outnumbered British defenders were unable to defend against the raiders. British Captain John Cochran and his five men were overwhelmed, and the patriots captured sixteen light cannons and ninety-seven barrels of gunpowder and captured the King's flag. Much of this bounty was used against the British at the Battle of Bunker Hill in June 1775. The British responded by sending two warships with more than one hundred marines to secure the fort and prevent a third raid. The British collected the remaining cannons and munitions and brought them to Boston. The raid on Fort William & Mary is considered the first act against of aggression against the British in the Revolution. The raid can be attributed to the planning by John Sullivan and John Langdon. The fort was renamed in 1808 as Fort Constitution.

Newington

Marker # 0151: Newington

Location: Shattuck Way (southeast corner of NH Route 16 bridge overpass) next to bike path

Sign Erected: 1985

GPS Coordinates- N 43° 06'.912″ W 70° 49'.397″

"Boundary disputes among the early river settlements caused this area to be called Bloody Point. By 1640 Trickey's Ferry operated between Bloody Point and Hilton's Point in Dover. In 1712 the meeting-house was erected and the parish set off, named Newington for the English village, whose residents sent the bell for the meeting-house. About 1725 the parsonage was built near the town forest, considered one of the oldest in America."

This marker is in a spot which may be difficult to find. The best approach is to use Exit 4 (Newington Village). Sign is at the bike path at the underpass of Exit 4. If you walk up the bike path until you see the waterfront, Trickey's Cove is to your left. On the other side of the highway (through the underpass), you will come to Bloody Point (Bloody Point Road). Trickey's Ferry extends from the spit of land known as Bloody Point to Hilton's Point.

The name is derived from a feud that occurred in 1631 between Captain Walter Neal and Captain Thomas Wiggin. Both men were sanctioned by John Mason to manage their respective land grants of lower and upper settlements. Captain Neal had responsibility of what was the lower settlement-Odiorne's Point (Rye, Portsmouth, and Newington). Captain Wiggin had responsibility of the upper settlement-Hilton's Point (north from Dover).

While the men escalated their argument of this boundary dispute, it did not result to the level of bloodshed as the name suggests. The boundaries have been in dispute between Dover and Portsmouth in later years as well. In 1643, a dispute took place regarding the ownership of Bloody Point and it was deemed part of Dover. Newington was originally part of Portsmouth and Dover. The town was incorporated in 1764 and named for an English village.

In 1712, the meetinghouse was built, and the townspeople of Newington, England donated a bell to be installed in their sister town in America. The Newington Historic District which is comprised of the Town Forest, Parade grounds used by the colonial militia, the 1725 parsonage, meetinghouse, buildings and homes can be seen around Nimble Hill Road and north of Arboretum Drive. The district was listed on the National Register of Historic Places in 1987.

Newmarket

Marker # 0209: Wentworth Cheswill (1746-1817)

Location: NH Route 152 at 206 South Main Street

Sign Erected: 2007

GPS Coordinates- N 43° 04'.557" W 70° 56'.608"

"One of the earliest students at Governor Dummer Academy in Massachusetts, Cheswill was among Newmarket's best-educated and most prosperous citizens. He was entrusted with many offices, including justice of the peace, selectman, town clerk, moderator, and representative. He amassed a noted private library, helped found the Newmarket Social Library, corresponded with Jeremy Belknap (1744-1798), New Hampshire's first historian, and conducted pioneering archaeological investigations. His father, Hopestill, was a noted housewright. His grandfather, Richard, was listed as "Negro"."

Wentworth Cheswill (also known as Cheswell) was born in Newmarket on April 1, 1746. Considered the "Father of Newmarket", Cheswill served his community in several roles. U.S. Representative Jeb Bradley stated on the floor of the US Congress "Wentworth served his town in varied capacity every year from 1768 to 1817" and "During the Revolutionary War, Wentworth acted as the town's messenger, delivering messages between Exeter and Newmarket in a duty quite like Paul Revere's." The New England Historical Society claims that

Wentworth Cheswill accompanied Paul Revere on his ride to Portsmouth on December 13, 1774.

At the age of 22, Cheswill served in his first elected position as town constable. According to George Mason University, he is considered the first African-American citizen elected to public office in America. Wentworth's grandfather Richard was believed to have been the first African-American to have owned land in New Hampshire. Deed records show that he purchased twenty acres from the Hilton Grant in 1717. By 1770, Wentworth owned more than one hundred acres of land. Wentworth married Mary Davis in 1767. They had thirteen children.

During the Revolution, Cheswill also served his country as member of the militia and fought under the command of Colonel John Langdon at the Battle of Saratoga. Wentworth Cheswill accomplished a great deal for any man of that time. While being biracial, the accomplishments achieved by Wentworth Cheswill makes them even more impressive. I believe that Newmarket is proud to call Wentworth Cheswill the father of their town.

North Hampton

Marker # 0062: Breakfast Hill

Location: US Route 1(Lafayette Road) at Rye/North Hampton Town line (mile marker 10.2)

Sign Erected: 1970

GPS Coordinates- N 43° 00'.068″ W 70° 48'.668"

"On the hillside to be seen to the north of this location a band of marauding Indians and their captives were found eating their breakfast on June 26, 1696, following the attack and massacre at the Portsmouth Plains. When confronted by the militia the Indians made a hasty exit leaving the prisoners and plunder. This locality still enjoys the name of Breakfast Hill."

Settlers had amiable relationships with the local Indians in most cases. These relationships were centered on trade. King William's War, the first of the French and Indian Wars, pitted the French against the English settlers in the New England colonies. The French based in Quebec, Canada paid Indians to capture English settlers. French missionaries (Catholics) also convinced the Indians that the English (Protestants) were evil and only want to take their land. Typically, an Indian raid lead to the capture of prisoners as well as the confiscation of goods from the settlements. The Indians would move the prisoners to Canada where they would be ransomed back to the colonies by the French. The massacre at Oyster River (marker #0050 in

Durham) which occurred in July 1694 made the local settlements uneasy of the neighboring Indian tribes.

Portsmouth Plains (marker #0075) was a site of a massacre of local settlers on June 25, 1696. Excerpts from Charles Brewster's "Rambles about Portsmouth" (1869) read: *"The raiding party made their way to Portsmouth Plains during the night. Just before dawn they set fire to the barns and outbuildings of the village, only then screaming their war cries to wake the people. They charged the houses, looting anything that could be easily carried and killed as they went. The women and children that could escape while the men put up a defense ran for the garrison house just north of the Plains. The elderly and injured attempted to hide in the nearby woods."*

Once enough men were gathered to defend the settlement, the raiders had left with prisoners and captured goods. The men from the Portsmouth Plains settlement led by Captain William Shackford pursued the retreating raiders. The hunting party found the Indians at this site the morning of June 26, 1696. Shackford had caught up to the Indian raiders and surrounded the hill they were encamped on. The Indians placed the hostages on the perimeter to deter an attack. As Captain Shackford's men charged the hill the Indians fled to the marshes and escaped.

Portsmouth

Marker # 0075: Portsmouth Plains

Location: NH Route 33 (Middle Road) & east of Islington Street at Plains Field Park

Sign Erected: 1971

GPS Coordinates- N 43° 03'.461″ W 70° 47'.025″

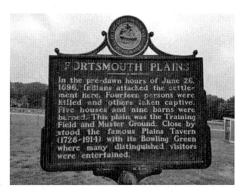

"In the pre-dawn hours of June 26, 1696, Indians attacked the settlement here. Fourteen persons were killed and others taken captive. Five houses and nine barns were burned. This plain was the Training Field and Muster Ground. Close by stood the famous Plains Tavern (1728-1914) with its Bowling Green where many distinguished visitors were entertained."

The Portsmouth Plains massacre is related to the Breakfast Hill marker in North Hampton. The Indians had traveled south from York, Maine /Nubble Point area and were seen paddling up the Piscataqua River from Portsmouth. With the recent unrest between settlers and Indian tribes, there was a sense of alertness. An excerpt from Charles Brewster's "Rambles about Portsmouth" (1869) read: *"That afternoon at Portsmouth Plains the livestock came out of the woods where they had been grazing and seemed somewhat agitated. Was it just the storm, or were there Indians waiting to attack? The villagers suspected Indians but decided to stay in their homes for the night instead of seeking the safety of the nearby Garrison."* The following morning the

Indian raiders attacked the settlement burning buildings and killing settlers along the way. Before the settlers could muster a group of men to defend, the raiders had departed with prisoners and supplies.

The Plains continued to be a focal point for early Portsmouth. The marker denotes that the plain was used as a muster and training ground for militia and New Hampshire soldiers. President George Washington first arrived here in Portsmouth at the Plains on October 31, 1789 during his four-day tour of New Hampshire.

On this site is the World War I Plains Memorial marker. This marker was dedicated on August 10, 1919 with remarks given by Governor John H. Bartlett, a descendant of New Hampshire's first Governor Josiah Bartlett.

Portsmouth

Marker # 0114: North Cemetery

Location: 119 Maplewood Avenue & Vaughn Street at Old North Cemetery

Sign Erected: 1976

GPS Coordinates- N 43° 04'.722″ W 70° 45'.782″

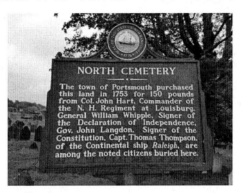

"The town of Portsmouth purchased this land in 1753 for 150 pounds from Col. John Hart, Commander of the N.H. Regiment at Louisburg. General William Whipple, Signer of the Declaration of Independence, Gov. John Langdon, Signer of the Constitution, Capt. Thomas Thompson, of the Continental ship Raleigh, are among the noted citizens buried here."

Having the opportunity to find and view each of the 255 New Hampshire historical markers was rewarding. This marker intrigued me as much as any other more popular sites. To stop and read about the number of influential individuals of our state history buried here was incredible. I believe this burial ground is as significant to New Hampshire as the Granary Burying Ground along the Freedom Trail is in Boston.

The Old North Cemetery was the third public burial ground in the city of Portsmouth in the Colonial Era. The cemetery is not the oldest public cemetery, but it is the largest of the 18th century cemeteries. It covers an area about 1.5 acres. The first burials occurred as early as 1751. Colonel John Hart sold the plot to the city in 1753. The graves in the northwest section is the Union cemetery which was established in 1844. The boundary is the row of maple trees.

This cemetery is the resting place of many notable people. Captain Thomas Thompson was the commander of the vessel *Raleigh*, which is the frigate depicted on the New Hampshire State flag. Other notable military members include crewmembers of Captain John Paul Jones, commander of *Ranger.* Brigadier General William Whipple was a Signer of the Declaration of Independence. Six-term Governor John Langdon, Signer of the Constitution and organizer of the raid on Fort William & Mary. A placard at the entrance lists the many influential people interred in this cemetery. From artisans, stonecutters, freed slaves, poets, authors, judges, doctors, and even a sheriff who holds the notoriety of hanging Ruth Blay; Sheriff Thomas Packer (see Packer's Falls marker #0154 in Durham). The Old North Cemetery was listed on the National Register of Historic Places on March 8, 1978. I recommend a stop to visit and walk of this historic site.

Portsmouth

Marker # 0127: John Langdon (1741-1819)

Location: 33 Elwyn Road in front of NH Urban Forestry Center building (east of Grant Ave)

Sign Erected: 1978

GPS Coordinates-N 43° 02'.664″ W 70° 46'.013"

"John Langdon, merchant and statesman, was born June 26, 1741, on this farm which was first settled by the Langdon family about 1650. With his brother Woodbury, he became a successful trader and shipbuilder. During the American Revolution, he supervised construction of the Continental warships Raleigh, Ranger and America at his Portsmouth shipyard, was in active military service, and personally financed General John Stark's expedition against Burgoyne in 1777."

"John Langdon had a long and distinguished career in public life, which included service in the New Hampshire House of Representatives, the New Hampshire Senate, and the Second Continental Congress. He became President of New Hampshire in 1785 and 1788, and was later elected Governor of the state six times, in 1805, 1806, 1807, 1808, 1810, and 1811. A close friend and advisor of Thomas Jefferson, John Langdon was a delegate to the Federal Constitutional Convention in 1787 and was elected the first president of the United States Senate."

I will start by stating that John Langdon's influence in the history of New Hampshire is evident that it requires two sides of this marker to touch upon his accomplishments. The Langdon family were one of the original settlers to Portsmouth having arrived from England in 1660. As a young man, John Langdon established himself as a skilled businessman and merchant. After grammar school, he and his brother Woodbury became apprentices of naval merchants. This led to his expertise in shipbuilding and seamanship. By the age of twenty-two, John was a captain of a cargo ship named Andromarche. In less than ten years, John Langdon had acquired his own fleet of vessels and became a prominent shipbuilder and sea merchant.

John Langdon used his wealth and influence to support the Revolutionary cause. Langdon and Colonel John Sullivan of Durham organized the group of men who raided Fort William & Mary in December 1774. While John Langdon supported the movement for independence from Britain with his wealth and construction of warships. In 1775, Langdon became a member of the First Continental Congress but resigned in June 1776 to oversee the production of Continental Army warships. The more famous vessels were the *Raleigh* which is depicted on the New Hampshire state flag, the sister ship *Ranger*, commanded by Captain John Paul Jones, and *America*.

Langdon returned to politics at the end of the war in 1783. In 1787, he returned to the Continental Congress and was a representative to the Constitutional Convention in that same year. John Langdon was elected to the U.S. Senate in 1789 and was elected as the nation's first President of the Senate. Locally, John Langdon served the state as a member of the New Hampshire General Court in 1801 to 1805. He served the last two years as Speaker of the House. In 1805, he began his unprecedented six terms as New Hampshire governor. What this marker does not reveal is that John Langdon declined an invitation to run as Vice President of the United States in 1812 on the Democratic-Republican ticket.

Langdon retired from political office in 1812 and quietly lived in his hometown of Portsmouth until his death on September 18,

1819. He is buried in the Old North Cemetery. John Langdon lived a distinguished life and his accomplishments have made a significant impact on our state and country. The Governor John Langdon House is where he lived most of his life. This home is located at 143 Pleasant Street in Portsmouth. It was listed on the National Register of Historic Places in December 1974. It is open to the public for guided tours and operated by the non-profit organization Historic New England.

Portsmouth

Marker # 0194: Wentworth-Coolidge Mansion

Location: NH Route 1A and Little Harbor Road (marker site)/Mansion- 375 Little Harbor Rd.

Sign Erected: 2005

GPS Coordinates- N 43° 03'.646″ W 70° 45'.219"

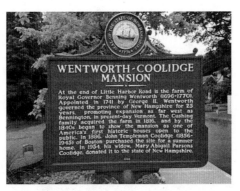

"At the end of Little Harbor Road is the farm of Royal Governor Benning Wentworth (1696-1770). Appointed in 1741 by George II, Wentworth governed the province of New Hampshire for 25 years, promoting expansion as far west as Bennington, in present-day Vermont. The Cushing family acquired the farm in 1816, and by the 1840s began to show the mansion as one of America's first historic houses open to the public. In 1886, John Templeman Coolidge (1856-1945) of Boston purchased the site for a summer home. In 1954, his widow, Mary Abigail Parsons Coolidge, donated it to the state of New Hampshire."

Governor Benning Wentworth was appointed the first Royal Governor of New Hampshire on June 4, 1741. Much of our earliest charters were granted under Benning Wentworth. As you may read throughout this book, the incorporated names of settlements were typically granted under the names of friends of the Royal Governor. While Benning Wentworth was influential in the expansion of the Province of New Hampshire, much of the land grants were given to people who had never, nor would ever visit their namesake. Benning Wentworth was born in Portsmouth and died here on this estate on October 14, 1777.

The Wentworth-Coolidge Mansion is a 40-room 18th century home located on the banks of Little Harbor. Original construction is believed to have occurred in 1695 with the main section added in 1730. In 1753, Royal Governor Benning Wentworth moved the seat of government from Portsmouth to his home at this site. It is believed that the lilac bushes onsite were planted by Benning Wentworth. J. Templeman Coolidge, who acquired the Wentworth Mansion in 1883, renovated the mansion and installed a modern-era kitchen. In 1916, he added the one-story western wing containing two additional bedrooms and two baths. The New Hampshire Division of Parks was gifted the house from widower Mrs. Coolidge in 1954.

Portsmouth

Marker # 0234: U.S. Route 1 Bypass of Portsmouth, NH (1940)

Location: US Route 1 Bypass Traffic Circle at NH State Liquor Store (500 Woodbury Ave.)

Sign Erected: 2013

GPS Coordinates- N 43° 04'.435″ W 70° 46'.881″

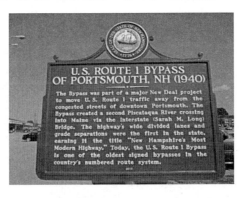

"The Bypass was part of a major New Deal project to move U.S. Route 1 traffic away from the congested streets of downtown Portsmouth. The Bypass created a second Piscataqua River crossing into Maine via the Interstate (Sarah M. Long) Bridge. The highway's wide divided lanes and grade separations were the first in the state, earning it the title "New Hampshire's Most Modern Highway." Today, the U.S. Route 1 Bypass is one of the oldest signed bypasses in the country's numbered route system."

Prior to 1956, the United States did not have the Interstate Highway System that we frequently use to travel. President Dwight D. Eisenhower signed into law the Federal-Aid Highway Act on June 29, 1956. Automobile travel was increasing, and we were in the middle of the Cold War with the Soviet Union. Interstate travel provided accessible thru-ways that could accommodate a high volume of traffic. Prior to the interstates (in this location is Interstate 95), the main arteries were coastal highway US Route 1 and US Route 4. Prior to the construction of the US Route 1 Bypass, travelers drove on the north/south route from Maine and points south via US Route 1 through downtown Portsmouth. The non-linear streets of Portsmouth combined with the narrow streets and commercial centers caused major congestion through the city.

Following the Great Depression of 1929, President Franklin D. Roosevelt took office in 1933 and established his economic policy of putting Americans back to work with domestic projects. President Roosevelt's program was named the New Deal. Under the New Deal's Works Progress Administration, projects included highways, bridges, schools, and public parks. The US Route 1 Bypass was one such project.

Prior to the US Route 1 Bypass, travel north to Maine was routed over the Memorial Bridge to Kittery Maine through downtown Portsmouth. After construction of the bypass, a new route was made over the Sarah M. Long bridge. This allowed for traffic from US Route 1 and US Route 4 to access a north/south route easily. Traffic shifted away from the Bypass after the completion of the more modern highway, Interstate 95 in 1957.

Rollinsford

Marker # 0088: Charles Cogswell Doe (1830-1896)

Location: NH Route 4 (Portland Road) and Sligo Road

Sign Erected: 1972

GPS Coordinates- N 43° 13'.494″ W 70° 48'.865”

"Rollinsford was the home of Charles C. Doe, Jurist, Judge of the Supreme Court and Chief Justice from 1876-1896. Upon graduation from Dartmouth College in 1849, he studied law at Harvard. His outstanding opinions as Chief Justice indicate his unusual legal attainments and left an indelible impression on the law of New Hampshire."

Charles C. Doe was born April 11, 1830 in Dover. He grew up in Somersworth and attended local Berwick Academy in Maine. Charles was the 4th son and youngest of six children born to Joseph and Mary Doe. Charles went on to Harvard in 1845 and only attended that one year after leaving for a suspicious occurrence related to a hazing incident against Charles. He continued his education by attending Dartmouth College where he graduated in 1849.

Charles returned to study law under the mentorship of attorney Daniel Christie for the next three years. In 1854, Charles Doe practiced law in Dover with local attorney and close friend Charles Woodman. Charles began his law career as a pro-unionist democrat but later changed his party affiliation to republican due to the Dred Scott decision. This US Supreme Court decision affirmed the rights of slave owners to take their slaves to Free-states without fear of loss of property.

Charles C. Doe served thirty-seven of his forty-two years of law as a member of the New Hampshire Supreme Judicial Court. He was appointed an Associate Justice to the New Hampshire Supreme Judicial Court in 1859 at the young age of twenty-nine. He served as an Associate Justice until 1874. The Court was dissolved for two years and established as the New Hampshire Supreme Court. He served as Chief Justice from 1876 to 1896.

Charles Doe died March 13, 1896 at the Rollinsford Railway station on his way to Concord. His sudden death is the reason no painting of Doe is displayed at the Supreme Court. Some of Charles C. Doe's judicial accomplishment include the reforming of the rules of evidence and the simplifying of rules of pleading. He abhorred the ceremonial and formalities of English Common Law. He believed the rule of law should be simple, commonsensical, and clearly defined. He is best remembered as a man of simplicity.

Rye

Marker # 0018: Isle of Shoals

Location: NH Route 1A at Rye Harbor State Park

Sign Erected: 1963 & 2006

GPS Coordinates- N 43° 00'.091″   W 70° 44'.671″

"About six miles offshore, these nine rocky islands served Europeans as a fishing station before the first mainland settlements were made in 1623. Capt. John Smith (1580-1631) named the group "Smith's Isles" in 1614. The codfish that "shoaled" or schooled there in huge numbers were a prized delicacy that supported 300 to 600 inhabitants before the revolution. By the mid-1800s, new hotels attracted a summer colony of writers and artists, chief of whom was poet Celia Thaxter (1835-1894). The islands have supported religious conferences since 1897 and marine research since 1928."

Prior to the arrival of Europeans, the Isles of Shoals was frequently used by Indians for fishing. Before Captain Smith arrived, records indicate that French explorers visited the islands as they sailed the Atlantic coast. On a clear day, visitors from this point can see the chain of islands on the horizon. Here is a short back story of Captain John Smith and his adventures in the New World.

Captain John Smith spent his lifetime at sea, but not always for good. He fought as a mercenary against Spain and Turkey. In 1606, he joined the Virginia Company of London to sail to the New World and colonized Jamestown, Virginia in 1607. Smith was not one to sit idle. He set off to explore and chart the eastern coast. In 1614, Captain Smith was mapping the New England coast for viable harbors, riverways and natural resources. He came upon the cluster of rocky islands and named them Smith Isles. He realized that these rocky outcroppings offshore were excellent for fishing. Smith took this information back to London where plans were made for future settlements.

The islands are split between the state of Maine and New Hampshire. The largest island Appledore is in Maine. The second largest island, Star, is in New Hampshire. Today, the Isle of Shoals is a popular destination for many interests. Star Island is home of the Oceanic Hotel and many artists visit the islands for its exceptional beauty.

Rye

Marker # 0063: Atlantic Cable Station and Sunken Forest

Location: NH Route 1A north of East Atlantic Avenue

Sign Erected: 1970

GPS Coordinates- N 42° 59'.584" W 70° 45'.542"

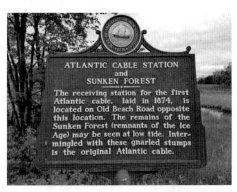

"The receiving station for the first Atlantic cable, laid in 1874, is located on Old Beach Road opposite this location. The remains of the Sunken Forest (remnants of the Ice Age) may be seen at low tide. Intermingled with these gnarled stumps is the original Atlantic cable."

The marvel of the technology in 1874 to lay a transatlantic cable from Rye, New Hampshire to Europe is quite impressive. On the southerly side of Locke's neck, the Direct United States Cable company constructed a cable station as the terminus on the United States telegraph communication cable. The transatlantic cable was the first of its kind that ran directly from Europe to the United States. Earlier cables had been installed from Britain to maritime provinces of Canada such as Nova Scotia and Newfoundland.

The steamship *Ambassador* designed for this cable installation laid the cable from this point off Old Beach Road out to the Isle of Shoals. Another section of cable ran from the Isle of Shoals northerly to Halifax, Nova Scotia and onto Ballenskelligs, Ireland;

more than 2,500 nautical miles. The section of cable from Isle of Shoals and beyond to Ireland was installed by the steamship *Faraday.*

On July 15, 1874, the *Ambassador* laid the short section from this point to the connection point at the Isle of Shoals. The *History of the town of Rye, New Hampshire* (1905) reads: "*On Wednesday morning the shore section of the cable, weighing about fifteen tons, was loaded from the steamer upon a platform laid upon two steam launches, and at about three o'clock in the afternoon the shore end of it was successfully landed, amid the booming of cannon and the enthusiastic cheers of the faithful few who had remained to see the work completed. It took about an hour to place the cable in the trench that had been dug to receive it, quite a number of ladies taking hold of the rope attached to the cable and assisting to drag it to high water mark; and the work of splicing took about two hours more. Then the Ambassadors guns replied to the ones on shore, rockets were sent up from the ship and blue lights burned, and there was hearty cheering by the crowd that had again been attracted to the beach.*"

The telegraph cable provided a means to transfer messages via Morse Code between two continents. The Atlantic Cable Station was manned by four workers around the clock. Two to receive messages and two to send messages. The cable still lies in place. Scuba divers can still observe the cable which was installed nearly 150 years ago.

The sunken forest that is depicted on this marker is one of two in the area. One is located at Odiorne's Point and is referred to as the "Drowned Forest". After the receding of the glacial shelf, the trees were immersed in the saltwater. Unable to survive, the stumps that remain are all that are visible. The larger remains are located here near Jenness Beach. The Sunken Forest is rarely seen unless during periods of exceedingly low tides. The stumps of these trees range from eight to ten feet in diameter and are carbon dated as nearly 3,500 years old.

Rye

Marker # 0078: Odiorne's Point

Location: NH Route 1A at Odiorne Point State Park boat launch (not at Fort Dearborn)

Sign Erected: 1971 & 1983

GPS Coordinates- N 43° 02'.905″ W 70° 43'.633″

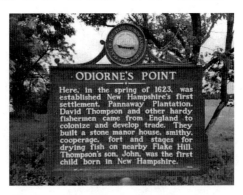

"Here in the spring of 1623, was established New Hampshire's first settlement, Pannaway Plantation. David Thompson and other hardy fishermen came from England to colonize and develop trade. They built a stone manor house, smithy, cooperage, fort and stages for drying fish on nearby Flake Hill. Thompson's son, John, was the first child born in New Hampshire."

In 1622, the Plymouth Council (a company established by King James of England) granted John Mason and Sir Ferdinando Gorges land between the Merrimack and Kennebec Rivers. These two men created the "Laconia Company". Captain John Mason granted six thousand acres to David Thompson to settle and establish trade. Thompson hired men to help establish this settlement to include the Hilton brothers Edward and William. Thompson arrived on this ridge of land in 1623 and established the settlement of "Pannaway" an Abenaki word meaning "place where the water spreads out". This settlement was also known as "Lower Plantation". David Thompson sent the Hilton brothers upstream of the Piscataqua River to establish a settlement at

Plantation". Cocheco Plantation is New Hampshire oldest permanent settlement.

Fish caught off the Isle of Shoals and from Hilton's Point were brought here to be dried on racks. Fishing and trade were the main commerce of this settlement and it continued for nearly four years. Trade continued with the Indians and much of the bounty caught was shipped to England. In 1626, David Thompson abandoned Pannaway and moved to his namesake Thompson Island in Boston Harbor. By 1630, most of the settlers abandoned Pannaway as well and settled at Strawberry Banke in what is now Portsmouth.

By 1629, settlers from the Massachusetts Bay Colony came and settled along land between the Piscataqua and Merrimack Rivers. Pannaway did not survive as a permanent settlement. Today, the tracts of land known as Pannaway Plantation comprise the Odiorne Point State Park. The name Odiorne Point was derived from the Odiorne family that settle here in 1660.

Seabrook

Marker # 0103: Shapley Line

Location: NH Route 1 and Rocks Road

Sign Erected: 1975

GPS Coordinates- N 42° 53'.827″ W 70° 52'.205″

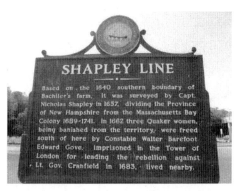

"Based on the 1640 southern boundary of Bachiler's farm, it was surveyed by Capt. Nicholas Shapley in 1657, dividing the Province of New Hampshire from the Massachusetts Bay Colony from 1689-1741. In 1662 three Quaker women, being banished from the territory, were freed south of here by Constable Walter Barefoot. Edward Gove, imprisoned in the Town of London for leading the rebellion against Lt. Gov. Cranfield in 1683, lived nearby."

The feud between the Province of New Hampshire and the Massachusetts Bay Colony over their shared boundary started as early as 1629. King Charles I of England had granted land to two colonies; the Province of New Hampshire and Massachusetts Bay. The New Hampshire grant claimed the southern boundary was the center of the Merrimack River. The northern boundary of Massachusetts Bay was three miles north of the Merrimack River. This boundary dispute caused havoc between the towns of Hampton (Seabrook was not incorporated) and Salisbury, Massachusetts.

According to Joseph Dow's book, *History of Hampton* (1988), *"Soon after the settlement of Hampton, a controversy arose with Salisbury about the line between the two towns, which was the beginning of a controversy between New Hampshire and Massachusetts, that vexed the colonies continually and has but recently ended. These towns were granted about the same time, and it was intended that the southerly boundary of the former should be at the distance of three miles north of the Merrimac river, while the latter should embrace all the territory between Hampton and the river. At the same session of the General Court, in which Mr. Bachiler and his company had obtained permission to form a plantation here, measures were taken to run out and establish this line."*

It was not settled until May 1657, when Captain Nicholas Shapley was commissioned to survey the boundary and it was accepted by the Massachusetts General Court as the official boundary between Hampton and Salisbury. The stone at this marker denotes the western boundary of the surveyed line. Originally, this point was marked by a tree.

Seabrook

Marker # 0120: Bound Rock

Location: Woodstock Street in vacant lot near Ocean Drive

Sign Erected: 1978

GPS Coordinates- N 42° 53'.469″ W 70° 48'.821″

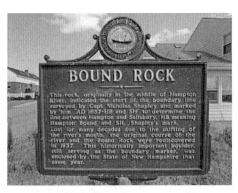

"This rock, originally in the middle of Hampton River, indicated the start of the boundary line surveyed by Capt. Nicholas Shapley and marked by him "AD 1657-HB and SH" to determine the line between Hampton and Salisbury. HB meaning Hampton Bound and SH, Shapley's mark.

Lost for many decades due to the shifting of the river's mouth, the original course of the river and the Bound Rock were rediscovered in 1937. This historically important boulder, still serving as the boundary marker, was enclosed by the State of New Hampshire that same year."

This marker coincides with the previous marker of the Shapley Line. The disputed land between New Hampshire and Massachusetts was due to the conflicting land grants made by King Charles I. Both towns claimed the right to tax the residents under their land charter and set out to imprison those who did not pay. Ultimately, residents owed taxes to both colonies.

In 1656, the Court appointed Captain Shapley to survey the boundary. Shapley began his survey on a section of ledge in the center of the Hampton River and marked this point, "H.B." for Hampton Bounds. From that time on, this rock was known as Bound Rock. This point denoted the easternmost boundary of the Shapley Line. Shapley engraved this boulder in 1657.

As decades past, the boulder was covered by sand and over time ocean currents and winds shifted the flow of the river. Today, the river flows nearly one mile north of this point. The boulder was not discovered again until 1937. The Army Corps of Engineers were excavating in the area and came upon this rock with markings.

When Seabrook was incorporated in 1768, the town claimed their boundary with Hampton as the shore of the Hampton River. A dispute ensued over the ownership of the Bound Rock.

In 1953, the NH Supreme Court ruled in favor of Hampton which read, "*a fixed and immovable bound and remains in the same position, whether it be covered with sand as it now is or whether it be in the harbor's mouth with water on all sides as it was in 1908-1910.*" The lot which the Bound Rock is located was purchased by the town of Hampton in 1956 for $2,000. Bound Rock is the second oldest boundary marker in the United States.

Notable Reference Sites

Each page required specific references to complement the information found on the historical markers. There were several resources that were available online and at the New Hampshire reference room at my place of employment that provided the information needed. Here are a few of the most useful references that I hope the reader may be able to visit and get more information from.

Great North Woods and White Mountains Regions:

Berlin and Coos County Historical Society. (2017). *Berlin and Coös County Historical Society | Preserving the past for the future.* http://berlinnhhistoricalsociety.org/

Harris, J. R., Morgan, K., Dickerman, M., Monadnock Institute of Nature, & Place and Culture. (2011). *Beyond the notches: Stories of place in New Hampshire's North Country.* Littleton, NH: Bondcliff Books.

North Country Chamber of Commerce. (n.d.). *North Country Chamber of Commerce - North Country Chamber of Commerce.* www.chamberofthenorthcountry.com

White Mountain Art. (2017). White Mountain Art & Artists- History. http://whitemountainart.com/about-3/history/

White Mountain History.org. (2018). http://www.whitemountainhistory.org

Lakes Region:

Lake Winnipesaukee Historical Society. (n.d.). *Lake Winnipesaukee Historical Society.* http://lwhs.us/history.htm

Mayo, L. S. (1921). *John Wentworth, Governor of New Hampshire, 1767-1775.* https://archive.org/details/johnwentworthgov00mayouoft

Dartmouth/Lake Sunapee:

New London Historical Society. (n.d.). Area Historical Societies, Historic Sites, and Museums. http://www.newlondonhistoricalsociety.org/visiting-new-london.html

Monadnock Region:
American Revolution.Org. (2017). Last Men - Samuel Downing. http://www.americanrevolution.org/last_men/lastmen1.php

Historical Society of Cheshire County. (n.d.). Research - Historical Society of Cheshire County. https://hsccnh.org/education/research/

Library of Congress. (n.d.). Edward Alexander MacDowell (1860-1908) | Library of Congress. https://www.loc.gov/item/ihas.200035715/

The Lexington Minute Men. (2013). William Diamond - The Lexington Minute Men. http://www.lexingtonminutemen.com/william-diamond.html

Merrimack Valley Region:
Canterbury Shaker Village. (2015). The Shakers. http://www.shakers.org/education/the-shakers/

Federal Writers Project of the Works Progress Administration. (1938). *New Hampshire. A guide to the granite state.* https://archive.org/details/newhampshireguid00federic

Manchester Historic Association, S. (2018). Research Center | Manchester Historic Association. https://www.manchesterhistoric.org/research-center

State of New Hampshire. (n.d.). NH General Court. http://www.gencourt.state.nh.us/

Seacoast Region:
Belknap, J. (1812). *The history of New-Hampshire. Volume I: Comprehending the events of one complete century from the discovery of the river Pascataqua.* Library of Congress.

Dow, J. (1988). *History of Hampton, New Hampshire, 1638-1988.* Portsmouth, NH: Published for the Town of Hampton, New Hampshire by P.E. Randall Publisher.

Lane Memorial Library. (n.d.). History of Hampton, New Hampshire | Lane Memorial Library. http://www.hampton.lib.nh.us/hampton/history.htm

Mike in New Hampshire | Exploring New Hampshire History, one Road Side Marker at a time. (2010). https://mikenh.wordpress.com/

Speare, E. A. (1967). *New Hampshire's historic seacoast.* Littleton, NH: Courier Print. Co.

Statewide Resources:
Marsh, Richard. (n.d.). Images of New Hampshire History.www.images-of-new-hampshire-history.com/

McGee, W. (2007). *Men of granite: True stories of New Hampshire's fighting men.* Portsmouth, NH: Peter Randall.

New England Historical Society. (2016). *New England Historical Society - New England History.* http://www.newenglandhistoricalsociety.com/

New Hampshire Public Radio. (2018). Marking History | New Hampshire Public Radio. Retrieved from http://nhpr.org/topic/marking-history

New Hampshire Division of Historical Resources. (n.d.). New Hampshire Covered Bridges. https://www.nh.gov/nhdhr/bridges/

New Hampshire Division of Historical Resources. (2018). New Hampshire Historical Highway Markers, New Hampshire

Division of Historical Resources.
https://www.nh.gov/nhdhr/markers/

New Hampshire Union Leader. (2017). Historical Markers - unionleader.com - Manchester, NH. http://www.unionleader.com/section/NEWHAMPSHIRE0310

Northern New England Villages. (2017). *Historic Markers | Northern New England Villages.* http://northernnewenglandvillages.com/road-historical-markers/

Speare, Eva A. (1938). *Colonial Meeting-Houses of New Hampshire.* Littleton, N.H.

State of New Hampshire. (2012). NH.gov - NH Cities and Towns. https://www.nh.gov/municipal/index.html

U.S. Department of the Interior-National Park Service. (2011). National Register of Historic Places Database and Research Page -- National Register of Historic Places Official Website--Part of the National Park Service. https://www.nps.gov/nr/research/

United State Library of Congress. (2018). Research and Reference Services: Access to Library of Congress Collections and Research Tools. http://www.loc.gov/rr/

Wetherbee, F. (2005). *Fritz Wetherbee's New Hampshire.* Concord, NH: Plaidswede.

Wetherbee, F. (2007). *Fritz: More stories from New Hampshire Chronicle.* Concord, NH: Plaidswede.

Wetherbee, F. (2008). *Fritz Wetherbee: Taken for granite.* Concord, NH: Plaidswede Publishing.

Whitney, D. Q. (2008). *Hidden history of New Hampshire.* Charleston, SC: History Press.

Wikoff, J. (1985). *The upper valley: An illustrated tour along the Connecticut River before the twentieth century.* Chelsea, VT: Chelsea Green.

Wood, F. J. (1919). *The turnpikes of New England and evolution of the same through England, Virginia, and Maryland.*

ABOUT THE AUTHOR

Michael was born and raised in the Lakes Region of New Hampshire. After serving in the U.S. Army for more than 23 years, Michael returned to New Hampshire in 2009. Michael has been a JROTC Army Instructor at White Mountains Regional High School in Whitefield since his military retirement. Michael attained an Educational Specialist (Ed. S) degree in Curriculum and Instruction from Liberty University in Lynchburg, VA. Michael resides in the historic mountain community of Bethlehem where he is actively involved in town government.

In 2017, Michael wrote and sponsored an historical marker commemorating Frances Glessner Lee, who made significant contributions to the study of forensics. Michael is also a certified New Hampshire Granite State Ambassador. In his spare time, Michael enjoys hiking in the White Mountains and riding his motorcycle with his wife Kristin along the country roads of New Hampshire.   Contact Michael at NHMarkers603@gmail.com